REVOLTING FAMILIES

Revolting Families

Toxic Intimacy, Private Politics, and Literary Realisms in the German Sixties

CARRIE SMITH-PREI

UNIVERSITY OF TORONTO PRESS
Toronto Buffalo London

© University of Toronto Press 2013
Toronto Buffalo London
www.utppublishing.com
Printed in Canada

ISBN 978-1-4426-4637-7 (cloth)

Printed on acid-free, 100% post-consumer recycled paper with
vegetable-based inks.

Library and Archives Canada Cataloguing in Publication

Smith-Prei, Carrie, 1975–
Revolting families : toxic intimacy, private politics, and
literary realisms in the German sixties / Carrie Smith-Prei.

Includes bibliographical references and index.

ISBN 978-1-4426-4637-7

1. German fiction – 20th century – History and criticism.
2. Families in literature. 3. Germany (West) – In literature.
I. Title.

PT405.S57 2013   833'.91409355   C2013-901733-X

University of Toronto Press acknowledges the financial assistance to its publishing
program of the Canada Council for the Arts and the Ontario Arts Council.

Canada Council   Conseil des Arts
for the Arts   du Canada

ONTARIO ARTS COUNCIL
CONSEIL DES ARTS DE L'ONTARIO
50 YEARS OF ONTARIO GOVERNMENT SUPPORT OF THE ARTS
50 ANS DE SOUTIEN DU GOUVERNEMENT DE L'ONTARIO AUX ARTS

University of Toronto Press acknowledges the financial support of the Government of
Canada through the Canada Book Fund for its publishing activities.

For my family, Doreen and Leopold

Contents

Acknowledgments

A great many people supported me throughout the inception, research, and writing of this book, whether directly through their careful reading and feedback or indirectly through their support of me in my early career. I am indebted to Sarah McGaughey who has read, reread, and reread again the chapters as they evolved into a book. Without her insight, encouragement, friendship, and task-mastering over a period of many years, this publication would never have been possible. Many thanks to my PhD student and RA Barbara Pausch: not only did she have the dreary task of quote checking the manuscript, but also her talented translations of the German quotations formed a starting point for my own translations. My gratitude also extends to my colleague Raleigh Whitinger, who carefully read and edited the individual chapters, and to my RA Olena Hlazkova for reading the final proofs. Thank you also to the anonymous readers for University of Toronto Press whose excellent comments helped me to craft the final manuscript. My greatest appreciation should also be known for editor Richard Ratzlaff for supporting me in this first book venture with patience and enthusiasm. I also thank managing editor Barbara Porter for shepherding the manuscript through the production process and copyeditor John St James for his careful eye. Finally, I am grateful to the Faculty of Arts at the University of Alberta for their support of this work through the Publication Subvention Program.

This book represents the mentorship of many people during my studies and the initial stages of my early career. Thank you to those who guided me throughout my MA and PhD studies, especially Lutz Koepnick, Erin McGlothlin, Stephan Schindler, Lynne Tatlock, Gerhild Williams, and my tireless supporter Paul Michael Lützeler, as well as my BA mentor Leslie Morris. Thank you also to my Irish colleagues, who gave me an institutional home during my first two years as a newly minted PhD, particularly Moray McGowan, Gilbert Carr, and Jürgen Barkhoff at Trinity College Dublin and Valerie Heffernan, Florian Krobb, Jeffrey Morrison, and Arndt Witte at the National University of Ireland Maynooth. My appreciation also goes out to fellow Gisela-Elsner scholar Christine Künzel for her intellectual support. Huge thanks to my colleagues at my current institutional home, the University of Alberta, particularly to those in German studies: Jennifer Dailey-O'Cain, Elisabeth Herrmann, Claudia Kost, Helga Mitterbauer, and Raleigh Whitinger. Special mention is reserved for those collaborators who, while not involved in this project, have formed much of my thinking for past and upcoming projects: Hester Baer, Cordula Böcking-Politis, Gwyneth Cliver, Valerie Heffernan, and, finally, Maria Stehle, who continues to be an inspiration daily. This book ultimately represents the good fortune I have had to receive constant love and support throughout the years from many friends around the world and, most importantly, from my mother, father, stepmother, and stepfather. This book is dedicated to my wife, Doreen, to whom I owe everything and to my son, Leopold, who was born during the book's writing and thus helped to keep it all in perspective.

REVOLTING FAMILIES

Introduction: On Realism, Negativity, and Intimacy

Das Private ist diesem Verständnis nach nie und nimmer das politisch nur Marginale, sondern gerade das Gegenteil – der Ursprung allen Protestes und aller Revolte, die Quelle jeglicher Art von Veränderung, auch der politischen. (Tschierske 17)

The private is never merely the politically marginal, but exactly the opposite – the source of all protest and all revolt, the source of any kind of change, including political change.[1]

This study is located at the crossroads of the normative 1950s and the radical 1960s and early 1970s in West Germany. It looks backwards and forwards from the vantage point of 1968, the year that functions as a milestone for the coming-into-being of a socially and politically motivated cultural consciousness.[2] It discusses texts that are a product of the earlier part of the decade, but it does so with the social and political awareness of the end of the decade in mind. In line with historian Martin Klimke's claim that 1968 is now being understood as a "social departure that was experienced by all parts of West German society," this study contributes to the establishment of a "plethora of new ways of narrating the German 'Sixties'" (Klimke 250). In this narration of the "German 'Sixties,'" I argue that the representation of the private sphere in literary works of realism provides an avenue through which to access a shared public imaginary of postwar West German cultural identity, not the least because this avenue leads to a wide variety of non-literary contextual sources. My overarching literary argument is that these forms of realism use the negative workings of the body as a narrative aesthetics through which to express socio-political concerns related to the 1960s private sphere. By so doing, I also develop a theoretical apparatus for approaching the appearance of negatively coded bodies, an apparatus that is sensitive to bodies' narrative-aesthetic potential and to their attunement to a historical present that is located in a specific moment of cultural change.

This study pivots around the cultural imaginary of 1968 intellectually, thematically, historically, and aesthetically by developing upon two key aspects of the symbolic capital carried by the notation 1968: the politicization of the private sphere and the mobilization of literature and art for immediate critical change. The year 1968 marks the shift in public perception on aspects of intimacy and interpersonal relations, specifically with regard to sexuality (from the sexual revolution, to second-wave feminism, to the gay rights movement) and family structures (from the founding of communes to the establishment of storefront day-care centres known as *Kinderläden*). Keeping this shift in mind, the study examines the interplay between the literary depiction of familial and intimate relations and the public discourse on the political import of the private sphere throughout the 1960s leading up to 1968. I focus on debut literary works by so-called New and Black Realists Dieter Wellershoff, Rolf Dieter Brinkmann, Gisela Elsner, and Renate Rasp. Into these literary analyses I weave contextual discussions on the private sphere from these authors' intellectual and political contemporaries. The study thereby offers a broad and synthesized reading of writings on the private sphere across disciplines and shows how these offer up an intimate portrait of West Germany in the 1960s.

In the literary texts, the social and political implications of the private sphere are communicated through the body. The four chapters identify how these authors mobilize negative corporeal realism in their family novels. I borrow the term "corporeal realism" from Richard Langston, who in *Visions of Violence* coins it to reference the characteristic manner in which post-fascist avant-gardes ethically approach "categories of totality and fragmentation" of the body in order to "demarcate their claims to reality from those of the historical avant-garde" (19).[3] I use Langston's term to describe how the body communicates these literary texts' "claims to reality" with regard to contemporaneous discourses on the private sphere, specifically discourses on the subject in the family. I add the descriptor "negative" to characterize the manner in which these realisms can be understood in terms of their critical intentionality towards their readers. Negativity points to the corporealities depicted in and guiding the narratives at the levels of plot and poetics. It resonates within the literary texts primarily from unpleasant corporeal representations. These, in turn, construct the poetic language of the narratives and thereby unsettle the reader. The texts call readers to political, social, or ethical action through their affective reaction to each author's respective depiction of negative emotions and sensations caused by neurosis, disgust, vertigo, or violent love.

Not only is 1968 a watershed year for the politicization of the private sphere, it also denotes the apex of the decade-long calling-to-task of literature's social and political relationship to reality. The literary texts discussed in this study assume a socially and politically conscious readership. Negative corporeal realism prompts, enacts, engages, or stages the reader's psychosocial and socio-political awareness. The texts thus take on a literary-aesthetic posture that is negative rather than affirmative. By so doing, they remain in keeping with much writing published or read in the 1960s, from the Frankfurt School to the Konstanz School. The interaction between textual body and contextual discourse is revealed to be a key factor in the authors' development of a narrative strategy based in negativity. Through the analysis of these texts, a theoretical concept of intimate and body-based negativity emerges as a narrative-aesthetic model for inciting socio-political engagement in the reader. The texts develop a socio-politically charged relationship with the reader by crafting a literary narrative out of the negative corporeal effects of society's repressiveness in the private sphere. Negativity therefore also describes the psychosocial development or misdevelopment of the fictional subjectivities that reflects on the repressive socio-political contexts. It also constitutes the reader's experience with text and context. Owing to this study's focus on realism, context here must be understood simultaneously as the text's context – that is, the context out of which the text grows, within which it acts, and with which it engages – and the reader's context. Author and text imagine these contexts to be identical. Realism in this sense is so bound to everyday experience of both author and reader that the texts themselves call up that sense of immediacy. In the trifold sense of context-based, text-based, and reader-based, negativity is at once structured by both cultural and literary frameworks and experienced by the reader physically and emotionally.

The literary texts examined in this study thus resonate within, react to, and reflect the "social-cultural-political-intellectual-psychic orders" of the 1960s (DeKoven 18). In her study of the emergence of the postmodern, *Utopia Limited*, Marianne DeKoven chooses Raymond Williams's phrase "structure of feeling" to discuss these orders (18). Williams's original use of the term describes cultural experience in particular, for such experience "is as firm and definite as 'structure' suggests, yet it operates in the most delicate and least tangible parts of our activity" (48). In Williams's formulation, cultural experience is at once concrete while also engaging affective connections at the physical level of human emotions. DeKoven sees the utility of Williams's concept for the 1960s because he implements it to work against the clear distinction between the political and the personal in cultural analysis. The eradication of this distinction, DeKoven notes, is at the core of many transformations taking place during the decade (19). Used in this manner, the "structure of feeling" points to the subjective, emotional, and private experience bound up with dominant institutions and structures that make up the public sphere. This study takes up DeKoven's considerations and allows Williams's term to serve in the organization of the following introduction. My object of study, like DeKoven's, is concerned with the "relation of the social to the personal" that is fundamental to the manner in which the individual, subjective, intimate, and libidinal body is mobilized in a variety of 1960s public discourses, including politics, psychoanalysis, sociology, and philosophy (19). While DeKoven examines these discourses in terms of the emergence of the postmodern during the decade, I do so for their convergence within the field of literature.

Beginning with "structure," this introduction provides an overview of the literary development of realism as both politically engaged and linked to contemporary banalities by tracing the variety of voices on literature's relationship to reality heard throughout the decade. It then turns to the manner in which the term negativity was used specifically for literature. In this discussion, the writings of Konstanz School co-founder Wolfgang Iser are of importance, in particular because of his interests in identifying literary-aesthetic negativity to describe the structuring of the reader's engagement at the level of text as well as context. The second section, "feeling," explores negativity as a politically, socially, and culturally engaged concept that is based nevertheless in corporeal subjectivity and aesthetics. This section begins by elucidating how negativity arises directly from within the discursive context of the 1960s in a variety of ways beyond the structured relationship between literature and the reader. Negativity also surfaces in the discourse of the psychosocial constitution of the individual subject, in the development of socio-political critical practice, and in resistance to historical and cultural expectations. Here, Herbert Marcuse's writings are the primary focus. The final section connects negativity to libidinal, emotional, and affective responses found in the private sphere. It approaches intimacy and the private as the most emotional aspects of this study, but also the most political. Thus, it brings "structure" and "feeling" back together by connecting the political and the personal central to Williams's term through a brief overview of the political mobilization of the private sphere and the family in Germany since the postwar period. The three sections of the introduction set the contextual discursive stage for the literary analysis in the chapters while at the same time providing the correct "feeling tone" for the study as a whole (Ngai, *Ugly* 29).[4]

Structure

Realism and Literary-Political Engagement

As early as 1970, Renate Matthaei summarizes the production of contemporary literature in the 1960s as vehemently reacting to the constraints produced by a backward society, claiming that the decade challenged German literature like no other before it (13).[5] In no other decade was it "so irritierbar, so unsicher und zugleich angereizt, unentwegt effektiv zu sein" (as puzzling, as unsettled yet motivated to be consistently effective; 13). She sees the passionate interest in society as the literary decade's unifying feature, and authority and the perversion of society through repression as the focus of literary-political critique (16). This passionate interest translated into a fundamental debate as to how best to represent reality in literature and to what aesthetic, moral, or political end.[6] In these discussions, realism is defined as displaying an attention to details, a keen awareness for the aspects of reality that are experienced by the senses, and a focus on the banal and immediate experience of the West German context.[7]

Walter Höllerer stresses these features in a 1964 edition of the journal *Akzente*, in which he presents what he sees as the emergence of a new type of realism, based partially on the readings of the Gruppe 47 (Group 47) at Sigtuna, Sweden, in the same year.[8] The journal issue introduces a series of German and international authors whom the editors felt were representative of this new literary direction, Wellershoff among them. Höllerer writes in the introduction that in these new writings, realism manifests itself as a detailed description of everyday surroundings. He asks rhetorically: "Auf welche seltsam-fremdartige Weise erscheint das Detail aus dem Alltag in der Prosa?" (In what strange way does the everyday detail appear in prose? 386). Höllerer answers his own question by claiming that this strange appearance of detail arises in the authors' pairing of language and image to create what he calls a "Bewußtseinslandschaft" (landscape of consciousness) that not only represents facts, but also factual untenability, performability, and impermanence (387). For Höllerer, those authors writing in this new realistic style, which he terms "der '*neue Realismus*'" (the "new realism"), work not with a preconceived and fixed image of reality, but instead one that is indeterminate and in flux (394; emphasis in orig.). They thus mould their experience of reality to fit with their creative imagination. This new realism is more closely linked to fantasy than to mimetic repetition, for that which is represented is not identical to tangible experience, despite its clear origination in that experience. As perception moves away from mimesis and towards aesthetic abstraction it is not distanced from everyday experience. Höllerer explains that fantasy is dictated by familiar banalities, even if these appear in ironic or grotesque form (394). He also places the emphasis on change or transformation taking place in this new realism, and thus he cautions that his musings should not be taken as theory. Realism is a process, for authors use the tools of "taste and see" in order to seek out or close in on reality (398). Therefore, Höllerer views in contemporary literature a tendency to portray the everyday not as a fixed reality, but instead as a changeable and sensory-oriented process.[9]

It would be this concrete description of the everyday that Peter Handke would criticize at the Group 47 meeting at Princeton in 1966.[10] His outburst during a reading by Hermann Piwitt focuses on this new realism, which, as Handke complains in an interview with John Alexander of *The Daily Princetonian*, "has no metaphors, no imagery, no interest ... It is meaningless and idiotic." Handke later elaborates that the problem is that critics see social engagement of the author in the objects described in the texts, and not in the language used for the descriptions. He uses the example of a story that references a computer to deal with the present or a slideshow depicting travels to Poland to overcome the past (182). In Handke's summation, the new direction in realism links present and past issues to familiar everyday objects and devalues language and poetics (181).

A very different attack on realism and the everyday in literature came in that same year, this time in the form of Emil Staiger's acceptance speech for a literary prize given out by the city of Zurich on 17 December 1966. His speech unleashed a debate across Switzerland and Germany, and the scandal was given its own special issue of the journal *Sprache im technischen Zeitalter* (Language in the Technical Age) in 1967. While highly reactionary in content, the speech illustrates well the manner in which literary aesthetics was endowed with moral weight across the board. In it, Staiger laments literature's turn away from humanity through a turn towards the vulgar that is without moral reflection. He warns that the path that begins in an admiration for the unusual continues to the bizarre, and ends ultimately in the criminal. Such a path does not evoke "höheres Dasein" (higher existence) in the literary imagination of the reader (qtd. in Jaeckle 19).[11] Literature's task, according to Staiger, is not to depict reality, but instead, with "Machtvollkommenheit des Schöpferischen" (absolute authority of creation), to create reality as a moral and ethical model for humanity (24).[12]

Of course, Staiger's demand for a return to the beautiful in literature out of consideration for the morals of humanity is overhauled by the dominant discourse on aesthetics in the postwar period that rejected a view of literature that privileged beauty. Theodor Adorno captures the reason behind much of this sentiment of rejection in 1949 in his famous dictum that writing poetry after Auschwitz is barbaric.[13] His contemporaries into the 1950s and 1960s (and beyond) would reduce this truncated quotation to the impossibility of literature and art to exist after the Holocaust. Within the context of the original citation, however, Adorno criticizes cultural production and critique as tainted both by their manipulation and support of National Socialist ideology and by the primary role they played after the war in facilitating a forgetting of the past through cultural consumption. Adorno returns to similar themes throughout his work. At the core of these is his critique of literature and art's utility in communicating moral values through a poetics of beauty.

In 1974, R. Hinton Thomas and Keith Bullivant remark that, for 1960s literature, the beautiful is associated with the "maintenance of power and authority" (77). By extension, the ugly works to dismantle that power and authority. Nowhere is this more explicit than in Christian Enzensberger's *Größerer Versuch über den Schmutz* (*Smut: An Anatomy of Dirt*, 1968), which is a poetic treatise on the social relevance of cleanliness and dirt. The text begins:

> *Sauber ist schön* und gut. Sauber ist hell brav lieb. Sauber ist oben und hier. Schmutzig ist häßlich und anderswo. Sauber ist doch das Wahre, schmutzig ist unten und übel, schmutzig hat keinen Zweck. Sauber hat recht. Schmutzig ist demgegenüber, sauber ist da denn doch, schmutzig ist wie soll man sagen, schmutzig ist irgendwie unklar, schmutzig ist alles in allem, sauber ist wenigstens noch, aber schmutzig das ist also wirklich. (9)

> [*Cleanliness is well* and good. Cleanliness is light proper dear. Cleanliness is above and here. Filthy is ugly and elsewhere. After all, cleanliness is true, filthy is below and evil, filthy has no use. Cleanliness is right. Filthy is in contrast, cleanliness is there then after all, filthy is how do you say, filthy is somehow unclear, filthy is all in all, cleanliness is at least still, but filthy, that is, I mean really.][14]

C. Enzensberger's work characterizes a variety of bodily excretions, the contact between bodies, and interpersonal communication as well as existential reality, all of which are related to concepts of filth. The poles of filth and cleanliness stand in here for the ordering structure of dominant society, which produces fear and violence (48). Personal cleanliness is connected to conformity, totalitarianism, and authority, and filth – or the negative – to personal freedom and rebellion (55).[15] The negatively represented bodies in the texts of Wellershoff, Brinkmann, Elsner, and Rasp are directed by, confronted with, or control such "filth," whether it comes from their own bodies in the form of sweat, excrement, and waste, or the "filthy" is created in the confrontation with repressive society, often in the form of repressive family structures.

The literary-aesthetic representation of the filthy, base, banal, or grotesque elements found in the 1960s everyday therefore take on obvious political dimensions. Thomas and Bullivant suggest that this emphasis came about because literature itself was seen as an institution and as an instrument of authority (65). The germination of literature's political function begins in an understanding of realism as directly connected to the (negatively coded) present and thus deeply rooted in the social concerns of the period. Confirming this in 1976,

Wolfgang Powroslo writes that literature can become critical only if it depicts contemporary society through the use of realism and, in doing so, grows out of the prevailing social situation. Because of this, literature is able to engage with, denounce, and even destruct that social situation through direct and intensive contact (109).

Thus, when Hans Magnus Enzensberger proclaimed literature dead in *Kursbuch 15* (1968) he was in actuality demanding it be stripped of its privileged status and its distance from social praxis corrected, both marks of the literary establishment. He opens his *Kursbuch 15* essay with a tolling of the bells for literature ("Gemeinplätze" 187). With this often-used metaphor, he suggests that change needs to occur in literary production, which since 1945 has increasingly become linked to a normative and non-critical society: "Die Literatur sollte eintreten für das, was in der Bundesrepublik nicht vorhanden war, ein genuin politisches Leben" (Literature was to stand in for that which was missing in the Federal Republic, genuine political life; 190). Calling the history of missing political opposition in West Germany a literary history, he suggests that literature functioned to bolster the establishment. Because of this historical dampening of a critical approach to reality, contemporary literature has no apparent social utility (195). This lack of social and political awareness produced in and through literature can be corrected only if, first, the writers themselves are politicized: "[Die politische Alphabetisierung] hätte selbstverständlich, wie jedes derartige Unternehmen, mit der Alphabetisierung der Alphabetisierer zu beginnen" ([The development of political literacy] must naturally begin, as is the case with all such projects, with the development of this literacy in the litterateurs; 197). The political enlightenment of literary Germany can take place only when both author and reader agree on its necessity, which begins a unified drive towards shared political praxis.

Many authors and critics weighed in on the discussion resulting from H.M. Enzensberger's essay. Brinkmann responded by attacking his assessment, calling *Kursbuch 15* a fad-driven shock of the forty- and fifty-somethings, which affects a younger generation already stuffed to the gills with abstractions, and ends this attack with the question "doch was soll das?" (but what's the point?; "Einübung" 147). The bite in this sentiment makes clear his disdain not only for H.M. Enzensberger's generation, but also for those members of the student movement who jumped onto the political bandwagon. Brinkmann suggests that if literature begins by studying the present, then it would instead become a "Transportmittel der Entdeckung des eigenen Selbst, der Verrücktheit des Schreibers, seiner Konfusitäten, seines eigenen Wirrwarrs" (means of transportation to the discovery of the self, the madness of the writer, his confusions, his own muddle; 151–2). Here, his interest in subjectivity comes through in his belief in literature's ability to function as a tool for the author's and the reader's self-discovery. This self-discovery does not imply a disconnect with the text's contemporary – including political – context, but instead suggests an individual and subjective focus on context instead of a broad-brushed approach. Self-discovery places emphasis on poetic creation and language in the shaping of how context appears in literature, and not merely on the production of content-based politics. Further, it highlights the reading act itself. Wellershoff also criticizes *Kursbuch 15* in the opening of the essay "Fiktion und Praxis" (Fiction and Praxis) contained in the collection *Literatur und Veränderung* (Literature and Change): "Die Literatur steht wieder unter Anklage" (Again literature is being accused; 9). Like Brinkmann, he sees poetic creativity not to be at odds with literature's social function and political validity. Literary production cannot be reduced to a specific model but instead must attend to individual experience. It is here that political praxis in literature meets with and changes the everyday. The subjective and individual attention to literature's social and political potential is located in a redefinition of the reader's experience of the text in conjunction with the reader's recognition of that context as his or her selfsame reality.

Wellershoff's and Brinkmann's interest in the reader suggests the importance not only of literary production for the discussion of this new realism in the 1960s, but also of literary reception. That this reception – whether professional in terms of critical reception or non-professional in the reader's individual experience – is recognized as being indivisible from context is noted by another 1968 literary moment: Leslie Fiedler's era-defining speech at the University of Freiburg, "Close the Gap, Cross the Border."[16] In this lecture, Fiedler attacks not literature but literary criticism and therefore the literary market as perpetuated in and by the academy. He calls for the invention of a new kind of criticism, one that is contextual rather than textual, not concerned with diction or syntax because these "assume that the work of art 'really' exists on the page rather than in a reader's apprehension and response" (230). Fiedler continues to explain that literary criticism should take into account the words as they resonate in the author's imagination and not how they exist on the page. Critics should consider not the author's, but the reader's biography when examining texts, that is, the way the reader reacts to texts should be seen in conjunction with the reader's own life experience. Again, this does not suggest disengagement with politics, but instead an engagement with society through the reader's experience in and beyond text that the reader brings to the text. In this manner, Fiedler's lecture supported many in the overall feeling in West Germany that literature did have a role to play in social and political change (Thomas and Bullivant 163).[17]

This sketch shows that the two strongest tendencies of the literary debates of the 1960s were a keying of realist aesthetics towards the everyday and a focus on social or political problems. The former is based on the reader's recognition of context. The latter is located in the author's political commitment, the text's reflection of socio-political realities, or the reader's experience of text and context. Wellershoff's writings on realism, later termed *Neuer Realismus* (New Realism), sometimes also *Kölner Realismus* (Cologne Realism), channel these two tendencies into individual subjective experience. Moritz Baßler says of New Realism that it contains antirealistic features, primarily because it does not formulate the known in text through established codes. It therefore is able to describe "Konstellationen von Wirklichkeit" (constellations of reality) in a manner that is anti*bürgerlich* or antibourgeois (23). For Wellershoff, the constellations of reality describe subjective experiences of the everyday contained within the private sphere. New Realism envisioned as such is a tool for social change in that it portrays socio-political problems resonating in the private sphere. In his introduction to the 1967 collection of commissioned short stories entitled *Wochenende* (Weekend), Wellershoff explains how he sees the portrayal of the private sphere in literature to be indicative of the reality of 1960s life:

> Die zunehmende Penetranz des Subjektiven, Intimen, die fortschreitende Psychisierung des Lebens, seine Distanz- und Formlosigkeit, seine neurotische Labilität, aber auch seine Beweglichkeit, das sind Sachverhalte, die unter den verflüchtigten allgemeinen Inhalten und den sich auflösenden traditionellen Daseinsstilisierungen neu auftauchen, selbstverständlich auch in der Literatur erscheinen, dort vielleicht am deutlichsten sichtbar werden. (11–12)

> [The growing persistence of the subjective, the intimate, the increasing tendency to subject life to psychological speculation, its lack of distance, its formlessness, its neurotic instability, but also its mobility – these are the issues that resurface as universality of content and traditional modes of stylizing existence fade. Of course, these issues also appear in literature, where they are perhaps most visible.]

Literature is the space for the concentration of social and individual experience Wellershoff sees around him. He considers the private sphere in literature not as separate from social structures but rather as the space in which public desires are repressed and come out as symptoms in the individual. Further, the reader's participation in this literature leads to change – a change in the perspective of and relationship among the author, text, reader, and context.

The novels and short stories examined in the following chapters were chosen not because they fall unequivocally under the rubric of New Realism, but because they germinate within this thinking. Scholars have often debated the viability of using the term New Realism to describe the collection of texts written by those 1960s authors often found under this heading in literary histories. These scholars come regularly to the conclusion that New Realism is not to be seen as an imperative, since the term originates as Wellershoff's working hypothesis.[18] It is true that New Realism is not a literary prescription; Wellershoff himself never identified New Realism as a movement, seeing it to be a term of introduction for a group of authors he edited in the 1960s who displayed similar narratological interests. As a literary term, however, New Realism does capture a set of aesthetic and political considerations at the root of certain texts appearing at a certain time in history. I use the term throughout this study as a blueprint for understanding those issues at stake in this literary moment in West Germany leading up to 1968. With this blueprint in hand, I can better trace the relationship between those literary and public spheres claiming that the private sphere and the family has greater importance in 1960s West Germany.

Texts that correspond to the New Realism blueprint narrate intimate, private, and everyday experiences and show the political significance of these experiences by using the negative workings of the body to guide their narrative structures. In *Visions of Violence*, Langston highlights the emphasis on the body as the precise difference between New Realism and the French *nouveau roman*, which appeared in the previous decade. Langston writes that the Germans, unlike the French, "indulged in 'subjective idealism'" and continues: "This divide served as a powerful differential that eventually enabled one episode of West Germany's postfascist avant-gardes to reclaim realism as a tool for constituting a historical consciousness through the body" (98). This is true for the depiction of violence and the negotiation with the past, as Langston's study shows, but also for constituting a politically engaged private consciousness in the present, as argued here.

Beginning from the assumption that 1960s literary realism reflects or engages with the individual's everyday private experience, these texts portray reality not mimetically, but instead sensually and emotionally, and thus as formulated and experienced by the body. This body includes textual bodies and the reader's body. The literary texts in this study correspond to Wellershoff's New Realist ideas in terms of aesthetics and social engagement. More specifically, they follow a New Realist approach to relating author, text, and reader in a critical manner through the negative representation of the body as it acts within or is constituted by the private sphere recognizable in the 1960s context. That Wellershoff, as editor for Kiepenheuer & Witsch during this decade, was formative also for the literary market helps to determine the interplay between market and consumption. This interplay is explored here in chapter 1 through a further analysis of Wellershoff's three literary roles: editor, essayist, and novelist. Brinkmann's "In der Grube" (In the Ditch), the text at the heart of chapter 2, was commissioned by Wellershoff and published in his 1962 anthology *Ein Tag in der Stadt* (A Day in the City). Wellershoff's second commissioned anthology, *Wochenende*, provided the forum for the 1967 debut of Renate Rasp, whose work is the focus of chapter 4. Gisela Elsner, whose first novel is discussed in chapter 3, is the outsider to this group, for she was never published by Kiepenheuer & Witsch, but instead made her debut at Suhrkamp in H.M. Enzensberger's collection of texts by young authors, *Vorzeichen* (Signals), also published in 1962.[19] For each of these authors I utilize the term realism, although, like many literary historical surveys outlining the period, distinguishing between New Realism (Wellershoff, Brinkmann) and its darker offshoot, Black Realism (Elsner, Rasp).[20] Concerned with the same issues of the private sphere and everyday subjective experience as New Realism, Black Realism displays a marked aesthetic shift towards the grotesque and the satirical in its socio-political engagement.

In keeping with the political and social understanding of 1960s discussions on reality and literature's commitment to the everyday, both realisms make noticeable "die alltäglichen Grausamkeiten und zwischenmenschlichen Deformationen der Gesellschaft" (society's daily cruelties and interpersonal deformations) in the wake of the 1950s economic miracle and the Adenauer and Erhard governments (Ernst 32). Each of the texts examined in this study shows interest in interpersonal concerns as reflecting this deformation of society, particularly as created within the family as a political and social imaginary microcosm of West German society.[21] These texts constitute a private sphere in which the "soziale Kitt brüchig geworden ist und familiäre und andere Bindungen Löcher bekommen haben" (social cement has become fragile and familial and other ties have frayed; Jung 144–5). The texts, therefore, attend to the social and psychological effects of authority, excess, and repression of the 1950s on the private sphere in the 1960s. They critically comment on these effects through the negative workings of the body, intending that the reader be mobilized by the resulting negativity.

Engaging the Reader in Text and Context through Negativity

Negative, negation, and negativity describe, like the above discussion of the filthy or ugly, a fundamentally critical approach to dominant beliefs, mindsets, and structures of society. As discussed by Adorno and Max Horkheimer in the *Dialektik der Aufklärung* (*Dialectic of Enlightenment*) and furthered in Adorno's *Negative Dialektik* (*Negative Dialectics*) as well as in Herbert Marcuse's *One-Dimensional Man*, the negative and negation are essential to critical thinking and therefore to the critical dialectic. In this sense, the negative and negation are oppositional positions, countering dominant thinking, normativity, or passively accepted practices; the negative and negation destabilize the status quo. Negativity is the mode of nonconformist critical thinking, the negative posture that the subject takes towards societal norms. These conceptions find their place within aesthetic frameworks for art and literature, and also with regard to the realities of the political atmosphere of the 1960s. In his post-humously published *Ästhetische Theorie* (*Aesthetic Theory*), Adorno links the negative and negativity to art's relationship to reality. With regard to abstraction, he writes:

> Um inmitten des Äußersten und Finstersten der Realität zu bestehen, müssen die Kunstwerke, die nicht als Zuspruch sich verkaufen wollen, jenem sich gleichmachen. Radikale Kunst heute heißt soviel wie finstere, von der Grundfarbe Schwarz. (65)

> [To survive reality at its most extreme and grim, artworks that do not want to sell themselves as consolation must equate themselves with that reality. Radical art today is synonymous with dark art; its primary color is black. (*Aesthetic* 39)][22]

Art, according to Adorno, should not merely mimetically represent an already dark or black reality, but it also has the potential to radically resist, not affirm, normative expectations that are presented as positive for society. The critical approach to society that is inherent in the authentic artwork is "unvereinbar mit dem, was die Gesellschaft sich selbst dünken muß, um so fortzufahren, wie sie ist" (incompatible with what society must think of itself if it is to continue as it is) for the dominant mentality cannot be freed of its ideologies, "ohne die gesellschaftliche Selbsterhaltung zu schädigen" (350) (without endangering society's self-preservation; *Aesthetic* 236). Although this reading could assume art's utility for social transformation, Adorno cautions that art cannot be linked to "gesellschaftliche Zweckmoment" (375) (social function; *Aesthetic* 253). This, he warns, merely popularizes art, turns it into a commodity, and diminishes its negative critical power. Art must instead take up a position that is critically distant from society in order to mobilize the dialectical engagement with the dominant mentality.

While Adorno's understanding of negation as the root of all art here serves as a starting point for this discussion, it does not capture the full significance of the role of the viewer or reader in the formation of negativity. Wellershoff sees negativity as a literary-aesthetic concept that both engages the reader as well as affects the reader's experience with society. His understanding is outlined in his paper for the volume *Positionen der Negativität* (Positions of Negativity), published in 1975 as the proceedings of the 1972 meeting of the research group *Poetik und Hermeneutik* (Poetics and Hermeneutics). The volume speaks specifically to negativity as a literary or poetic category.[23] In his paper, entitled "Die Verneinung als Kategorie des Werdens" (Negation as a Category of Becoming), Wellershoff uses psychoanalysis, literature, and reception theory to examine the manner in which negation in literature functions to bring subjects into being. He discusses negation in terms of loss, writing that following loss, the subject directs his drives towards those goals approved by culture (225). In this manner, negation is a foundational experience for the subject in the act of becoming, for negation leads to new experiences (225). At the same time, if in its form as loss negation is not compensated, then fear and regression take over, leading to the development of the authoritarian character. Fear destroys the "Fähigkeit, Bestehendes zu kritisieren und Neues zu erfinden, sie engt die Kommunikation ein, verteufelt das Fremde, sie ist erstarrte Negativität" (ability to criticize that which exists and to invent the new, it constricts communication, demonizes the foreign, it is ossified negativity; 225). The way to neutralize this fear and release this stagnant negativity lies in literature as a space for "Probehandeln" (the rehearsal of behaviour),[24] where new forms of behaviour can be practised without consequences (226).

In the same volume, reception theorist Wolfgang Iser engages with Wellershoff's paper and identifies the experience of literary imagination through the reading act as compensation for that negation. In his commentary, Iser expands on Wellershoff's concept of *Probehandeln*, writing that literature must open up possible routes for action ("Negativität" 530). In order for the reader to recognize and understand these routes, Wellershoff writes in his response to Iser, distance – not identification – must be created so that "gefährlichen und verborgenen Möglichkeiten" (dangerous and hidden possibilities) are revealed ("Identifikation" 550). Fictionalization in this sense is an expression of the reader's recognition of those hidden, inner, negative, and repressed possibilities in society open to him or her in the text.

Iser's own writing on negativity and reader-reception elsewhere builds on Wellershoff's understanding of the essential role negativity plays in establishing the relationship between reader and text. Winfried Fluck notes in "The Search for Distance: Negation and Negativity in Wolfgang Iser's Literary Theory," that *Rezeptionsästhetik*, or reader-response theory, founded by Iser and Hans Robert Jauss in Konstanz in 1968, grew out of the countercultural atmosphere of the West German student movement, despite common assumptions of the theory's apolitical characteristics. In the 1960s, the "negating potential" of literature proposed by members of the Frankfurt School was politically mobilized, and Adorno was criticized for not defining negation in aesthetic theory as political enough (Fluck 197). Negation counters not only aesthetic, but also social and political structures, and is therefore seen by the New Left as effective societal criticism (ibid.). For Iser, negativity is a literary device that engages the reader in this critical practice through the process of reception, without losing sight of the aesthetic dimension of literature (Fluck 199).

In *Der Akt des Lesens* (*The Act Of Reading*, 1976), Iser clearly delineates the terms negation and negativity as they apply to literature. Negation he understands as a blank in the text, or that which remains unwritten. Iser sees blank spaces, or negations, to initiate interaction between text and reader, asking the reader to engage critically and imaginatively with a world that is foreign. The reader does so by projecting imaginary experience into the negation, which produces a second unformulated text as a double. Iser calls that text double negativity (*Akt* 348; *Act* 226).[25] Important in this conception of negativity is the reader's inability to identify with the text as a result of his or her creative engagement with its negations. Fluck writes that the text becomes a "training ground for the ability to correct or revise our interpretations of reality" (Fluck 189), a formulation reminiscent of Wellershoff's concept *Probehandeln*.

Iser explains that there are three aspects to negativity. The first is the formal interaction between text positions that occurs in the act of reading. Because negativity is created in the nothingness between text positions, it functions as a symbol for that which is not said or remains unsayable (*Akt* 349; *Act* 226). The second aspect is content-based, and occurs when negations, the blank spaces, of the text underscore or neutralize a specific repertoire of knowledge. This repertoire includes the social or historical context on which the text draws or which the reader brings with him or her to the text (*Akt* 350; *Act* 227). The negation marks "eine Verdeckung am bekannten Wissen" (a deficiency in familiar knowledge) and therefore questions the truth-value of that repertoire, including its norms, characters, and their actions (*Akt* 350; *Act* 227). These aspects point to, but do not articulate, underlying causes for such problems, which in turn create the text's double, negativity:

> Die in Deformation und Mißglücktsein gebotene Welt des Textes weckt zugleich die Aufmerksamkeit für die virtuell gebliebene Verursachung solchen Deformiertseins ... Die Negativität ist damit bedingende Ursache und mögliche Aufhebung der Deformationen zugleich. (351)

> [Failure and deformation are surface signs that indicate a hidden cause, and the presentation of these signs in the literary text alerts the reader as to the unformulated cause ... Negativity is therefore at one and the same time the conditioning cause of the deformations and also their potential remedy. (*Act* 227–8)]

The reader must interact with the hidden cause pointed to by deformity through imagination (*Akt* 352; *Act* 228). The reason behind this deformity is not contained in the text as the mere opposite of negativity. In this way, the reader is called upon not only to engage with representation in text, but also to critically examine his or her real context, representation and context not being identifiable as a congruous match (Iser, "Play" 326). That which is not said gives birth to a critical-dialectical relationship between text and reader, and reader and context. The text remains open because it demands that the reader engage with the production of negativity through the doubling of the text in the reading act.

This brings Iser to the third aspect of negativity. He claims that texts communicate that which is unknown or which is not yet in the world. As Fluck explains: "Constituted by negation (and turned into an aesthetic experience by negativity), the literary text can never be identical with 'the real'" (193). As such, literature is constituted as difference. Through the contents of the text, the reader is offered a way of transcending the world, but at the same time realizes that the world cannot be transcended. Negativity as Iser defines it, then, is not part of a concept of radical resistance, but instead a communicative method that enables the reader's aesthetic experience and self-reflection (Iser, *Akt* 354; *Act* 230).[26] This communicative aspect suggests that negativity and the reading act can also be applied to the performative act and body language.[27] In the negative corporeal realisms of this study, the body acts as that negativity by undoing what is uttered in text (Iser and Budick xvii). These "modes of negativity" are in constant transformation, and do not merely represent the polar opposite of the affirmative (xiii). Negativity demarcates a trifold of relationships between text and reader, between the text and its contextual reality, and between the reader and his or her experiential reality, all of which are in process.

If negativity is in constant transformation, this quality also affects the reader's experience with the extraliterary context as repertoire – that is, the text and reader's shared social, historical, or political context. Iser's colleague Jauss, in particular, criticized Adorno for seeing negativity at the root of all art and not dependent on historical flux and change (Fluck 187). In a 1967 acceptance speech to his appointment at the University of Konstanz, Jauss claims that the functional relationship between literature and society occurs when the reader's experience enters his or her expectations for their "*Lebenspraxis*" (life practice) and thus impacts his or her social behaviour (Jauss 63; emphasis in orig.). In this manner, the reader's experience with negativity through the reading act not only relies on the text's critical reference to its context, but also has a direct effect on the reader's own ability for imaginative world making. Both aspects – context and ability – are not fixed, but instead are fluid.

This discussion of "structure" has focused on the manner in which literature affects and is affected by social, historical, and political context as well as the use of negativity as a literary-aesthetic concept related to the reader's critical, but also imaginative, faculties. However, the understanding of negativity as mobilizing the critical dialectic is not reserved only for literary or creative work. Negativity, which is essential to the reader's critical reception of both text and context, is also a sensual, libidinal, and emotional position. For this reason, the discussion of literary content and aesthetics as related structures of 1960s socio-political thought is connected also to corporeal subjectivity and "social aesthetics" (Highmore, "Bitter") as they relate to the dominant feeling tone of the 1960s. This feeling remains critically negative.

Feeling: Negativity, Corporeal Subjectivity, and Social Aesthetics

In the "structure of feeling" of the 1960s, "feeling" highlights the experiential aspect of the decade, the personal on which the social is dependent (DeKoven 19). Herbert Marcuse's postwar writings, the majority of which were crafted and first published in English in the United States, exemplify and extrapolate upon this dependence. This Frankfurt School outsider is a theoretical informant for this study in two ways. He theoretically informs the cultural contextual pool from within which the examined texts are generated in that his writings were widely read during the 1960s.[28] Most important, however, he theoretically informs the approach to that context as it emerges from within literature through his useful connection among negativity and corporeality, subjectivity, and aesthetics. Prolific Marcuse scholar and editor Douglas Kellner writes that "Marcuse offers a notion of a corporeal subjectivity with an emphasis on its aesthetic and erotic dimensions" that includes also a "critique of the tendencies toward conformity and normalization" as well as a "notion of transformation and emancipation" ("Quest" 96). Corporeal subjectivity is based for the most part in the senses and the manner in which the senses are involved in constituting experience, including both aesthetic and libidinal experience. Moreover, corporeal subjectivity is linked to freedom and socio-political transformation as well as recognition of negativity. These aspects make Marcuse foundational for a discussion of New and Black Realism as using engaged literary aesthetics that locates narrative subjectivity in the body.

At the core of Marcuse's writing of this period is a belief in the ability of non-repressive sublimation to free society. In *Eros and Civilization* (1955), a text that is formative for his later 1960s writings, Marcuse undertakes a philosophical rereading of Sigmund Freud's analysis of the integral connection between Eros (the life drive, synonymous with libidinality and sensuality) and Thanatos (the death drive, which guides aggressive and destructive instincts). Marcuse postulates that culture and civilization are founded on a false understanding of progress, which is facilitated by repression and lack of freedom. He explains further that pleasure is seen as negative by a repressive society: "In a repressive order, which enforces the equation between normal, socially useful, and good, the manifestations of pleasure for its own sake must appear as *fleurs du mal*" (50). Thus, all libidinal relationships are threatening and channelled away from society into the private sphere (50). This is what Marcuse calls repressive sublimation, and he notes that it occurs collectively, as more and more institutions in contemporary society penetrate and replace the family (97). He also explains how the repressive sublimation of sexuality into private relations transforms the realm of the family into the space where desire is trained and managed, which has an effect on the body as a libidinal instrument for satisfaction (200).

Marcuse believes that Eros must take on a more primary role in all aspects of society if the balance between Eros and Thanatos is to be reinstated: "The notion of a non-repressive instinctual order must first be tested on the most 'disorderly' of all instincts – namely, sexuality" (199). Were the body resexualized, he claims, libidinal energy would unseat institutions because it would enter public spheres from which it was repressed. This would allow the body to change the structure of the private sphere, for it would "lead to a disintegration of the institutions in which the private interpersonal relations have been organized, particularly the monogamic and patriarchal family" (201). In his formulation, the liberation of Eros functions as critical negation of repressive reality (95). Moreover, Marcuse notes that in this negation, the "roots of the aesthetic experience reemerge" in existence (223). Elsewhere, in an essay entitled "Cultural Revolution," he explains that aesthetics is to be understood "in the dual meaning of pertaining to the senses and pertaining to art" (132). In a repressive society, Marcuse sees the "erotic-aesthetic drive" to be sublimated into a traditional concept of culture, which separates the two by channelling the erotic (Eros) into sexuality and the aesthetic into art (133); non-repressive sublimation through the reinstatement of Eros in the public sphere would correct that split. Revolutionary thinking, according to Marcuse, must harness both Eros and aesthetics in terms of the sensuality and corporeality contained in the two terms: "The sensuous need for revolution is the expression of a sensitivity which sees, hears, smells, tastes, and touches the injustice, exploitation, ugliness, the cheat and the stupidity of established society – not only as one's own, but also as the other's doing and suffering" (135). That he believes in the senses and their libidinal counterpart to make this revolutionary change possible suggests that, for Marcuse, aesthetics is highly political. This is substantiated in his 1966 "political preface" to *Eros and Civilization*: "Today the fight for life, the fight for Eros, is the *political* fight" (xxv; emphasis in the orig.).

Marcuse expands on the above approach to Eros and aesthetics in *One-Dimensional Man* (1964). In this later text, he uses the relationship between the two to apply to freedom from conformity through negativity that would transform the one-dimensional society focused solely on progress. Kellner explains in his reading of the text that, in such a society, all forms of critical thinking are eradicated through consumption and a perception of progress, which leads to control in all social institutions, such as workplaces, schools, the state, and the family ("Introduction" 5). Marcuse claims in *One-Dimensional Man* that this progress unseats opposition and criticism because of its increasing ability to only seemingly satisfy the needs of its individuals. The loss of the dimension of critical thinking, or the "power of negative thinking," is the "ideological counterpart to the very material process in which advanced industrial society silences and reconciles the opposition" (11). This is the one-dimensionality in the one-dimensional society: the missing critical dialectic. Marcuse advocates for the pairing of critical reason with Eros, which he sees as "two modes of negation," to reinvigorate two-dimensional thought, or negativity (127). However, like Adorno before him (and Wellershoff and Iser after him), Marcuse makes clear that negativity cannot be understood as the flip side of affirmation; negation cannot be used as a positive remedy (253).

Marcuse's conception of negativity and critical thinking is deeply rooted in individual freedom, which is founded on subjectivity, or "being a self" ("Cultural" 156). However, if the negative dialectic, or critical thinking, can be mobilized in the subject by aesthetic experience and if aesthetic experience is clearly tied to the senses and therefore to Eros, then this mobilization of subjectivity has a specific effect on the private. DeKoven notes that in *One-Dimensional Man*, subjectivity, as the "primary agent of social change," is located in inner freedom that designates a "private space" to be configured towards "oppositional consciousness, out of which a new society could be built" (33, 37). This is because the one-dimensional society affects the relationship between the private individual and social processes by inserting the social into individual concerns (*One* 8). Marcuse questions the manner in which a society that cannot protect the privacy of the individual can stake claim to being a free society: "Massive socialization begins at home and arrests the development of consciousness and conscience" (245). For this reason, he sees protest to be both ineffective and dangerous because it pretends that democratic sovereignty still exists in a one-dimensional society (256). Despite all social and political claims that the private sphere is a locus of individual agency, it is not just ineffectual in developing democratic individuals; it prevents that development.

This desolate image of social repression can be countered. Marcuse finds hope for change in groups that are marginalized:

Underneath the conservative popular base is the substratum of the outcasts and outsiders, the exploited and persecuted of other races and other colors, the unemployed and the unemployable. They exist outside the democratic process; their life is the most immediate and the most real need for ending intolerable conditions and institutions. Thus their opposition is revolutionary even if their consciousness is not. (256)

His belief in the socially marginalized to effect revolutionary change shows Marcuse's clear use-value for the variety of bourgeoning movements across the Western world in the 1960s, specifically for racial equality and gay rights. Despite the hope that bubbles under their surface, these closing words should not be read as positivistic, but rather as marked by pessimistic idealism. Illustrating this, *One-Dimensional Man* ends on a highly negative, ambivalent note: "The critical theory of society possesses no concepts which could bridge the gap between the present and its future; holding no promise and showing no success, it remains negative. Thus it wants to remain loyal to those who, without hope, have given and give their life to the Great Refusal" (257). The Great Refusal does not provide answers, but instead is a positioning of the subject with respect to the experience of repressive reality. Kellner notes of the Great Refusal that it means rebellion towards existing oppression, "artistic revolt" that envisions an alternative culture, and "oppositional thought that rejects the dominant modes of thinking and behavior" ("Introduction" 10). This refusal, while ambivalent, is not disengagement, but instead political commitment at the level of the sensual subject. As Kellner explains elsewhere, Marcuse sees only "an emancipation of the senses and a new sensibility" to bring about social change ("Quest" 90). Part of this new sensibility, Kellner continues, is Marcuse's development of reason that is "bodily, erotic, and political" (91). What Marcuse calls new sensibility is a political force and factor that combines critical theory with concepts of a free society and that valorizes life instincts such as love, community, and Eros.

This development of a new sensibility can happen only through aesthetic education, which, moreover, must go hand in hand with a reconfigured conception of moral and political categories. Marcuse writes in *An Essay on Liberation* (1969) that contemporary Western society must forge a new "Reality Principle: under which a new sensibility and a desublimated scientific intelligence would combine in the creation of an *aesthetic ethos*" (24; emphasis in orig.). Instead of "aesthetic ethos," contemporary cultural theorist Ben Highmore uses the umbrella term "social aesthetics" to describe the "cross-modal investigation" of emotions, passion, major and minor affects, forms of perception, the senses, and the body ("Bitter" 120–1). The term describes those aspects key to the original meaning of aesthetics and connects "perception, sensorial culture, [and] affective intensities" with their social and cultural contexts (128).

Using an anthropology of cleanliness as illustration, Highmore writes: "Ethos (or social aesthetics) ... links the perception of cleanliness and dirt, or purity and impurity, to orchestrations of shame and comfort, to resonances of other sensual worlds, and on to the social ontology of bodies" (129). Interchangeable with Marcuse's term "aesthetic ethos," social aesthetics describes the social utility of and cultural context behind the sensual experience.

In Marcuse's writings from the 1950s to the end of the 1960s, he merges the possibilities for political and social transformation with the development of critical and negative subjectivity. Further, the senses and corporeality dominate Marcuse's understanding of subjectivity, freedom from repression, as well as his notion of aesthetics. Negativity as it is used in the following chapters is a socially critical and aesthetic concept, aesthetics in these literary texts working both as the unification of the senses – or the physical, emotional, and visceral experience of objects and others – and as the narrative-poetic production of literature. As seen in Marcuse's Great Refusal, the sensual experience inciting socio-political change as it appears in literature can also be negatively ambivalent. In *Ugly Feelings*, Sianne Ngai examines the "politically ambiguous work" of an "aesthetics of negative emotions" in a variety of cultural products (1). Emotional negativity is critically productive even as it is ambiguous, for it can be "thought of as a mediation between the aesthetic and the political in a nontrivial way," because it illuminates how "sociohistorical and ideological dilemmas, in particular, produce formal or representational ones" (3, 12). In keeping with Marcuse's understanding of corporeal subjectivity and taking feeling-cues from Ngai's belief in the political utility of negative emotions, this study pursues the politics of ambivalence of negative corporeality in New and Black Realism. It does so through an interrogation of their aesthetic ethos, or their social aesthetics. The social aspect of negative corporeal aesthetics comes from the context, or the repertoire (Iser), of both text and reader, but also from within the text itself. This context is built around the intimate subject constituted in the private sphere. Moreover, negativity is linked to two aspects of corporeality: to the physical or external experience of the body and to the body's senses and emotions or its inner experience. Both of these experiences reflect the cultural context of the 1960s and together create the social aesthetics of the texts with critical effects. That cultural context is comprised of the intimate, subjective, and familial experiences in the private sphere.

Structure of Feeling: The Politics of the Private Sphere as West German Intimate Family History

The symbolic year 1968 denotes the moment when, to utilize the often-quoted battle cry, the private became political. Because of its origins in protest and radicalism, and most particularly in second-wave feminism and the gay rights movement, the battle cry could be seen as a purely countercultural concept. Quite the contrary, however, many all along the political spectrum led discussions on just how the private was political: those wielding hegemonic power to those at the intellectual and cultural margins of hegemony. The family was considered the "Inbegriff des Privaten" (epitome of the private), the private space for the development of intimate subjects, and as such a socio-political institution (Rölli-Alkemper 22).[29] Jaimey Fisher writes in *Disciplining Germany*, that the "family and the social norms circulating not only around it but also through it form the foundations of bourgeois society" (41). These norms are constituted in a variety of spaces, including the political, the social, and the domestic. The following chapters formulate a literary history of the private sphere as a further space in which cultural-political conceptions of the development of intimate subjects emerge.

The "intimate" and the "private" are two different, yet highly interconnected concepts. These two terms are essential to understanding the relationship between the discussion of corporeal subjectivity (intimacy) and social aesthetics (the private). The intimate is a category of the subject and of psychoanalysis, whereas the private is a social, or asocial, category. Julia Kristeva defines the intimate in *Intimate Revolt* to be essential to revolt, for "the intimate is where we end up when we question apparent meanings and values" (43). Defining the term using the Latin *intimus*, or "the most interior," she notes that it is often defined dialectically in opposition to "social or political action" (43–4). Lauren Berlant brings these two spheres together in her own analysis of the term in the edited volume *Intimacy*. She notes of the intimate that it is private as well as shared. Although it describes inner "zones of familiarity and comfort ... the inwardness of the intimate is met by a corresponding publicness" ("Intimacy" 1). Intimate lives both "absorb and repel the rhetorics, laws, ethics, and ideologies of the hegemonic public sphere, but also personalize the effects of the public sphere and reproduce a fantasy that private life is the real in contrast to collective life" (2–3). Berlant sees the push and pull of discourses from the outside to work on configurations of intimacy within but also on private spaces. Both the rejection and consumption of such discourses feed into the constitution of the intimate subject. In *Ordinary Lives*, Highmore suggests the term "public intimacy" to describe the material and theoretical collapse of the separation between public and private (16). In a similar manner, Berlant writes in *Cruel Optimism* that the public is always made up of "affect worlds" that bind people to them through "affective projections of a constantly negotiated common interestedness," which she calls an "intimate public" (226). This interconnectedness between intimacy and public has consequences for a politically engaged literature that uses as its narrative authority a subject constituted through intimate experiences. Kristeva writes that she sees "the intimate as representation of the subject on the way to constitution and revolt," commenting that the imaginary provides us with the "most immediate, most subtle, but also most dangerous access to the intimate" (*Intimate* 63). She locates the deployment of intimacy in literature. In the literary texts examined here, the appearance of a sense-based and critical corporeal subjectivity as understood by Marcuse is created through intimacy.

Whereas the intimate is a concept that is rooted in subjectivity and is deployed in the imaginary that reverberates publicly, the private requires a concretely demarcated public against which to be defined (Warner). German sociologist Wolfgang Sofsky defines privacy in *Verteidigung des Privaten* (*Privacy: A Manifesto*), as "Festung des einzelnen. Sie ist ein machtfreies Terrain, das einzig der Regie des Individuums unterliegt" (18) (the individual's fortress. It is an area free of domination, the only one under the individual's control; *Privacy* 12).[30] The word *Festung* (fortress) displays the manner in which Sofsky sees the definition of the private sphere to be dependant upon the protection of the individual. The walls of the fortress are simultaneously built and torn down by the public sphere: "Die Grenzen des Privaten sind die Grenzen des Politischen" (23) (The limits of the private are the limits of the political; *Privacy* 17). He sees the defence of privacy from within to be the only tool the individual has to counter universal power (23; *Privacy* 17). Both the home and the body belong to the private sphere. Whereas the intimate offers us access to the literary development of a corporeally based subject, the private comprises the social sphere that is politically engaged by these texts. This social sphere is the family, whether present or absent. The two concepts are ultimately tied to one another, for intimacy is constituted within the private, and the private is constructed as a realm – whether as home or body – for intimacy.

In 1968, the government, made up of a coalition formed in 1966 (and ending in 1969) between the CDU/CSU (Christian Democratic Union/Christian Social Union) and the SPD (Social Democratic Party), published the first federally commissioned report on the state of families, entitled *Die Familie heute* (The Family Today) and prepared by Max Wingen for the family ministry. The preamble to the report states that its goal is for the federal government to inform the public about the "*Struktur und die Lebensbedingungen der Familie*" (family's structure and conditions of life) in a society under transformation (2; emphasis in orig.). The report closes with the statement that family politics is not only relevant to government, but also of import to various organizations belonging to the public sphere (32). The family-political genealogy of the West German politicized private sphere begins, however, much earlier than 1968.

The conception that the family as an institution is decisive for the formation of political subjects is a postwar German continuity.[31] Beginning at the end of the war and well into the late 1960s, public figures, sociologists, and psychologists alike defined the family in terms of its political worth; each saw in the solidification, or conversely, eradication, of the normative West German family the site upon which the reconfiguration of national identity could take place.

A large number of publications produced on both sides of the political spectrum, that is, by both governmental agencies as well as countercultural intellectuals, articulated the family as a site for the re-establishment of norms in the postwar period and into the 1950s, and as a hotbed of repression a decade later. In all cases, the attempt to define the family in conjunction with larger social institutions and structures was fraught with ideology. The conservative Catholics argued for a stronger family structure in order to strengthen the country, while the New Left and liberals suggested that it was exactly this repressive structure of the family that came from or resulted in a repressive society.

The politicized focus on the family begins in the immediate postwar period when the *Frauenüberschuss* (excess of women) and *Männermangel* (scarcity of men) as a result of internment, imprisonment, battles, and bombings led to a concern for misaligned gender normativity in the family.[32] The interest is in a return to normativity in familial configurations that was often related to a perception of reverting to existing structures and morals in pre-fascist Germany and was therefore seen as a return to values that were deemed truly German.[33] Women's central status in the period of rebuilding raised fears surrounding the social, economic, and moral fates of those left as single mothers, which also had particular effects on children; women and children were key targets of moral discourse (Moeller 32).[34] Robert G. Moeller compellingly argues in *Protecting Motherhood* that the postwar family became a national body through a politicized discourse on the woman's role in private life: "[West Germans] renounced a past in which they had sought political stability in *Lebensraum* (living space) in Eastern Europe; they replaced it with a search for security in the *Lebensraum* of the family, where a democratic West Germany would flourish. At the center of this construction was the German woman" (5). Those policy decisions linking the family to postwar security of the nation had the effect of narrowly defining the rights of West German women. Nick Thomas asserts in *Protest Movements in 1960s West Germany*: "Defending paternalism benignly ensured the protection of traditional female roles, as well as encouraging the population growth deemed necessary to defend the West German 'national spirit' from communist hordes" (223). In positioning women in their traditional role as mothers within the normative family, the West German government intended to ensure population growth inspiring national stability, both at the political and identity-political levels. Or as Moeller writes, women were seen as "best serving Germany by best serving German families" (141). This national approach remained in effect throughout the 1950s and well into the 1960s, despite the reforms of family law. Of course children, too, were surrounded by prohibitions and susceptible to compulsory morality. In his examination of the trajectory of youth crises in the immediate postwar period, Fisher notes, "youth crises are deployed in order to redraw old boundaries or explore new ones" (90). Representations of youth also show the manner in which Germany attempted to come to terms with challenges of the present, one of these challenges being the rebuilding of the family.

On the other hand, the worrisome crisis of manhood also contributed to discourse on the family as fathers and husbands returned home from imprisonment. Fisher argues that the representation of the *Heimkehrer* (soldiers returning home) in films of the time placed the "weakening of traditional social relations" on display (179). The weakened family as well as the "society and nation that the family underpins" is shown in the weakened body of the man (179). Writing in the postwar period, psychologist Joachim Bodamer illustrates this sentiment in *Der Mann von Heute: Seine Gestalt und Psychologie* (Today's Man: His Figure and Psychology, 1956). He claims that the male ideal of physical and emotional hardiness is lost through man's experience in concentration camps, war, and prison. The man returning to his home is either too authoritative with his family to compensate for this lost manhood or is unable to be authoritative in his castrated feminization. Historian Frank Biess suggests that this problem of masculinity is reflected in the high number of documented sexually pathological behaviours of returning prisoners of war and their feminization in public discourse. This in turn formed how the men were accepted into postwar society: "It transplanted the primary locus of their readjustment to a civilian environment from society at large into the families" (71). He continues to suggest that the remasculinization of West Germany, or rather the recasting of German manhood, reflected a broader recasting of society as a familial unit (73).

In reaction to the messy state of sexual morals, marriage, and children in the wake of the NSDAP (National Socialist German Workers Party) policies towards sexuality, childbearing, and youth mobilization and to postwar trauma of German motherhood and manhood respectively, the Christian conservatives fought for the institution of policies that were later seen as socially repressive.[35] Through Franz-Josef Wuermeling, who held the newly formed post of family minister from 1953 to 1962, the ruling CDU/CSU party defined the relationship between family and state. In a 1954 essay, Wuermeling explains his understanding of this relationship as symbiotic:

Wenn die Aufgaben der Familie mißachtet und ihre Ordnungsgesetze verkannt werden, kann die Familie ihre unentbehrliche Funktion im Dienste am Menschen und an der Gesellschaft nicht mehr erfüllen. Dann verliert der einzelne Mensch seinen natürlichen Halt, und es zeigen sich bald Krankheitserscheinungen an den Lebenswurzeln von Staat und Gesellschaft. Die Familie ist eben lebensnotwendig auch für Staat und Gesellschaft. ("Aufgabe" 11)

[If the tasks of the family are neglected and its regulatory laws misunderstood, the family can no longer fulfil its indispensable function in the service of humanity and society. Consequently, individuals lose their natural support system and soon the life-giving roots of state and society show signs of disease. After all, family is vital, also for state and society.]

When the family is shaken in its moral foundations, society feels the results. By using the metaphor of disease, Wuermeling suggests an integral relationship between family and state as that of two interdependent organisms. For this reason, the cultivation of morals and ethics in the family through government support carries national weight. The family is the basic unit (*Urzelle*, literally primordial cell) of the state. Accordingly, Wuermeling identifies only the normative family as deserving of state protection and support (Moeller 126).[36] He writes in another essay entitled "Zur inneren Ordnung der Familie" (On the Inner Order of the Family), also from 1954, that the family is a community made up of husband, wife, and children and notes that the marriage between a man and a women has as its primary purpose the creation of life and the rearing of children (15).[37] The role of the family as such is described in more detail in "Die Aufgabe der Familie" (The Purpose of the Family) and is trifold: the family is the "unersetzliche Schule für Charakter und Leben" (irreplaceable school for character and life), the "Träger und Übermittler unserer Kultur" (bearer and transmitter of our culture), and the "natürliche Lebensquell des Volkes" (natural source of life for the people; 11–13). His primary understanding of culture and character lies in his patriarchal-ethical belief in Christian faith, or even the Catholic religion, as the foundation of the family and thus national identity.

Because of the interdependence of society and the family, the family must be protected from the dangers of society, as Wuermeling elucidates in a 1960 essay entitled "Der besondere Schutz der Familie durch die Staatliche Ordnung" (Special Protection of the Family through the State). The concept of protection is particularly important, according to Wuermeling, as the family maintains a hierarchy of values between the public sphere and the individual (86). Through nurturing the subject within this sphere, the family helps to regulate the social order. For this reason, it must be protected from external disturbances and offered "*Freiheitsraum*" (freedom of space) in order to allow it to develop in the proper manner (87; emphasis in orig.). Wuermeling claims that aside from financial support, the ethical and moral protection for the family is the most important type of protection. The state must be willing to erect a "Schutzwall" (protective barrier) around the family (88). In a later speech from 1963 entitled "Die Kinder von heute sind die Ernährer von morgen" (The Children of Today Are the Providers of Tomorrow), he speaks even more specifically of family politics as geared towards protecting the "Lebensraum der Familie in der Industriegesellschaft ..., um des einzelnen Menschen und um des Staates und der Gesellschaft willen" (family's living space in the industrial society ... for the sake of the individual, the state, and society; 3). Here, as in the other essays, Wuermeling deepens his notion of the family as formative for the character of individuals and for their role in the future German nation.

While these essays all clearly outline the social and ethical value of the family for the family ministry and its policies, Wuermeling's conception of the relationship between family and national stability becomes explicitly political in a 1961 speech. In it, he claims the nation becomes weakened,

> wenn unsere Familien innerlich nicht in Ordnung sind, wenn nicht die rechte Ethik und das Verantwortungsbewußtsein vor Gott die Lebensgestaltung unserer Familien bestimmen ... Die sittlichen Kräfte gesunder Familien sind und bleiben die beste Sicherung gegen die drohende Gefahr aus dem Osten. ("Acht" 170)

> [if our families lack inner order, if our families' way of life is not controlled by the correct ethics and a sense of responsibility towards God ... The moral strength of healthy families is and will remain the best protection against the looming danger from the East.]

The moral strength of the family is intended as a political shield for the nation, here against communism. In this manner, family politics function as the Adenauer era's antifascist and anticommunist platform. In 1963, Wuermeling expands the family's political reach to Europe. He describes the government's goal of maintaining the family as a "Hort und Schutzraum sittlicher Ordnung, menschlicher Freiheit und Selbstverantwortung" (refuge and shelter of moral order, human freedom, and self-determination) through economic security as essential not only to family politics, but also "um der Freiheit Europas willen" (for the sake of Europe's freedom; "Kinder" 6; emphasis in orig.). Such families become a precious inner "Bollwerk" (bulwark) against eastern threats (6).

The relationship between the family, state, and religion in Wuermeling's ideology sets up a paternalistic hierarchy that directly mirrors society, for the family is the basic unit of society ("Aufgabe" 14). It is this type of moralization that calls forth a negative response in countercultural and New Left discourse on the private sphere and the family. When the 1960s anti-authoritarian movement criticized the government's policies, they targeted the family in particular as the stronghold of the perceived perpetuation of National Socialist values and repression. But even here, the family remained a place of ethical and national import. Writing retrospectively about the 1968 movement in 1988, Reimut Reiche identified the family and "Triebverzicht" (renunciation of drive) as the "Medium und Agentur der Repression" (medium and agency of repression; "Sexuelle" 52). The New Left and the members of the student movement considered the family as an authoritarian structure that perpetuated the repression of sexuality. This, in turn, led to the creation of a society of Germans willing to bend to authority, as is clear in Reiche's own writings on the subject during the decade.[38] New Left discussions on the family were guided not only by the questioning of normative expectations and freeing of sexual repression, but also by politicizing the child and childrearing. Almost in agreement with Wuermeling that the family is the basic unit of the state, left-leaning sociologist Dietrich Haensch sees the family not as a source of control, but as a force of change. He writes in *Repressive Familienpolitik* (Repressive Family Politics, 1969): "Insofern ist die Familie eine repressive Institution; eine Politik, die diese Familie stärken und fördern soll, ist eine repressive Politik" (Insofar as the family is a repressive institution, a politics intended to strengthen and support this family is a repressive politics; 7). He places the blame for these politics on the repression of sexuality, which replaces the individual's tendency towards rebellion with general passivity and apathy. He strongly criticizes Wuermeling's family politics and his use of the family as political propaganda. Haensch's own demand for change in the sexual morals of the family to transform the politics of the state, however, has a similar, albeit socially liberalized, intention. Haensch, like Wuermeling, implies that the family is steeped in a political agenda, but he focuses on its repressive characteristics and how these affect or create the repression also seen in society. A loosening of sexual mores in the family would, according to Haensch, create a freer society. In contrast, the public sanctioning of state-induced authority in the private sphere would, through the raising of passive children, eventually lead to a resurgence of fascism in Germany.

What this overview of the political landscape of post–Second World War discourse on the family displays is the high political and moral value placed on the private sphere.[39] The individual chapters that follow further illustrate how the psychosocial context is part of the historical trajectory of the politicized West German private sphere, which includes discourse ranging from ideological public policy and counter-revolutionary writing to the psychological and pedagogical. In these chapters, the private sphere is understood as primarily familial, even if the family proper is absent. Because the private sphere is the place for the development of intimate subjects, it also includes physical and emotional workings of the body and the psyche. The chapters thus trace the manner that the history of the private sphere as a national space for the development of intimate subjects in the second half of the twentieth century resonates negatively within literary corporeal realisms.

Of course, this history is not disengaged from the history of Germany's National Socialist past. Langston writes that past studies on the body in postwar Germany "concur that the body in postfascist culture occupies a decisive role in mediating and framing the historical experience of fascism, an experience otherwise inaccessible to cognition alone" (*Visions* 17). Langston examines the manner in which fractured bodies in the texts of this period are "flagged as the loci of real historical violence" (20). The following examinations of negative corporeality constituted in the private sphere and politically mobilized through realism's relationship to the reader joins this analysis of the appearance of the past and its resonances in the present to the negatively represented body. The focus shall be on how this legacy was perceived to be at work in the private sphere in the form of the individual results of repression and violence on corporeal subjectivity.

The Chapters

The following does not take a chronological approach to the presentation of materials. Instead of seeing the discourses as responses and reactions that build upon one another, the chapters present discourses from the 1950s and into the early 1970s as an atmosphere of thinking – social-, political-, and psycho-revolutionary – out of which the literary texts are born and within which they are read. The texts found in the literary corpus making up the bulk of this study are joined not only in their literary-historical collection under the broad umbrella of 1960s New and Black Realism, what I term negative corporeal realisms. More specifically, they share the use of corporeal subjectivity and a politically charged understanding of social aesthetics to guide the content and the form of their narratives. Each text tackles the negative development of a corporeally based subjectivity in the private sphere, this private sphere being readable for the social, political, and psychological contextual discourses. Moreover, whether explicitly or implicitly, the texts communicate with the reader those possibilities for socio-political engagement in the private sphere of the reader's contemporaneous reality.

Chapter 1 considers Wellershoff's theoretical and literary texts, focusing on his interest in using negative corporeal realism to incite the reader to political and social action. It outlines Wellershoff's New Realist theories, emphasizing his investment in the reader, the politics of the private sphere, and the function of the body in narrative, and then turns to an analysis of individual neurosis in his novel *Ein schöner Tag* (A Beautiful Day, 1966). Chapter 2 analyses Brinkmann's characterization of the effects of societal repression on the body in the story "In der Grube" (In the Ditch, 1962) and the collection *Die Umarmung* (The Embrace, 1965). It focuses on the poetic-subjective experience of post-adolescent men as they grapple with memories of growing up, their disgust towards the changing sexual body, and the repressively formative private sphere. The chapter also examines Brinkmann's thoughts on the textual-aesthetic possibilities of freeing the reader from the repressive constraints of reality. Chapter 3 shifts to the Black Realism of Elsner's debut novel *Die Riesenzwerge* (The Giant Dwarfs, 1964). Differently from her contemporaries, Elsner mobilizes corporeally based visual modes in order to criticize middle-class institutions, primarily those related to the economic-miracle family. The chapter concludes by examining how the reader's uneasy vertigo brought on by this visual world insists on the reader's critical recognition of the parasitic nature of intimate, familial, and private institutions. An examination of Rasp's parabolic novel *Ein ungeratener Sohn* (*A Family Failure*, 1967) and the authoritative family constitutes the final and most political chapter of the book. The novel will be read in chapter 4 for the manner in which it satirically prefigures late 1960s discourse on anti-authoritarian childrearing and the political economy of the child's body. The chapter suggests that the negative language of the satirical parable challenges the reader to immediate political action in the private sphere. This final chapter ascertains the literary reach of family politics for the construction of postwar West German identity on the cusp of 1968.

Chapter One

Trauma, Neurosis, and the Postwar Family: Dieter Wellershoff's Politics of Reading

The writer Dieter Wellershoff was, in his function as the editor for publishing house Kiepenheuer & Witsch from 1959 to 1981 and as founder of New Realism, also always a professional reader.[1] Conversely, his work as editor, as professional reader, inspired him to write on the subject of writing, a move that occurred parallel to his own literary production. In the 1960s alone, Wellershoff published numerous essays on literature, edited two volumes of short stories by new German authors, and wrote two novels, all the while introducing new authors to the West German reading public. Bernd Happekotte notes in his study of Wellershoff that the rare unification of publisher, editor, theoretician, and novelist predetermines the reception of his literary work (31). Critics see the theoretical works as "verderbliche Einmischung" (corruptive interference) in his literary production or his literary activity as transgressing "theoretischer Enthaltsamkeit" (theoretical austerity; Happekotte 31). This simplification does Wellershoff's work as editor, his essays, and his novels no justice. Instead, the theoretical and literary texts should be read for the manner in which they archive Wellershoff's reading act.

Wellershoff's diverse body of work is united by a firm commitment to the cultural context from which it springs. The texts produced as a result of these roles display clear traces of 1960s social concerns in the form of allusions, paraphrases, or citations of non-literary 1960s discourses, particularly psychological texts on repression that were popular to the New Left and that were conceived or read as a direct reaction to the political and social conservatism of the 1950s. Most specifically, private experiences, in keeping with the developing intellectual and political jargon of the time, have a very public dimension also when it comes to literary production, the literary market, and literary theory. Wellershoff's focus on personal, intimate, and private experiences in his novels finds resonance in his theoretical essays, where he elucidates on his literary-theoretical model for a New Realism and explains how the private sphere in the literary text is a space for political change. The model, moreover, serves as a conduit to understanding the public-private discussions found in the cultural context. And conversely, following the traces of contextual discourse on the private sphere in his theoretical essays leads to a social understanding of the private as formulated in his novels. But because Wellershoff is very concretely interested in new aesthetic models for addressing these concerns, these traces also craft his corporeal-narratological approach to the aesthetics of his novels. In Wellerhoff's first novel, *Ein schöner Tag* (A Beautiful Day, 1966), the bodies' display of neurotic and pathological symptoms as a result of social repression resonating in the familial structure creates a neurotic narrative. The symptoms and resulting negative corporeal aesthetics point readers to discourses of the 1960s cultural context found also in Wellershoff's literary essays. Ultimately, Wellershoff's corporeally based aesthetic negativity has utopian political intent.

Dieter Wellershoff's Essays on Literature and New Realism: Towards a Political Theory of Corporeal Narratology

Wellershoff's understanding of the relationship between literature's public-political utility and what he views as a corporeally defined private sphere is outlined in his literary-theoretical essays. While most of the relevant theoretical essays were written or appeared well after all of the fictional works analysed here, his reflections on literature in general and New Realism in particular formulate a retroactive blueprint for the analysis of the realisms appearing in this study. Wellershoff initially sketched his thoughts on what he considered authentic literature in a brief essay entitled "Neuer Realismus" (New Realism), published in 1965 in Kiepenheuer & Witsch's in-house magazine *Die Kiepe*. It therefore appeared three years after the publication of the short story collection *Ein Tag in der Stadt* (A Day in the City) had already introduced to the West German reading public those authors now widely associated with New Realism. He refined these thoughts in several essays published between 1967 and 1969 and collected in *Literatur und Veränderung* (Literature and Change, 1969), this time after the publication of the second volume of short stories by New Realist authors, *Wochenende* (Weekend, 1967). Based solely on publication dates, then, Wellershoff's theoretical writings follow or spring from his work as editor and do not work as a prescriptive formula. In these essays, Wellershoff defines and refines New Realism as an "Arbeitsrichtung" (working direction) meant to counter standard models prescribed by the literary establishment, including fantastical and escapist literature divorced from present-day reality ("Neuer" 843). His working direction provides the reader with a "sinnlich konkrete

Erfahrungsausschnitt, das gegenwärtige alltägliche Leben in einen begrenzten Bereich" (sensual and concrete slice of experience; today's ordinary life in a narrowly defined space; 843). This new type of realism should not present the reader with idealized reality, but instead offer up a specific snapshot of experience that the reader emotionally and viscerally encounters but does not, at least initially, cognitively process.

New Realism, as Wellershoff first conceives it, therefore, describes a world very much part of the reader's own immediate surroundings. The New Realist author should focus on specific and subjective descriptions matching the reader's concrete experiences, although this does not mean that literature should reflect only the familiar. In the later essay collection, he expands upon the term to explain that realism, understood in this manner, does not merely repeat and thus underscore expectations and patterns used in literature for the mimetic replication of reality. Instead, New Realism dissolves established terms "um neue, bisher verbannte Erfahrungen zu ermöglichen, das Gegenteil also einer Wiederholung und Bestätigung des Bekannten" (in order to facilitate new and hitherto banned experiences, thus it is the opposite of a repetition and confirmation of the known; "Wiederherstellung" 87). Banned experiences include both those repressed in the reader's subconscious because of their social or political non-viability, as well as those that are considered taboo to literature, which he sees to be the case with the category of the private.

Because of this emphasis on the reader's personal experience, subjectivity is essential to the narrative perspective of New Realism. Wellershoff compares the New Realist subjective technique to that of the extreme close-up used in film, which allows for a careful examination of detail by the photographer or cameraperson and, in turn, by the viewer. These close-ups are hyperreal depictions of reality that render the objects in the viewfinder new and strange ("Fiktion" 26). Taking a cue from this filmic perspective, the author should pay close attention to the "Störungen, Abweichungen, das Unauffällige, die Umwege" (distractions, deviations, the unremarkable, the detours), which in turn allow for an "Inflation der sinnlichen Einzelheiten" (inflation of the sensual details) of the narrative ("Neuer" 843). The extreme standpoint allows for the influx of stimuli, which should not be controlled and ordered, but instead exacerbated and allowed to multiply ("Instanzen" 58). This filmic approach brings those banned experiences or taboo elements mentioned above to the foreground. Wellershoff's realism is therefore not to be understood as mimetic reproduction, but instead as a hyperdetailed projection of concrete experiences in which sensory elements communicate the text's meaning. This subjective approach should increase the sense of realness in the text, while at the same time making that reality uncomfortable for or foreign to the reader. Along these lines,

New Realism forgoes all conventional knowledge in favour of highlighting the world's strangeness in order to increase the "Wirklichkeitsdruck" (pressure of reality) and thus produce discomfiture or agitation in the reader ("Wiederherstellung" 88).

To underscore the reader's unease at experiencing the familiar in an unfamiliar fashion, literary praxis must be marked by "Störungen und ruinöse Abweichungen, in Dienst genommene Automatismen und Zufälle, abnorme und pathologische Sichtweisen, gelenkte Psychosen und Tagträume" (distractions and ruinous deviations, enlisted automatisms and coincidences, abnormal and pathological perspectives, controlled psychoses and daydreams), prompting the reader to re-evaluate and change his or her perception of reality to include the chaotic, the absurd, the chance, and the disparate ("Instanzen" 58). In so doing, literature can better portray problems related to the normativity enforced by societal structures and public institutions. Literature that refuses to conform to reader expectations by dismantling standard methods of classifying experiences and by presenting that material in its negative form – such as unpleasant, painful, or disorienting experiences – challenges the reader to apply that same process to his or her reality. This literature approaches marginalized or deviant behaviour as a "Vehikel der Veränderung" (vehicle for change). Wellershoff adds: "Und auch die ruinöse und katastrophale Veränderung steht, wenn auch als deren Negativ, für die Befreiung ein" (And even ruinous and catastrophic change advocates freedom, if even as its negative; "Nachhausekommen" 162–3). Marginal behaviours and figures in literature become the vehicle for social change as they model for readers how to destroy standard paradigms and destabilize normative expectations placed on them by society. The subjective perspective, therefore, is ultimately a critically negative one, for it represents resistance through specific critique ("Wiederherstellung" 96).

Negativity thus plays a primary role in Wellershoff's critical approach to literature's political potential. The narrative-aesthetic vehicle for communicating this negativity is the body. The text's subjective point of reference is dictated by corporeal processes that highlight the body's negative actions, reactions, and emotions that guide the New Realist narrative perspective and upstage the figures' spoken communication, thereby filling in the negative blanks in the text as Wolfgang Iser proposes (Wellershoff, "Wiederherstellung" 93; Iser, *Akt* 348, *Act* 226). The word "experience" refers not to the cognitive but to the visceral and the corporeal, and describes the experience of the figures in the texts as well as that of the reader. These corporeal processes function as the text's subdialogue, a term Wellershoff consciously borrows from French *nouveau roman* proponent Nathalie Sarraute. Wellershoff understands this subdialogue to describe the movements and the physical unrest behind, under, or even carrying the written words. The subdialogue is a form of communication that provides language with its sensual nuances and gives meaning to or often replaces spoken discourse while it at the same time directs plot ("Wiederherstellung" 92). Literature can become productive only when

> viel mehr, als es in der Literatur bisher üblich ist, die Körperreaktionen der Menschen in die Aufmerksamkeit gerieten. Bisher waren sie gelegentliche Ausdruckserscheinungen, die zur Bekräftigung an Handlungshöhepunkten zitiert wurden. Da konnte dann jemand erbleichen, schwitzen, zittern oder in Ohnmacht fallen. Aber es wäre auch denkbar, daß diese Vorgänge, die ja, kaum bewußt, immer ablaufen, die Wichtigkeit einer zweiten selbständigen Sprache bekämen, die das bewußte Handeln, Denken und Sprechen dauernd begleitet. (93)

> [human bodily reactions receive more attention than they have in literature till now. Thus far, they have been occasional forms of expression that were used for emphasis during plot climaxes. In those moments, characters would turn pale, sweat, tremble, or faint. But it could also be imaginable that these processes, which are happening unconsciously all the time, might acquire the importance of a second, independent language that constantly accompanies conscious behaviour.]

Wellershoff conflates narration from the subjective perspective with narration from the perspective of the body. The direction of the narrative hinges upon the bodies in the texts, their actions and reactions playing a more decisive role than the characters' speech acts. Because the body is the central narrative element in Wellershoff's New Realism, the subjective gaze is trained on, or more accurately originates from, not only the figure's immediate experience of reality, but also the internal workings of the figure's body. The subjective gaze looks "mit neuer Aufmerksamkeit für die Dunkelzonen des Vorbewußten und der Körperreaktionen oder für die flüssigen und flackernden Gestalten des Tagtraums" (with new attention to the dark areas of the preconscious mind and bodily reactions or towards the fluid and flickering shapes of daydreams; "Fiktion" 27). These external (communication as subdialogue) and internal (daydream) corporeal dimensions are often interchangeable or indistinguishable from one another. Moreover, the corporeal is linked to the marginal because the individual physical experience as described in text moves away from mutual social assurances of normalcy ("Fiktion" 29). Through the narrative's corporeal and subjective gaze, the figure – and with him or her, the reader – is cordoned off from the rest of society.

The analysis of the body in text as described here should not be understood as running parallel to and thus supporting plot, dialogue, or character development. Instead, the body constitutes a language integral to the text. Corporeal subjectivity is Wellershoff's guiding narrative perspective. In a singular look at the relationship between narratology and the representation of the body, Daniel Punday argues in *Narrative Bodies* that the culturally and historically specific understanding of the body has influence over "narrative worlds" and, moreover, that the "human body provides a metaphor for thinking about the relation between text and reader" (12). Narratives can be considered corporeal not only because of the existence of embodied characters within stories, but also by virtue of the simple question as to how the "text can be meaningfully articulated through the body," in a way that the contextual understanding of the body elaborates on and better illuminates the text's historical and cultural implications (15). Corporeal narratology unlocks the way in which the body works within the narrative, but also how stories are made "meaningful to readers" (ix).

This describes almost precisely Wellershoff's narratological approach to the body's importance in New Realism, and how the body works throughout the narratives examined in this study. His negative corporeal realism uses the body to drive the narrative, but also links the reader specifically to text and, through it, to the text's context – which is, at least in Wellershoff's formulation and at the time of publication the reader's selfsame contextual reality. Wellershoff intends the body's negative physical reactions to psychic stress as depicted in fiction to display the adverse effects of society on the individual in the private sphere, which he understands to be formed by socio-political concerns, thus inspiring the reader to rethink the effects of repression on his or her own private life ("Zu privat" 34). The private sphere is therefore the focus of Wellershoff's socio-political and narrative interests, becoming the place where what Richard Langston calls the "thoroughly political form of writing" offered by German New Realism can truly unfold into a utopian aesthetic formula (*Visions* 106).

True to Punday's assessment of corporeal narratology, the above discussion of New Realism implies a constructed self-referentiality to Wellershoff's emphasis on corporeal subjectivity that prescribes both the reader's role in literary production as well as the author's critical intent. Wellershoff describes literature here as a "Simulationsraum" (space of simulation), which is a space in which the reader (with the author) practises breaching the borders of experience by entering new and negative subjective dimensions and therefore becomes less willing to conform to societal expectations ("Fiktion" 22). Although the narrator's and the reader's shared subjective, intimate, and visceral experience of reality takes the foreground, this experience should not imply the reader's passive identification with the subject in the text. Through the use of the third person, a mixture between third and first person, or a strangely distanced "I" that is entirely divorced from the first person as traditionally associated with the subjective, the New Realist text establishes an anonymous voice that permits the reader to make a personal connection between textual and everyday reality but also to retain a level of distance. This distance, in turn, allows for the reader's critical approach to the reading experience. Or phrased differently, the reader is not allowed to identify with the figures of the novel, and instead is encouraged to read the figures as a metaphor for the reader's reality. This commitment to the reader opens the door on an analysis of Wellershoff's fictional texts as written by the reader – not author – Wellershoff. His own readings of literature and other contextual discourses are laced with political intent, thereby allowing for an interpretation of his reading act as also political. The reading act is inscribed onto the narrative bodies, and offers access to the political thrust of the negative display of corporeal subjectivity.

From Professional Reader to Writer and Back Again: Reading/Writing the Private Sphere

The discussion regarding subjectivity, marginality, and the body's symptoms is, of course, not merely reserved for the literary market, criticism, or the publishing industry. Wellershoff's epigraph preceding the essays in *Literatur und Veränderung* reads: "Diese Aufsätze ... handeln von Literatur nicht so, als sei sie eine Sache für sich" (These essays ... do not treat literature as if it were a thing unto itself; 7). This claim can be read twofold: Literature is not self-evident and therefore cannot be encapsulated in one single theory, and, moreover, literature does not occur in a vacuum. Wellershoff's conception of the public importance of the private sphere in literature is very much in keeping with the contextual subtext of West German psychological and political discourses on the relationship between nation and family or the private individual. Like much New Leftist intellectual and radical thinking of the time, Wellershoff sees 1960s society to be repressive of individual freedom and writes often of the neurotic pathology of the private sphere resulting from such repression. Interwoven into his essays on literature and culture are the voices of those thinkers who were prominent or were read during the 1960s, whether in direct quotation, in paraphrase, or in statements that call up an entire psychopolitical atmosphere.

Wellershoff's corporeal emphasis in his literary theory originates in his persisting interest in the private sphere, which is a category that he bases on the individual psyche, but that has greater social and political meaning. In "Zu privat: Über eine Kategorie der Verdrängung" (Too Private: Regarding a Category of Repression), Wellershoff responds to the critical complaint following the publication of *Ein schöner Tag* that calls the novel precisely that, too private. He writes: "Privat – das ist offenbar immer ein Defekt" (Private, apparently, is always a defect; "Zu privat" 35). According to normative expectations, the private sphere is the space that should contain those individual problems not to be brought into the public sphere. Wellershoff uses Herbert Marcuse to explain that the taboo surrounding individual or intimate concerns stems from the fact that culture and subjectivity are at odds, for culture demands work in the place of desire fulfilment (36). Wellershoff sees individual (private) desire, drive, and ultimately identity formation to be incompatible with the collective (public) interests as presented by social, cultural, or institutional politics. This incompatibility, however, does not mean that the two spheres are mutually exclusive. Wellershoff would strongly agree with Marcuse's assessment in *Eros and Civilization* that psychological categories have become political categories and "private disorder reflects more directly than before the disorder of the whole" (Marcuse, *Eros* xi). Because society is repressive, the individual develops a disturbed subjectivity that shows in the body's actions and reactions in the private sphere. These, in turn, display the pathology of society.

The interlinkage between public and private in the broken development of the subject means, according to Wellershoff's assessment of his own readings, that the collective repression of desire by society or culture leads to the production of the superego, which channels repressed desires to the subconscious. The repressed desires "führen ein von der Person abgespaltenes Leben, das sich nur noch verschlüsselt äußert als Fehlleistung, Traum und neurotisches Symptom" (lead a life separate from the person, an encrypted life expressed only as failure, dream, or neurotic symptom; "Zu privat" 36). Taking his cues from Sigmund Freud's *Zur Psychopathologie des Alltagslebens* (*Psychopathology of Everyday Life*), Jürgen Habermas also describes this neurotic symptom in *Erkenntnis und Interesse* (*Knowledge and Human Interests*, 1968). Habermas explains that because the symbols that represent desire are removed from public circulation, they are transformed into unconscious desires that appear as distortions. He categorizes neurotic appearances of distortion into three dimensions, "den sprachlichen Ausdruck (Zwangsvorstellungen), Handlungen (Wiederholungszwänge) und den leibgebundenen Erlebnisausdruck (hysterische Körpersymptome)" (*Erkenntnis* 269) (linguistic expression [obsessive thoughts], actions [repetition compulsions], and bodily experiential expression [hysterical body symptoms]; *Knowledge* 219).[2] Habermas calls these symptoms the "Narben eines verderbten Textes" (scars of a corrupt text), scars that mark the disturbance of individual subjectivity, communication, and the understanding of the self (269; *Knowledge* 219).

An den Bruchstellen des Textes hat sich die Gewalt einer vom Selbst hervorgebrachten, gleichwohl ichfremden Interpretation durchgesetzt. Weil die Symbole, welche die unterdrückten Bedürfnisse interpretieren, aus der öffentlichen Kommunikation ausgeschlossen sind, *ist die Kommunikation des sprechenden und handelnden Subjekts mit sich selber unterbrochen.* (278; emphasis in orig.)

[The breaks in the text are places where an interpretation has forcibly prevailed that is ego-alien even though it is produced by the self. Because the symbols that interpret suppressed needs are excluded from public communication, *the speaking and action subject's communication with himself is interrupted.* (*Knowledge* 227)]

The scar or breakage in the text, forming in the literary text those blank spaces Iser describes as negative, results from the act of repressing desire in language and symbolizes the destruction of the individual's unified subjectivity. This estranges the individual not only from society, but also from the self.

Wellershoff, too, sees language to be essential for individual development of subjectivity in that language is used by society in a negative manner. He writes in another essay in *Literatur und Veränderung*: "Sprechenlernen als fortschreitende Sozialisation ist eine Einübung in die herrschenden Vorurteile, die die Konstanz und Konformität des Verhaltens sichern" (Learning to speak as a form of continuing socialization is practice in dominant stereotypes, which ensure behavioural continuity and conformity; "Instanzen" 48). In learning to speak, the subject agrees to participate in society by giving into a power that organizes sensory experience into language (50). This suggests that language follows normative cultural order, that is, the manner of communication accepted by society as a whole. When a subject's removal from society or public circulation as a result of marginalization triggers the chaos of sensory experience, then the subject can no longer connect thought with meaning, which leads to a loss of language, catatonic paralysis, and ultimately even death (52–3). However, this moment of paralysis, which acts in a sense as the inception of the individual's psychic destruction, becomes also the point at which the individual can in fact be reconstituted. Wellershoff summarizes his thoughts, implicitly inspired by Freud and Habermas, by discussing the manner in which repression results in a neurotic symptom that acts like a private and deformed language. The shared inability of the individual and society to see the source of original repression makes it impossible for either to read the symptoms of repression. Although the public facade of intact language remains, what is repressed rears its head as disturbance and causes aberrant behaviour ("Zu privat" 36–7). Society relegates the effects of repression to the private sphere, where the resulting neurotic symptoms play out: "Dauernd will abgewehrtes Leben sich zu Wort melden, will zur öffentlichen Kommunikation zugelassen sein und wird gewaltsam privatisiert" (The repressed life repeatedly tries to speak up, wants to be authorized for public communication but is forcibly privatized; 37). In this manner, the private sphere is the location for the neurosis that is symptomatic of society, for that neurosis is violently relegated to the private.

The narratological implications of this become clear when we remember that Wellershoff conflates the subjective perspective with the corporeal perspective ("Wiederherstellung" 92). Moreover, repression itself can function literarily through the use of conventional forms of writing and, by extension, critique ("Zu privat" 44). Wellershoff opens the essay "Zu privat" with the claim: "Zu privat. Das ist, wörtlich oder sinngemäß, eine geläufige Verdiktsformel des Literaturgesprächs" (Too private. This is, literally or figuratively, a common formulaic verdict of literary discussions; 33). Wellershoff explains that as a result of indirect and abstract relationships between industry, politics, and society that are felt or resonate in the private sphere, authors are unable to provide readers with a true panorama of society in their writing, for the scope of society is too broad and diffuse (39). The suggestion here is, therefore, that in order to grasp these multiple diverse relations, the author must take on the private sphere in or as literary subject matter. The individual as it is configured and acts within the private sphere becomes the focus for the literary critique of social and public praxis (43). Moreover, that which is taboo or repressed is identical with that which is relegated to the private sphere (as Marcuse claims of Eros in *Eros and Civilization*) and should be, according to Wellershoff, highlighted in New Realism.

For these reasons, Wellershoff calls the complaint that his literature's focus on the individual in the private sphere ignores political issues invalid and argues that those critics are unable to see that social, political, and public issues govern the private. He agrees that politics as such are not private, for everyone can feel their effects. However, he continues: "Sagen wir, die Folgen der Wohnungsbaupolitik, des Städtebaus, der Eigentumsordnung, der Markt- und Konkurrenzgesellschaft, des Bildungswesens, der Familienstruktur – die sind privat" (Let's say that the consequences of housing politics, city planning, property regulations, market and competitive society, the education system, family structure – they are private; "Zu privat" 34). The concrete effects of political decisions resonate in the private sphere. In turn, the corporeal and intimate reactions to such decisions resonate also in the public sphere. Connecting the term private to the individual experience of the body, he continues: "Beispiele für Privates: jemand schwitzt an den Händen, jemand stottert, jemand leidet an Schlaflosigkeit, jemand kann sich nicht konzentrieren, jemand hat Migräne" (Examples of the private: someone has sweaty hands, someone stutters, someone suffers from insomnia, someone cannot concentrate, someone has a migraine; 34). Politics affects individual private lives, which, in turn, has corporeal consequences for the individual. At the level of the subject, the neurotic symptoms are displayed in the figures' difficulty in linguistically expressing their thoughts or desires. The missing or distorted speech act highlights instead the physical appearance of neurosis. These physical or corporeal manifestations, in turn, dictate the narrative. The narrative, too, becomes hectic, feverish, and neurotically confused, breaking free from normative literary patterns. The individual neurotic breakage as well as the textual neurotic breakage, corresponding to the scar in the text out of which neurotic symptoms emerge that Habermas describes, reveal the problems with normative and repressive societal expectations working in the private sphere. This scar or blank in the text is where Wellerhoff's interest in the transformative power of the reading act lies (Sass 153), also because the scar denotes a true textual fissure occurring when the roles of reader and writer interlock. Entering through the scar of the text, its structural expression of negation, allows for the isolation of the symptoms of neurosis that indicate Wellerhoff's interest in psychology and discourse on the private sphere. The individual neuroses in Wellershoff's family novel *Ein schöner Tag* provide readers with just such an entry point.

The Novel *Ein schöner Tag*

Ein schöner Tag charts the physical ramifications of those private psychic disturbances resulting from repressive social expectations. The novel follows three members of a family – an aging father, son Günther, and daughter Carla – during roughly two weeks of the reportedly hot summer of 1965, which leaves the figures and the narrative feverishly unstable. In alternating chapters, the family members narrate their struggles with the feelings of dependence on, entrapment in, and alienation from the family nexus (Laing)[3] and normative society. These feelings translate into neurotic panic, hallucinations, delusions, and paralysis in both the father and the son, while the daughter wields the publicly powerful signs of language and money that mark the men as outcasts from society. These signs also serve to bind the family together in a system of entrapment. While Carla does not feel the same externally sanctioned societal repression as the men, she must regulate her self-repression in order to support the family in her job as a schoolteacher. The daughter's narrative thread functions to connect the men's pathological neuroses, the physical manifestations of which dictate the narrative.

The main plot of the novel finds Günther undertaking a trip, funded by Carla, in his father's stead to prove that a house in Pomerania, lost following the

Second World War, belongs to the family. Günther fails in his endeavour, as he spends the money intended for the trip on a detour to Bad Wildungen. When Carla must travel to bail Günther out and provide him with money for a trip home, she briefly flirts with embracing freedom from the responsibilities of her job as a teacher and taking care of her irresponsible brother and aging father. The book closes as the two grown-up children return home to celebrate their father's birthday.

In their various physical neuroses, the father and Günther each display Wellershoff's interest in diverse psychological concepts circulating in the 1950s and 1960s. In keeping with Punday's thesis that the culturally and historically specific understanding of the body is essential for understanding the meaning of stories, the negative corporeality found in Wellershoff's novel communicates politically charged and cultural-historically specific meaning to the reader. The bodies in *Ein schöner Tag*, therefore, offer a reading of both time (mid-1960s) and place (West Germany) through their discursive references, thereby displaying what the politicized reading act might look like in practice.

Carla's Public Body

An image dominates the opening of the third chapter of the novel. The interdependence of the family members bound to one another through the circulation of public signs is initially represented pictorially in the text in the form of a triangle. In this first chapter written from Carla's perspective, the reader finds her rushing to her classroom after lunch, late because she had been at the bank withdrawing money for Günther's trip to Pomerania. Upon entering her classroom, she sees a forest scene that a colleague has sketched on the chalkboard. A brown triangle in the centre of the picture draws Carla's focus, a sign that immediately calls to her mind the familial relationship. As if to underscore this even further, Carla, turning away from the chalkboard, looks out the window and sees her father, who is sitting outside the school building on a bench in his own "kleines bepflanztes Dreieck" (little planted triangle; 48). Through her gaze on the congruent triangles, the novel contrasts the forest scene with this cultivated patch of grass. The family structure penetrates her workplace doubly, first in the form of an unknown and untamed forest scene and then in the form of cultivated *bürgerliche* norms. Carla punctuates her resignation to the latter normativity by commanding one of the schoolchildren to clean the chalkboard.

Carla is a foil for the dominant and repressive society with which the men grapple. She holds the economic and linguistic power that is necessary for the individual's entry into society and that also defines the men's feelings of inadequacy. Because of their interdependence, the relationships between Carla and the two men underscore and question those gender-specific patterns seen in the West German postwar family – patterns fought against by Family Minister Franz-Josef Wuermeling – throughout the 1950s and well into the 1960s.[4] In her public function, Carla most broadly represents the economically and socially powerful woman working outside the home as contrasted to the weaker men bound to the home and haunted by their past, a past that is synonymous with Germany's recent past.

The text connects the two men to Carla through the symbols of her power, which are represented by signs that circulate in society, signs that the men seek to wield, but that constantly escape their grasp: money and language. Money moves between the family members symbolically and upholds the triangle on the chalkboard. Each man is connected to Carla first in his financial dependence on her: The father lives with his daughter and is supported in full by her, whereas Günther's financial dependence on Carla is represented in sums she logs into a small notebook (231–2). As a result, both the father and Günther are plagued by thoughts of achieving financial independence. The father wishes to achieve this independence by finding a witness to prove ownership of the lost Pomeranian house so that he may file for compensation. While the father accepts Carla's money to reach this goal matter-of-factly, in Günther's case, the act of accepting the money prompts in him feelings of inadequacy that produce anger and resentment directed at the entire familial network.

When Carla hands Günther the money, she does so at the precise moment that he crafts a long story to his father about his plans for the future, which include work and studies. The act of taking the money from her hands exposes these plans as a lie, highlights his ineffectiveness in the public sphere, and causes him to blame his dismal future on the family and, more specifically, on Carla. This blame has a direct effect on his body, for when she enters the room, his body goes into a slump (51–2). Her ability to uncover Günther's lies, including those lies he tells to himself, is located in her control of family money. Even as he thinks that he must earn or find money himself so that he can disentangle himself from the family, Günther also admits that "es verzerrt ihn, seine Angst, von ihnen getrennt zu sein" (his fear of being separated from them tears him apart; 53). These two competing thoughts – freedom from the family as well as fear of that freedom – are inscribed in the movement of money. Through the sign of money, the men are bound to Carla and experience the resulting family nexus as repressive.

Whereas the sign of money most notably directs the relationship between the siblings, the text marks Carla's relationship to her father also through grammatical exercise; Carla wields linguistic, not only economic, power. Returning to the opening scene of Carla's first chapter, when the chalkboard is cleaned of the symbolic triangle, she fills it with the following string of sentences:

> Wenn das Kind schläft, gehe ich aus. Weil das Kind schläft, gehe ich aus. Sobald das Kind schläft, gehe ich aus. Damit das Kind schläft, gehe ich aus. Sie überlegt, ob das genug sei, aber am unteren Tafelrand ist noch Platz, und sie schreibt in die letzte Zeile: Wenn das Kind schliefe, ginge ich aus. (37)

> [When the child sleeps, I go out. Because the child is sleeping, I go out. As soon as the child sleeps, I am going out. So that the child sleeps, I am going out. She wonders if this were enough, but there is still room at the bottom of the blackboard and so she writes in the last line: If the child were to sleep, I would go out.]

These sentences define the father–daughter relationship: Her father is the child who will not sleep, who she finally subjunctively wishes would sleep. The linguistic signs express her desire to free herself of her father by putting the father-child to bed. Pulling herself away from the window, she further defines the final sentence, saying to the children: "Schreibt euch zum letzten Satz in Klammern dazu: Das Kind schläft nicht. Ich gehe nicht aus" (Please add in parentheses to the last sentence: The child does not sleep. I am not going out; 39). The manner in which Carla explains the use of the subjunctive expresses her resignation in her relationship with her father. Seeing the father's body outside of the classroom window sparks the string of signs that, in turn, are a discursive formula for the father–daughter relationship.

The linguistically and visually depicted father–daughter relationship also has corporeal consequences for Carla. When correcting her students' grammar books at home, the irritation at the students' mistakes causes Carla to feel as if she were breaking out in a blotchy rash (133–4). This same feeling occurs when she sees her father, for the moment he appears in the hallway, she feels as if there were red blotches all over her body (134). The triangle that determines the familial relationship and that dominates the classroom inside (chalkboard) and out (grass) also brings the family into the daily lessons. Carla's experience of that relationship as oppressive and promoting self-repression is communicated by her body's negative reaction in the form of a red rash.

As a figure, Carla is a repeated reminder of the failure of the respective men to obtain and wield normative patriarchal power within the traditional hierarchies of the family and society. Her financial and linguistic competences allow her to participate in society productively and force their dependence on her. Through her, they are bound together in the family nexus in lieu of their own societal circulation. However, Carla is not the root of their marginalization from society, she merely serves as a reminder. Instead, the traumatic death of the wife and mother, a personal trauma that stands in for the larger traumas of the war, is what causes the respective men to recede or be shut out from society. This trauma results in both cases in the shattering of individual cohesive subjectivity that has linguistic, physical, and ultimately narratological consequences. Each lose their ability to communicate through language, replaced instead by a display of neurotic physical symptoms that guide the reader's experience of the text. Though the two men experience contemporary society as repressive, as is made apparent in the figure of Carla as a symbol for public or social power (money, language), it is their private historical trauma that makes them unable to cope with society's normative expectations.

Private Neurotic Bodies Part One: The Father's Existential Panic

Kaja Silverman uses the term historical trauma to describe the splintering of male subjectivity following a traumatic event (4). It directly relates to what she calls the dominant fiction, which she explains as how a society asserts itself by assigning meaning and "fostering collective identifications and desires" (*Ein schöner Tag* 54). Carla can be seen as wielding the dominant fiction in and of the novel. Psychological trauma of historical proportions ruptures collective acceptance of the dominant fiction (Silverman 55). In *Ein schöner Tag* historical trauma is a private event that stands in for the larger traumas of the National Socialist period, particularly the traumas brought about by the war. The death of the wife and mother is the historical trauma shared by father and son, the death occurring in the final days of the war and thus coinciding with the fall of the regime and the upheaval of established patriarchal power structures.

The trauma that the father experiences in his wife's death results from his passivity in his choice of Kläre as his wife solely because of her financial stability (89). This financial arrangement is carried on in their daughter Carla. As a result of the similar nature of this relationship, the identity of the man as father is located in his perpetual return to the scene of guilt in the form of memory. The memory of his wife's death is linked to her drawn-out illness. His experience of that illness is physical and immediate, for he envisions her bloated body in front of him and thinks he hears her pained groans in his apartment (78, 81). This recurring memory of her illness is linked also to Carla as well as to the war. "Wo war Carla an dem Tag? Er hatte sie rufen wollen. Kläre war eingecremt gewesen wie zur Nacht ... und einen Augenblick hatte er gezögert wegen der Uniform, dem dunkelblauen Tuch, das alle Flecken zeigte" (Where was Carla on that day? He had wanted to call to her. Kläre had been covered in lotion like at night ... and he hesitated for a moment because of the uniform, the dark blue cloth that showed all stains; 78). His fear of dirtying his uniform connects the individual guilt he associates with his wife's death to the collective guilt of war. He puts these two events into context with one another in the present when speaking to Carla. He refuses to accept agency for his current psychological state, blaming it instead on two wars that had ruined him. "'Es war auch die Ehe mit eurer Mutter,' sagte er" ("It was also the marriage to your mother," he said; 159). By marrying Kläre for financial security, he sealed his fate for his later decision to remain with his daughter for the same reason. He sees the adverse psychological results of this private fate to originate in war.

The father's relationship with his daughter perpetuates his historical trauma by allowing him to repeat it and, at times, attempt to rectify it through a desire for intimacy with his daughter, although this remains unfulfilled. Further, the fact that Carla's body is interchangeable with that of his dead wife allows for his relationship with Carla to be dominated by a profound fear that Carla, like his wife in death, might leave him. This profound fear results in a corporeal panic, or neurotic symptoms, that disrupts reasonable communication. The father's neurotic symptoms that express his historical trauma take two forms: the inability to communicate with his daughter through linguistic breakdown and the physical experience of hallucinations.

Throughout the first chapter of the novel, which is narrated from the father's perspective, conversation between father and daughter falters as he is unable to respond appropriately to her questions. For example, we are introduced to the father as he wakes up from a dream and cannot return to sleep. He wanders through the apartment to wake up Carla and when she asks why he has done so, he cannot answer because he stares at her mouth, distracted by its resemblance to her mother's (14). When a conversation does occur, the single meaning of words confuses the father, who then cannot uphold the communicative act. In a longer exchange, the daughter demands:

"Mach doch keinen Unsinn, geh ins Bett." "Wieso, ich beschäftige mich hier, was ist daran Unsinn?" "Es ist wohl Unsinn mitten in der Nacht." Sie schläft noch, denkt er, sie kommt nicht von dem Wort Unsinn los. Um nicht zu lachen, beugt er sich über die Akte, und dabei vergißt er sie fast; sie ist ein Fleck dort in der Tür, während er starr auf das Wort "Festellungsbescheid" blickt. (15–16)

["Stop this nonsense, go to bed." "Why, I am busy, why is that nonsense?" "It is nonsense in the middle of the night." She is still asleep, he thinks, she cannot let go of the word nonsense. He bends over the file in order not to laugh and almost forgets she is there; she is a spot in the doorway, while he stares at the word "notification of assessment."]

The word *Unsinn* becomes in repetition exactly what it is, nonsensical. In addition, the "notification of assessment" has financial and historical importance as the certificate of ownership for his wife's house in Pomerania, which they lost during their flight at the end of the war. His obsession with receiving compensation is equated in this scene with *Unsinn*; the house, representative of his wife's financial prowess and thus her ability to circulate in society, just as her daughter does over twenty years later, interrupts the conversation and causes the father's already tenuous hold on language to slip. The father's difficulty with speaking continues throughout the novel, at times leaving him to shake his head involuntarily in mismatched response to Carla's questions (20). At other times, he fantasizes about refusing to communicate: "Sie wird fragen: Kannst du keine Antwort geben? Und er wird nicht antworten" (She would ask: Can't you answer? And he would not answer; 23). The fantasy of chosen silence expresses defiance, whereas the real silence resulting from the loss of voice denotes powerlessness, a feeling that finds its roots in the trauma experienced at his wife's death.

In keeping with Wellershoff's theoretical essays on the subdialogue of texts, body language often replaces or disrupts linguistic communication. Corporeality or physical sensation thereby determines the motion of the narrative as can be seen in the following example: "Er spürt, wie sich sein Gesicht verzieht, spürt die Muskeln, die ein Grinsen bilden, und gleichzeitig erscheint es auch auf ihrem Gesicht, beginnt in den Mundwinkeln, bahnt sich einen Weg durch ihr noch immer wütendes Gesicht, bis sie sich beide hilflos anblicken" (He can feel his face distorting, he can feel the muscles forming a grin, and it appears on her face at the same time, begins with the corners of her mouth, making its way through her still angry face, until they look at each other, helplessly; 17). The narrative reflects the autonomy of the body over speech, each divorced from individual subjectivity, through the oddly distanced and familiar position of the subjective third person. This close corporeally subjective experience underscores the communicative act of the body, while the distancing suggests here the father's lack of control over this communication.

The father's identity as formed in the present depends on and is splintered by his memory of the past.[5] His historical trauma destroys the unification between identity and body and makes it impossible for him to separate past from present. This splintering affects his physical experience of trauma; each time he is left alone, he fears Carla has gone for good. In turn, he connects this fear to a fear of his own death and his body reacts in panic. As a result of this dependence on Carla for both money and companionship, the father is not part of a larger social system but is only contained in the private sphere of the family. As explained above, Wellershoff sees the logical extrapolation of the loss of language to be the loss of unity between body and self as the subject slips into a catatonic state. The father's profound isolation produced by the trauma of loss is narratively articulated in his tenuous hold on lucidity as he repeatedly falls into hallucinatory dream-states. The dream-states have visceral and corporeal dimensions that are internal and external; in these moments, the father is unable to distinguish between his internal workings (or the physical and biological aspects of the body) and how these reflect or are extrapolated onto external experience.

The novel's opening sequence displays the manner in which the father's different experiential states bleed into one another. The first lines describe the father waking up and seeing not his surroundings, but instead a landscape of bubbles moving through the air (7). He experiences this hallucinated reality internally, for it penetrates, or perhaps even originates in, his body: "Wenn eine der großen Blasen sich dehnt und zu glänzen beginnt, spürt er das krampfartige Ziehen von der Brust bis in den Arm" (Whenever one of the big bubbles expands and begins to shine, he can feel a cramping sensation from his breast down through his arm; 7). The visual images correspond to physical pain, but their causal relationship remains unclear.

This unclear causality between the father's hallucination and physical sensation displays at the outset of the novel the way in which sensory categories are melded in the father's subjective corporeal perspective. Moreover, the melding or blending of sensory categories has a similar negative aesthetic effect on the reader. The father cannot fully focus on what he sees: "Das Ganze steht dicht vor ihm in der Dunkelheit, zu dicht, er kann nicht die Ränder beobachten, wo es verschwimmt" (All of it is right in front of him in the dark, too close, he cannot see the edges, where everything becomes blurry; 7). This, in turn, does not allow the reader to make out a clear picture. Through the extreme subjective perspective, the reader experiences the father's awakening also as a feeling of hallucinatory entrapment. The effect is heightened by the use of the third person that does not provide the reader with a distanced view on the scene, but instead makes strange the reader's intimate connection to and entrapment in the figure's world view. As the first page continues, it is only the body that distils into a concrete object: "Einzelne Schweißtropfen beginnen auf seinem Gesicht zu laufen. Sie lösen sich vom Nasenrücken oder von der Oberlippe und der immer gleiche Weg, den sie nehmen, zeigt ihm sein Gesicht" (Several beads of sweat are beginning to run down his face. They break away from the bridge of his nose or the upper lip and always take an identical path, showing him his face; 7). The bubbles from the opening sentence are transformed into droplets of sweat. The use of the word *zeigen* (to show) to refer to how the sweat traces the shape of his cheek and chin, melds the visual experience with the tactile.

The mixing of the senses is made possible through the body's – the father's and the reader's combined – reaction to the hallucination.

The father experiences his surroundings as liquid and sticky as he transfers what he feels as the inside of his body to the visual perception of the outside world; he projects internal experience onto his external experience. Because of the connection between perception and physical feeling, it is fitting that the only way for the father to fully emerge from this dream-state is for him to touch his body, as he strokes his thighs, belly, and chest (8). The visual hallucinations move through the body to be mirrored in its functions. They end in the tactile reassurance of self-guided physical touch, incidentally also the first and one of the few autonomous decisions made by the father in the novel.

The first few pages of the novel set up the subject and the subjective experience of reality that is guided by the sensory workings of the body. The narrative is opened as body; the body narratologically guides the development of the figure. Daniela Dujmić and Dietrich Harth propose that this opening reads like a metaphor of rebirth, the fluidity of the images the father experiences or produces constituted of a sticky, neonatal-like fluid (285). The rebirth imagery paves the way for the father's perpetual state of child-like dependence. In the assessment of Dujmić and Harth, this scene displays an almost primal moment of subjective constitution, as the father moves through stations of physical decomposition and synthesis that mark his transition from subject-object confusion to the identification of subject-object difference (285). This slow crystallization of the recognition of the difference between subject and object occurs in stages. First, the father, and with him the reader, experiences a unity between internal and external perception, or between subject and object: The bubbles are found both outside and inside the body. Next, when the father questions what he sees, thus expressing a wish to cognitively process the experience, the unity begins to fall apart and manifests itself in sweat. The sweat finally clearly draws the borders of his body by tracing the outlines of his face, in this manner assembling a new unity of subject (internal) as opposed to object (external). But the fear of death adds an existential dimension to and complicates the visual-corporeal process of emerging subjectivity (*Ein schöner Tag* 8). Each time the thought of death surfaces, the hallucinations return, these bringing with them again their physical manifestations and the father's inability to maintain a separation of subject-object in sensory experiences.

The fear of death is ultimately the fear of dying alone. Later in the novel, a second scene of hallucination illustrates this fear. Arriving home after an outing to find Carla missing, he closes his eyes and feels as if his head were disappearing, the disembodiment occurring simultaneously with sounds of construction work outside, which he experiences as a swirling brown that he feels in his body

(100). This synaesthetic confusion is exacerbated by the preceding scene, during which the father recounts his wife's death to a distant acquaintance, which brings a sense of fearful guilt to the hallucinations. When he resurfaces to waking consciousness, he calms himself as best he can as he feels his chest begin to tighten again (101). The father's childlike fear of being alone triggers a physical reaction, which in turn places his body at the centre of his experience of fear.

The father also transfers his physical feelings of pain and fearing death to his environment. When Carla leaves her father to retrieve her brother from Bad Wildungen, the father sees around him only images of decay and rot. He stands in the bathroom and notes the filthy sink and mirror, adding: "Es war eine seltsame Idee von ihr, ihm zu sagen, stell dir vor, ich wäre tot" (It was a strange idea she had had, telling him: pretend that I were dead; 195). The father's dirty surroundings carry the mark of his daughter's absence, although the connotation in her statement is not her but his pending absence in death. This passage continues as the father turns to examine the rotting hair and soap scum, and thinks: "Er lebt, sie ist tot, er lebt weiter in der langsam verrottenden Wohnung" (He lives, she is dead, he continues on living in the slowly rotting apartment; 196). Here, the perceived failing internal workings of the body are transformed to the waste that he sees around him. The apartment gives him a taste of how it would be were Carla gone, but the rotten hair and food particles remind him of the passage of time and his own pending decay.

Throughout the chapters narrated from the father's subjective perspective, the repeated interchange between external and internal experience as well as the dissolve of the subject/object distinction is marked. In *Self and Others* (1961), R.D. Laing writes that culture "comes down very sharply on people who do not draw the inner/outer, real/unreal, me/not-me, private/public lines where it is thought to be healthy, right, normal to do so" (19). Laing explains that while the body is a shared, public object, it is also made up of a set of private events. However, when reality and fantasy become interchangeable, the absoluteness of this inner (private) outer (public) split is blurred (27). In *Ein schöner Tag* the blurring among the public and private nature of the body, its internal workings, and external symptoms are precipitated by trauma. This occurs within what Laing sees as a social fantasy system (the family), in which the untenable individual makes a mistake not of content, for he or she adequately identifies what he or she sees, but with modality, that is, takes the object for real or present when it is a dream or in the past (23). These confusions and blurring of lines between real and fantasy, between inside and outside, self and other, invisible and seen, and past and present all take place in the body of the father. The father's externalized corporeal processes represent an absolute breakdown of the division between the body's internal and external experience, as the internal is superimposed onto the external.

Private Neurotic Bodies Part Two: Günther and Psychotic Paralysis

Günther finds the division between inner/outer and real/unreal impossible. As in the case of his father, the historical trauma of losing his mother results in Günther's loss of unified subjectivity. The death of his mother robs him of language and results in his communicative paralysis. As a child, Günther had a speech impediment. On her deathbed, the mother helped him with his impediment by asking Günther to parrot back her corrections. This mirrored repetition forms what the father calls the "leisen Zwiegespräch" (quiet dialogue) between mother and son (83). When she died, she took with her Günther's capacity for language. The reader meets Günther at the newspaper where he works (50). Here, he does not write – that is, he does not create his own linguistic patterns – but instead cuts and pastes the day's articles and therefore repeats and retains the linguistic patterns of others. The repetitive archival act echoes the dialogue he held with his mother and therefore also replicates his historical trauma. However, Günther wishes for even more mindless repetition. While pasting the headline "Messe der kleinen Fortschritte und ausgebliebenen Sensationen" (Fair of Little Progress and Failed Sensation) to paper, he thinks: "Wenn es nach ihm ginge, brauchte nie etwas anderes in der Zeitung zu stehen. Dies und das Gegenteil in rhythmischem Wechsel" (If it were up to him, the newspaper would never have to say anything else. This and the opposite in rhythmic alternation; 53). The expressed desire to archive the same preprinted words displays Günther's lack of interest in autonomous expression. When Günther does try to construct his own language, the words he writes are as meaningless as the repetitive words in the newspaper. A postcard he writes to his colleague Froitzheim reads: "Im Augenblick verstehe ich mich selbst nicht, zum Beispiel verstehe ich nicht, daß ich Ihnen diesen Satz schreibe, der ja gar nichts besagt" (I don't understand myself right now, for example, I don't understand that I am writing this sentence, which doesn't even mean anything; 70). Günther feels compelled to explain himself but is unable to and the postcard ends in meaninglessness.

Because he cannot express himself and therefore cannot assert an intact subjectivity, Günther is excluded from society, unlike his sister, who commands both money and language and is therefore able to communicate publicly. To counter this exclusion, Günther attempts to alter his physical experience. This, however, merely repeats his historical trauma: Each time, he immediately suffers a renewed eradication of subjectivity in paralysis. When he enters a department store to try on suits, for example, the elation of the promise of external change quickly dissipates as he is wracked by the feeling "als ziehe sich die Kopfhaut zusammen oder als sträubten sich die Haare im Nacken" (as if the scalp were tightening or as if the hairs on the nape of his neck were standing up) as the salesman approaches with the suit jackets (64). Moreover, external change results only in an emotional numbness, for he feels "unfähig zu urteilen oder nur wach zu werden" (incapable of judging or even waking up) as he slips the jackets on (65). He blames his loss of agency over self and body on Carla, for it is her money that was earmarked for the trip to Pomerania that he spends instead buying an expensive suit.

While Günther's wish for change in physical experience is marked throughout the novel, equally as dominant is his desire to disappear. When he steps out onto the street, he catches his image in a department store window and thinks, "jetzt bin ich unsichtbar, denkt er, jetzt beginnt es" (now I am invisible, now it begins; 68). In his fantasy, he is part of the department store window display, invisible and transparent like the windowpane. Laing describes in *The Divided Self* (1960) the self-conscious person tortured with guilt and trapped in the dilemma of wishing to be seen and wishing to be invisible. This results from what he calls ontological insecurity, or rather, a person who is insecure in their state of existence and place in the world (40). The fears and anxieties this person experiences have much to do with an inability to possess a personal understanding of cohesion and cause the feeling of being divorced from one's own body. The resulting panic and terror comes with the fear of not existing. "The compulsive preoccupation with being seen, or simply with being visible, suggests that we must be dealing with underlying phantasies of not being seen, of being invisible" (121). Self-consciousness serves to stabilize this ontological security.

Günther's ontological insecurity as depicted by his excitement to disappear in the store window leads to his flight to Bad Wildungen, a healing spa, a place "wo ihn niemand vermutet, dann wird er verschwunden sein" (where nobody suspects him to be, then he will have disappeared; 74). Ironically, in this place of healing, he becomes increasingly more ill, his linguistic mistakes betraying this: "'Ich bin nicht für länger hier.' Er hat sagen wollen: Ich bin nicht krank" ("I am not staying here long." He had wanted to say: I am not ill; 108). As in the above, this physical change, this time of location not of appearance, results in catatonic paralysis, for he can do nothing but sleep all day and when he does awaken, he is covered in sweat (115). Similar to the sweaty film that covers his father's body in panic (7), the sweat found on Günther's body expresses his paralysis; his body's communication of inner imbalance and ontological insecurity is transferred from the inside to the outside. The flight to Bad Wildungen does not secure but instead exacerbates his paralysing ontological insecurity.

In those chapters narrated from Günther's perspective, change in external experience (appearance, movement) results in internal disruption and paralysis (sweat, sleep, catatonia). Conversely, when Günther attempts to change his inner experience, most often through erotic or autoerotic pursuits, he becomes physically disassociated from his body. When Günther masturbates, for example, the use of definite articles and not the possessive displays this disassociation: "Er streift mit der Hand über den Bauch, die Schamhaare, berührt das Geschlecht" (He touches the belly with the hand, the pubic hair, the genitals; 115). Masturbation, too, ends in paralysis. Günther reaches orgasm merely because he cannot stop and get out of bed (115). The active impulse that prompts Günther to transform his inner, emotional, or sensory experience is immediately replaced with paralysis.

This contradictory impulse – change and paralysis, or preservation and annihilation of identity – is the root of Günther's neurotic fever, ignited by trauma.[6] The symptomatic manifestations of fever – here sleep, sweat, and inertia – occur as experiential border crossings destroy the tenuous division between his internal and external subjective experience. In order to combat the total disillusion of these borders, Günther enacts purification rituals that attempt to put out the feverish repetition of historical trauma and re-establish the external/internal division between self and other. He obsessively washes his hands following each thought of physical change (54). Further, when he devises the plan to leave town, the reader finds him showering:

> Er steht unter der Dusche und sieht, wie das Wasser über seinen Körper läuft, hält sein Gesicht darunter, seine Brust, seinen Bauch, das Wasser ... hüllt ihn ein in das dauernde Fließen, den Dampf, durch den er die Kachelwände sieht, überzogen mit Tropfen und Wasserbahnen, grauweiße fließende Wände, zwischen denen er verborgen ist. (74)

> [He stands under the shower and sees how the water runs over his body, he holds his face under it, his chest, his belly, the water ... engulfs him in a constant flow, the steam, through which he can see the tiled walls, covered with drops and paths of water, he is hidden between the grey-white tiled walls.][7]

The water defines the contours of his body, the parts mentioned here in the possessive unlike in the scene of masturbation described above, and the steam and water droplets form a protective shield around his body to ward off society. Each moment of change and paralysis is followed by a cleansing act that reassures Günther of his body's external existence, a corporeal ontology that can be secured only through the cleansing ritual.

Eventually, however, Günther's neurotic symptoms take over. Looking again for erotic stimulation, Günther follows a woman to a swimming pool and dives into the water, swimming through the woman's open legs to the surface (126). What could be yet another purification ritual becomes here a violent act: She accidentally kicks him in the head, and he struggles with losing consciousness. Shaking and shivering, he lies down in the sun and immediately falls asleep only to awaken sunburned. Back in the hotel, the heat of the external burn is transferred to the internal red blood of a nosebleed that has its roots in trauma. Upon discovering the blood he thinks of his mother, "die nachts gekommen ist und sein Kopfkissen befühlt hat, ob es blutig war ... es wundert ihn, daß sie jetzt tot ist und nicht er" (who came to him at night and touched his pillow to see if it was bloody ... he is surprised that she is dead now instead of him; 132). In lieu of a command over linguistic communication, Günther's body expresses his inner distress – his historical trauma – in its fluids, first sperm and then the nosebleed, which seep through the breakage between internal and external subjective experience.

Günther's loss of internal and external control comes to a head in the final chapter narrated from his perspective, in which he oscillates between the states of sleep and nausea, so much so that the reader, too, must fight to retain narrative coherence. His body is repeatedly immobilized as he falls asleep, first in his room between the mattresses and then as he moves from bench to bench through town (162, 164–5). The culmination of Günther's loss of control is a hysterical fall, which results in a final shattering of any unity between body and self:

> Alles sieht er einzeln, die Schuhe, die schwarzen spitzen Schuhe, die Hose, das Gras zwischen den gespreizten Fingern ... Das Gesicht ist geschwollen, die Lippen, die Augenlider, und der ganze Körper fühlt sich an wie eine empfindliche gequollene Masse, überspannt mit dünner platzender Haut, eine entzündete Hautblase, er liegt darin ... die Sonne macht ihn zu einem unförmigen glühenden Körper, in dem innen ein Schmerz ist ... (188)

> [He sees everything individually, the shoes, the black pointy shoes, the trousers, the grass between his splayed fingers ... The face is swollen, the lips, the eyelids, and the entire body feels like a sensitive bloated mass, spanned with thin, ruptured skin, an enflamed blister in which he lies ... the sun turns him into a shapeless glowing body, with pain at the centre ...]

Treated as an object in which Günther is housed, the body is infected, swollen, and broken into disassociated parts. Upon falling, he experiences his self no longer as embodied, but as unembodied. In *The Divided Self* Laing describes the embodied self as the feeling that existence begins and ends with the body and the unembodied self as the feeling that the body is merely an object (71). In the hysterical fall, Günther has redrawn the boundaries of his self to exclude internal subjective identification with his external body. The chapter ends as Günther sets out on the road home, dreaming of a desired future of completed studies and a career (189). That future remains unfulfilled, for he finds himself not on the road home but at the entrance to Bad Wildungen again. He rolls down the side of the road, crawls into the bushes, and returns to his paralytic state (193).

Günther exemplifies Wellershoff's interest in the social roots of individual neurosis and psychosis; throughout the three chapters narrated from his perspective, Günther charts a course from neurosis towards an ever-increasing loss of connection with reality that ends in a near-comatose psychosis.[8] His perception of reality and his self as a subject within that reality is hindered by his internal imbalance and ontological insecurity, which, in turn, results in flight and the ensuing paralysis. His body expresses his inner confusion by sweating, swelling, and breaking out in rashes. Social pressures cause this imbalance, and they are locatable in Günther's obsession with money and search for sexual fulfilment. The manner in which Günther traverses Laing's categories of the embodied and unembodied self corresponds also to Laing's writings on schizophrenia.[9] In *The Politics of Experience* (1967), Laing describes how the schizophrenic "will find himself going, or being conducted ... on a journey" (126). According to Wellershoff's reading of Laing in the essay "Nachhausekommen" (Coming Home), if we take a closer look at the individual who is pressured by normativity, we see a catatonic body with no inner unity: Body, soul, and mind are torn apart by inner conflicts and the half-crazed person reflects the insane realities of the world (153).

Here the scars displaying the break between an internal and external corporeal experience of reality also show in the narrative itself. As stated above, the novel emerges from the same ground as many of the psychoanalytic texts that analyse repression, neurosis, and trauma in West German society appearing or proliferating in the 1960s. The novel acts as a literary foil for these discourses. While never referenced directly by Wellershoff in his essays, Alexander and Margarete Mitscherlich's *Die Unfähigkeit zu trauern* (*The Inability to Mourn*, 1967) represents the first attempt at understanding the National Socialist past in terms of the psychologically adverse effects resulting from the way in which individuals and institutions of the postwar period dealt with the aftermath and guilt of the war and the Holocaust. In it, they explain that their patients' individual neuroses are built on their past internalization of authority and the resulting fear, guilt, and shame cause either defensiveness or, conversely, inertia

(*Unfähigkeit* 17, 27; *Inability* 23, 28).[10] The neuroses express themselves physically in heart palpitations and sweat (40; *Inability* 33). Although Wellershoff's text precedes the publication of *Die Unfähigkeit zu trauern* by one year, the novel represents the fictional anticipation of some of the Mitscherlichs' findings.

Günther fits the Mitscherlichs' description of the adolescent individual, who, having experienced psychological trauma during childhood in National Socialist–ruled Germany, now resists or is excluded from social normativity. This causes the individual to react in an infantile manner and to frantically search for the lost object that represents the mother-child unity. The linguistic training Günther received from his mother results in his later inability to integrate himself into society after her death. The attempt to compensate for this trauma by asserting his identity through change causes the drastic divorce of self from body that ends in complete paralysis. All of this affects his relationship to society; he cannot control his primary or innate drives and as a result becomes asocial. The child also finds his relationship to the father who has lost his authority – both in terms of nation as "Vater Staat," or father-state, as well as the father in the family – difficult to define. This relationship has a direct effect on the child's identity formation:

> Das Bild der idealisierten Eltern und die Identifikation mit diesem Bild können zu früh verlorengehen, zu einer Zeit, in der das Ich in seiner Entwicklung nicht genügend gefestigt ist, um diese Enttäuschung ohne traumatisierende narzißtische Einbuße ertragen zu können. Dies kann ... eine lebenslange Labilität des Selbstwertgefühls verursachen. (*Unfähigkeit* 245)

> [The image of the idealized parent and the identification with that image can be lost too early, at a time when the ego is not sufficiently consolidated in its growth to bear the disappointment without traumatizing narcissistic damage. This ... [can] lead to life-long instability of self-esteem. (*Inability* 205–6)]

This early loss of identification with the parents results in a rupture of narcissistic identity construction and underdeveloped self-confidence in the child, something that is common, according to the Mitscherlichs, in the generation born during Hitler's rule, the generation to which Günther belongs. In his later analysis of the sons of the National Socialist generation, psychologist and therapist Tilmann Moser points to what he calls a borderline disorder, created in the grown child's inability to keep up with the social desire to conform, which results in the destruction of the unity of the family. This disorder affects both private and public spheres:

> In the era of National Socialism – that is, the war and the persecution – and in the postwar period it means this: the father's – or both parents' – sudden shift from

enthusiasm, fanaticism, fear, terror, and subservience to distancing, untruth-fulness, and silence, inhibited cohesive ego and superego constitution in their children. (46)

Moser's *Körpertherapie* (psychomotor therapy), developed for working with the sons of the National Socialist generation, involves physical touch, that is, the intimate body, to help heal the egos and superegos of these grown children. Returning to the Mitscherlichs' assessment, the male child, most likely having grown up partially without the presence of the father – the father first on the front and then a prisoner of war – experiences the double loss of identification, for that same male child was already primed early to identify with Hitler as the hegemonic ideal and the father as the soldierly embodiment of that ideal. Hitler's death and the father's return in failure destroy the child's possibility for healthy identification with paternity (*Unfähigkeit* 258; *Inability* 217). The adolescent or adult child

> neigt zur Regression, er zeigt ein Bedürfnis nach früher sozialer und materieller Sicherung. Er löst sich im Grunde von den Eltern, auch wenn er sie wenig achtet, nicht. Diese Fixierung erschwert und verzögert die Möglichkeit einer lebendigen Beziehungsaufnahme zu Menschen und Dingen der außerfamiliären Welt. (*Unfähigkeit* 262)

> [tends to regression, and shows a need for early social and material security. Basically, he does not detach himself from his parents, not even when he has little respect for them. This fixation makes it difficult for him to form vital relations with people and things outside the world of the family. (*Inability* 221)]

The lack of positive identification creates the adolescent's inability to sever the ties to the family nexus. This paradox describes Günther's neurotic relationship to his family and his marginalization from his social environment. Although the wish to flee from his family guides those chapters written from Günther's perspective, the absolute fear of being separated from them also causes his paralysis. The splintering of Günther's connection to the family through the loss of the mother and lack of identification with the father results in his drastic divorce of his identity from his body, as well as his stagnated, infantile, self-absorbed, and disturbed subjectivity. His and the text's hectic oscillation between moments of action and of paralysis narratologically reflect this split of identity and body.

Laing approaches the psychologically negative aspects of the family nexus in his 1969 collection of essays, *The Politics of the Family*. In an essay entitled "The Family and the 'Family,'" he suggests that the family is a fantasy structure of internalized relationships (5). Internalization, Laing writes, "means to map 'outer' onto 'inner.' It entails the transference of a group of relations constituting a set ... from one modality of experience to others: namely from perception to imagination, memory, dreams" (7). The subject internalizes patterns of relationships and thus forms the imaginary group structure that is the "family." Laing suggests that people can also reverse the internalization, that is, they reproject the internal object of family onto an external person. In the disturbed person, the projection and introjection are mismatched (9). The integrity of the self is dependent upon the integrity of the family as a shared imaginary. Because of this, the preservation of the imaginary family is equated with the preservation of the self, or conversely, for those that despise their imaginary of the family, "the world will collapse if the 'family' is not assassinated" (14). Projection and introjection map the family's neurosis. In the title essay, "The Politics of the Family," Laing explains further:

> Projection is a mapping of inside onto (or into) outside, and introjection a mapping of outside onto inside. Families are of peculiar significance because, more than any other social set, they are both domain and range, for projections *to* outside, introjections *from* outside, *and*, they are the range for *projections* to them *from* the members of the family itself, as they are the domain of introjections to individuals in the family. (117; emphasis in orig.)

The family as the domain and range for mappings of, in Wellershoff's novel, neuroses means that the family is both origin from which this mapping occurs and essentially the continuum onto which the neuroses from the outside are mapped. Laing suggests that the family also receives introjective mappings from outside the family in society (118). Interestingly, the body in this scenario is the range for introjections from all domains of society and "provides a 'pool' for projections in turn *to* any domains" (117; emphasis in orig.). The reflexive relationship of the body in the family also allows for repeated re-introjections and re-projections in a cycle. Because Wellershoff understands his figures to represent the effect of repressive elements in society, neuroses experienced or expressed by the bodies in texts are mapped by that society.

. In *Ein schöner Tag*, the physical manifestations of the neuroses are introjected and projected by Günther and the father in turn. Carla becomes the place of contact between these two types of mapping. Further, the father scrambles to preserve the "family" at all costs, whereas Günther wishes to destroy it in what he deems to be a move of self-preservation. In addition, the father projects his imaginary of family onto his children, whereas Günther internalizes his imaginary of family, intensifying his hate. The result of this mismatched projection and introjection is neurosis in both cases. Therefore, as the father projects his internal feelings onto the objects around him, he repeatedly experiences a sense of panic. Günther, by contrast, internalizes his experience of the outside world and thus becomes increasingly paralyzed. The narrative reflects these physical manifestations of crippling neurosis in its own paralysis; although exacting scrutiny of the family is the medium of social criticism in the text, no alternatives are provided (Jung 148). Ambivalence ends the novel *Ein schöner Tag*. The final chapter finds the three family members together at last, joined to celebrate the father's birthday. But while the father says, "jeder Tag ist neu, jeden Tag kann man neu anfangen" (each day is new, each day we can start fresh), his closing thoughts are bleak: "Er ist nicht enttäuscht, nur still und leer im Kopf" (He is not disappointed, his head is just quiet and empty; 282, 283). The text ends in an anaesthetic loss of feeling, a quiet numbness that has spread over the entire family.

"Anti-psychiatrist" R.D. Laing was profoundly influential during the 1960s, in part because he viewed change to come about only at the individual level through self-actualized liberation, and in this manner, according to DeKoven, "redefining politics as a question of subjectivity (consciousness) rather than structural social change" (201).[11] This assessment of the political power of individual subjectivity displays Wellershoff's indebtedness to Laing. Moreover, DeKoven notes that for Laing, it is the literary space that gives us access to our bodies and provides a potential for liberation (204). By placing the literary representation of the symptomatic results of repressive society on the individual in the private sphere in and on the bodies of his male figures, Wellershoff taps into this dialogue of self-determined political critique. Ulrich Tschierske claims that Wellershoff's realism expresses a critique of society not in terms of cause and effect, but rather in terms of symptom and sign, the body becoming language and, in turn, text becoming body (28). Wellershoff translates the body's symptoms into negative corporeal realism. The resulting text should be read in terms of the external display of the reader's internally fissured subjectivity. Because the figures' neurotic symptoms also provide access to Wellershoff's understanding of the political literary process, the marginalized familial figures serve as a subversive suggestion for the contemporary reader to forgo the dominant fiction and the perpetuation of power structures by critically engaging with his or her own marginalization or neurotic repression in the private sphere. Wellershoff's reading of the discourse on social repression is intended to become part of the reader's private vocabulary.

Moreover, Wellershoff sees literature that deals with "abweichenden Verhalten als dem Vehikel der Veränderung" (deviant behaviour as the vehicle for change) to present readers with possibilities for freedom from repressive normativity ("Nachhausekommen" 162–3). Wellershoff calls such a literary approach to deviant and dysfunctional behaviour and "das gefesselte, verstümmelte und scheiternde Leben" (repressed, mutilated, and failed life) negative anthropology ("Fiktion" 30). In illuminating the negative symptomatic results of societal pressure on individuals in the private sphere, the author undertakes a negative anthropology of the 1960s family. If in keeping with Laing's assessment of neurosis as the negative stress expressed by the psychotic individual that can ultimately be transformative or interpreted as a healthy attempt to cope with a psychotic society, then the neurotic family bodies in *Ein schöner Tag* are intended to be read in terms of their transformative power for the individual reader. Because Wellershoff writes himself as reader into the novels, the effect of the novel is therefore "the scene of reading it provokes and in which the reader is inscribed in advance" (Derrida 67). Wellershoff considers literature to be a "Spielfeld für ein fiktives Handeln, in dem man als Autor und als Leser die Grenzen seiner praktischen Erfahrungen und Routinen überschreitet, ohne ein wirkliches Risiko dabei einzugehen" (playing field for fictional action, where the author and reader can transgress the borders of their practical experiences and routines, without taking any real risk; "Fiktion" 22). The reader is invited to try on these neurotic bodies, not only to enter but also to become Wellershoff's archive of reading.

In keeping with 1960s critical theory and the understanding of the use-value of both utopia and negativity in resisting dominant structures and normativity, Wellershoff's belief in the reader to effect social change through the reading act is utopian.[12] In a 1968 English-language collection of essays entitled *Negations*, Marcuse introduces negation and negativity as essential components of utopia. He writes in the foreword to the volume that "thought in contradiction must become more negative and more utopian in opposition to the status quo ... This means, however, that freedom is only possible as the realization of what today is called utopia" (xx).[13] Throughout his struggles to theorize the preservation of utopian thinking in society and the eradication of domination, Marcuse increasingly saw negation – and therefore utopian critical thinking – to be truly possible only within literature and imagination (*One* 250).[14] In light of negative corporeal realism and its potential to communicate resistance to the reader through a literary-based social aesthetics, Wellershoff would agree.

Chapter Two

Repression, Disgust, and Adolescent Memories: Rolf Dieter Brinkmann's Ethics of Textual Freedom

Rolf Dieter Brinkmann's photo appeared alongside Wellershoff's essay "Neuer Realismus" in Kiepenheuer & Witsch's in-house magazine *Die Kiepe*, visually and conceptually aligning him with the new trend in German literature that Dieter Wellershoff identified and theorized in the mid-1960s.[1] Brinkmann traversed a number of literary phases in his short career. The first phase of his work, up to 1966, can be roughly aligned with Wellershoff's New Realism.[2] The second phase of writing, stretching from 1967 to about 1970, displays Brinkmann's emerging pop and postmodern sensibilities.[3] The final phase, which saw many texts produced that were published posthumously after his death in 1975, often falls under the category of New Subjectivity. What unifies Brinkmann's writing throughout each literary and creative phase is his narrative focus on the body and sexuality, his experimentation with medium and form, and his suspicion of all established or normative means for capturing, categorizing, and interpreting subjective experience. These questioned means range from literary genres to politicized psychoanalysis to standard linguistic formulas. Unlike Wellershoff, Brinkmann was decidedly apolitical and antiformulaic in his writings. Instead, he repeatedly highlighted the necessity to produce literary texts beyond all predetermined or intentional meaning. However, Brinkmann's written and visual texts – including his short stories, essays, collages, and poetry – display a social commitment to the reader, what Brinkmann scholar Jonathan Woolley has termed his "ethical project," which can be understood within the context of the public and literary discourses of 1960s West Germany as having a political dimension.

Brinkmann's short stories published by Kiepenheuer & Witsch in the early half of the 1960s focus on the very intimate and subjective portrayal of reality. In Wellershoff's novel, the private sphere acts as the place where the symptomatic results of the neurosis caused by society's repressive expectations plays out;

in Brinkmann's stories, the private sphere is the repressive institution. But as was also the case with Wellershoff's novel, these stories chart how repression affects the individual subject's experience of self. The 1962 short story "In der Grube" (In the Ditch), commissioned for Wellershoff's anthology *Ein Tag in der Stadt* and marking Brinkmann's first earnest debut on the West German literary scene, depicts the repressive and oppressive private sphere as represented by the family and the small home town of the protagonist. The second set of texts published by Kiepenheuer & Witsch, the 1965 cycle of short stories entitled *Die Umarmung* (The Embrace), examines life processes such as death, coitus, and birth from ever-aging narrative perspectives, from the child to the adult father-to-be. In all the stories, the male subject's disgust towards sexuality and life processes produces physical manifestations that guide the narrative's poetic structures. The repulsed language of the short stories uncovers evidence of categorical repression in and of the private sphere and the resulting production of "körperliche Starre" (bodily paralysis or numbness) in the developing subject ("Film" 241). *Körperliche Starre* can be broadly defined as the corporeal manifestations of the individual's experience of sexual, sensual, and habitual entrapment within middle-class structures. Brinkmann counters this entrapment by rewriting the phallic male body as a fluid narrative construction through which meaning is produced and experienced at a visceral, corporeal, and semiotic level.

These short stories, furthermore, must be understood as texts that fictionally approach what he later articulates in his non-fictional essays as the liberating aspects of the creative medium, these aspects often expressed through intimate negativity, or a negativity that is bound up in libidinal, sensual, and corporeal experiences originating in the private sphere. When considered in the post-publication context of late-1960s nonconformist antibourgeois movements and the debates on the political role of repressive sexuality within these, the creative process offers freedom from the *körperliche Starre* that is cultivated in and by the postwar family. This is not to suggest that Brinkmann's early writing should be taken as prefiguring any conception of a sexual revolution specifically, but instead that these texts literarily reflect the growing public and intellectual sense of the political implications of the private libidinal body. When taken together, literary-aesthetic form and private-intimate content offer the writer and reader a venue for identifying, approaching, and addressing the negative aspects of society working in and on the private sphere.

The Social Politics of Sexual Repression

Der Steuerungsmechanismus der einzelnen Gattungen wie überhaupt der großen künstlerischen Tätigkeitsbereiche ... wird heute mehr und mehr gesprengt in dem

Maß, wie körperliche Starre und damit ein starres Selbstverständnis spezifisch "männlichen" und spezifisch "weiblichen" Sexualverhaltens unverständlich wird. ("Film" 241)

[The mechanism that drives individual genres, like the greater artistic range of activities more generally, ... is being increasingly torn apart to the same extent as bodily paralysis and with it a rigid self-evident understanding of specific "male" and "female" sexual practices are becoming incomprehensible.]

In Brinkmann's writings, *körperliche Starre* as well as gender-specific sexual practices are related to predetermined literary and artistic categorization.[4] Textual production is a meaningful part of individual sexual identity construction, both text and sex to be understood each as a fluid, even hybrid, creative process. The declassification or implosion of those corporeally experienced sexual-textual categories expressed in this quotation is Brinkmann's social-literary project, and is thus intimately linked with realities of the 1960s West German context. Debates on sexuality and intimacy, the family, and social or political repression as they appear in Brinkmann's writings must therefore be considered in tandem with textual and creative freedom. Richard Langston writes of the "multimedial aesthetic" that is integrally part of this creative freedom, that it is here where Brinkmann pinpoints the "possibility of a radicalized and expanded consciousness" that "presupposed the social utopias endorsed by West Germany's political opposition" ("Roll" 186). An emphasis on the resensitization of corporeal experience and the decategorization of literary forms guides Brinkmann's ethically charged vision.

In narrative construction and content, the short stories tangentially reference contemporaneous and future public debate on the role of sexuality and the body in the private sphere. Debates regarding sexuality in the 1960s – both from the emerging countercultural political opposition as well as from the conservative status quo – associated sex with a critical understanding of cultural, social, and political structures as well as West Germany's historical past. Dagmar Herzog has made a clear link between the way in which sexuality and sexual mores were dealt with in the aftermath of National Socialism and how memory and antifascist politics were constructed.[5] She suggests that the examination of sexuality in the postwar period well into the 1960s provides the key to the "extensive emotional repercussions of Germans' military and ideological defeat in World War II, and its consequences especially for German manhood" (1). This direct relationship between the violent past and regulation of sexuality in West Germany is true also of public discussions relating to fertility, family, and demographics in the 1950s and 1960s, as Annette F. Timm has shown (293). Furthermore, Jennifer V. Evans has argued that the "moral economy of behavior," denoting characteristics of sexual practices in the landscape of the postwar period formed a "foundation for heterosexuality as a supposedly natural condition of successful social and political rebuilding" (13). Although the mastery of the National Socialist past through a discussion of sexual morals was in many ways successful in diverting much of the attention about the past from the public to the private sphere, this served only to thinly veil greater issues related to national guilt and trauma, and relegate these issues to the family and individual sexual health.

Herzog makes the claim that Konrad Adenauer's government used conservatively regulated sexuality as its antifascist platform. The Catholic conservatives, headed by Family Minister Franz-Josef Wuermeling, fought for the institution of policies directed at the private sphere that were later seen by the student movement of the 1960s as sexually repressive. Adenauer's government pronounced a supposed return to pre-fascist conservative values by demanding the reinstatement of normative family structures and by injecting the private sphere with national import. This public reinstatement of the normative family brought with it a politicized understanding of normative sexuality. In the 1960s, many members of the New Left saw in this normative regulation of sexuality relics of the National Socialist past. Although many nations in Europe and North America underwent a liberalization of sex in the 1960s and early 1970s, the liberal understanding that the National Socialists were sexually repressive was a feature particular to West Germany (Herzog 141–2). By suggesting a resemblance between the Catholic conservative government and the National Socialists in terms of their supposedly similar politics of intimacy, the left was able to put the former on the defensive.

The consensus among writers dominating New Left public debates on sexuality in 1960s West Germany was that a sexually repressive society is repressive and violent in other ways; conversely, the liberation of sexuality would free society on the whole. Inspired in particular by the writings of both Herbert Marcuse and psychologist Wilhelm Reich, the New Left believed that the control of genital sexuality through those normative morals upheld by repressive institutions would lead to neurosis and a deformation of character as well as a willingness to submit to authority (Herzog 159).[6] This is reflected already in Reich's early studies on the relationship between sexual and social bodies. In Reich's thinking, children particularly are affected by sexual repression in the family. In *Die Massenpsychologie des Faschismus* (*The Mass Psychology of Fascism*, 1933) Reich writes of the authoritarian family that it is one of the primary institutions supporting authoritarian society. He sees this in part to grow out of what he calls the family's treatment of sexuality, particularly in women but also children and young people. Number ten in his eleven-point summary of the authoritarian character and social processes in this text reads as follows: "Die Unterdrückung des natürlichen Geschlechtsle-bens der Kinder und Jugendlichen dient der Strukturierung williger Träger und Reproduzenten der mechanistisch-autoritären Zivilisation" (286) (The suppression of the natural sexuality of children and adolescents serves to mold the human structure in such a way that masses of people become will-ing upholders and reproducers of mechanistic authoritarian civilization; *Mass* 322).[7] He furthers this in the first volume of *Die Entdeckung des Orgons* (*The Discovery of the Orgone*), entitled *Die Funktion des Orgasmus* (*The Function of the Orgasm*, 1942). In the introduction, Reich writes that "die seelische Ge-sundheit hängt von der *orgastischen Potenz* ab" (psychic health depends upon *orgiastic potency*; emphasis in orig.), made possible by the ability to love, con-tinuing: "Die seelischen Krankheiten sind Ergebnisse der gesellschaftlichen Sexualunordnung" (15) (Psychic illnesses are the consequences of the sexual chaos of society; *Function* 6).[8] This sexual disorder is the product of an au-thoritarian civilization. The starting place for structuring a people to blindly follow authority is the authoritarian family. "Ihr Hauptmittel ist die Unter-drückung der Geschlechtlichkeit des Kleinkindes und des Puberilen" (*Funk-tion* 16) (The suppression of the sexuality of small children and adolescents is the chief means of producing this obedience; *Function* 8). The family, and therefore society, is negatively affected by compulsive sexual morality. Reich's focus in this and other writings read by the German New Left in the 1960s is the manner in which the control of genital sexuality through socially accepted morals and repressive institutions leads to neurosis and a negative deforma-tion of character. Reich utilizes the term sex-economy throughout these and other writings to explain the way in which a society regulates, promotes, or hinders gratification. The sex-economy reflects an individual's, and by exten-sion a society's, health by showing the way in which both approach matters related to sexuality.

According to Reich's thinking, then, the regulation of sexuality also has so-cial, cultural, and political consequences, for while an individual experiences repression that the private sphere carries out, it is society that determines the form of that repression. Expanding on this symbiotic relationship in *Eros and Civilization*, Marcuse writes of the social regulation of sex and pleasure that it is determined by the performance principle, or the organization of social labour and society's demand for performance that controls the time and energy spent on fulfilling drives and instincts. The performance principle alienates the individual through repressive sublimation of sexuality away from the sphere of work and into the private, thereby turning sex into a taboo and produc-ing aggression and guilt (80, 129). Non-repressive sublimation would free Eros from the constraints of repression: "The culture-building power of Eros *is* non-repressive sublimation: sexuality is neither deflected from nor blocked in its objective; rather, in attaining its objective, it transcends it to others, searching for fuller gratification" (211; emphasis in orig.). In this formulation, the biological drive becomes a cultural drive as it replaces the productivity principle with the pleasure principle. A reorganization of society to follow Eros instead of economic productivity – allowing Eros to direct the sex-economy – would free society from repressive domination.

In his publication with the telling title *Sexualität und Klassenkampf* (Sexuality and Class Struggle, 1968), New Leftist thinker and psychologist Reimut Reiche takes both Reich and Marcuse one step further for the West German counterculture by explicitly outlining his understanding of how sexual repression is a political tool wielded by authoritarian institutions.[9] Reiche sees his text as tackling the policy towards sexuality in bourgeois, late capitalist society by examining specific sexual practices along gender and class lines and the way in which media and other forms of social teaching are complicit in promoting sexual repression and conformity. In this text, Reiche discusses a variety of cultural and social issues regarding the regulation and repression of sexuality, including contemporary West German examples that counter such normativity (for example, *Kommune I*, the first commune). Discussing the importance of sexuality for capitalist repression, he claims that the control of sexuality also leads to the control of social abilities and cultural accomplishments (28). Like Marcuse, he sees the separation of work and Eros and the relegation of sex to the private sphere as the repressive functions of capitalism, even as sex takes on similar properties as work in the emphasis on reproduction and not pleasure (39). At the same time, this allows for love to be separated from sexuality as morally superior (40).

Further, reflecting Reich's earlier discussion of the social importance of children's sexuality, later writings on sexual repression in the late 1960s and early 1970s also turn to pedagogy. In the political booklet *Sexualität, Moral und Gesellschaft* (Sexuality, Morals, and Society, 1970), Reiche discusses in depth the pedagogical implications of normative and marginalized sexualities. The intention of the booklet is to make the pedagogue practising sexual enlightenment superfluous through a broader societal standard of "erotische und kulturelle Selbsterziehung" (erotic and cultural self-education) of all children and youth (2). Here, Reiche turns his sights entirely to the development of a sexualized and politicized anti-authoritarian youth movement. The widespread understanding that the sexuality of children was political is also seen in Doris and Thomas von Freyberg's *Zur Kritik der Sexualerziehung* (On the Critique of Sexual Education, 1971): "Sexualerziehung ist immer auch politische Erziehung" (Sexual education is always also political education; 9). The institutional structures of the family and the school create subjects willing to follow social norms communicated through sexual pedagogy (13). Such thinking is seen in practical application in the *Kinderläden* (storefront day-care centres) movement and in the communes, where caregivers encouraged children's free exploration of their own sexuality as well as that of the adults. The essay "Kindererziehung in der Kommune" (Childrearing in the Commune) printed in *Kursbuch 17* (1969) outlines, for example, how the children in the commune discover genital difference as hands-on, practical exploration. In one of the protocols included in the essay, commune member Eike recounts how she navigated the girl's (age three) and boy's (age four) reticence towards being touched by first stroking the naked boy herself, and then encouraging their curiosity through mutual genital touch, the protocol ending with the note: "Dann versuchen beide zu koitieren" (Then both attempt coitus; Bookhagen et al. 165).

Brinkmann's texts display what is at stake at the core of these debates. He "beschreibt die Normalität einer aggressiven und gewaltvollen Phantasie und ihrer alltäglichen Entladung, in der sich die sexuelle Frustration und Beschädigung des einzelnen ihr Ventil sucht" (describes the normality of aggressive and violent fantasy and its daily discharge in sexual frustration and damage to the individual; Herrmann 163). In the short stories, the sexual repression each protagonist experiences or remembers experiencing manifests itself in disgust towards all forms of corporeality, intimacy, and, at disgust's zenith, towards all life processes. This disgust, in turn, colours the subject's experience of and with his surroundings, these surroundings recognizable in true New Realist fashion as also those of early-to-mid-1960s West Germany of the stories' publication dates. With its corporeal narrative focus on negativity, the early fiction highlights not the celebratory destruction of categorical thinking, but instead the repressive aspects of categorical entrapment, by providing a critical approach to any possible sexual-textual utopia as envisioned by New Leftist thinkers. Disgust is offered as a creative tool for liberating the individual – the protagonist, the author, and the reader – from the *körperliche Starre* produced by normative, including intimate or sexual, expectations. The "poetics of disgust" (Ngai, "Raw" 164) originating from within the narrative body experiencing a repressive familial and intimate past opens a textual window onto Brinkmann's non-restrictive concept of cultural production.

Revolution in Poetic Disgust

Marcuse sees non-repressive sublimation going hand in hand with a pairing of Eros and the aesthetic, resulting in a new form of corporeal, or libidinal, subjectivity not bound by social normativity. Douglas Kellner notes of Marcuse's understanding that "aestheticized and eroticized subjectivity preserves the connotation of *Sinnlichkeit* as pertaining to sensuality, receptiveness, art, and Eros," thus liberating body and senses from "repressive reason" ("Quest" 88). Brinkmann's short stories utilize the body and its senses in just this manner; the aesthetic engagement with the effects of *körperliche Starre* on the subject in text also offer up a manner of resistance against repressive reason through a poetics of disgust as a negative-critical impulse.

Disgust, like neurosis, is a negative emotion, an "ugly feeling" that, when viewed in terms of the social aesthetics of a literary text, engages a reader's critical awareness of societal normativity surrounding the regulation of the senses. In her conclusion to *Ugly Feelings*, Sianne Ngai notices that while theories of desire abound, there is no theory of disgust separate from desire (332). She sees the two emotions to be radically different, particularly in their impulse: Disgust contains an urgency or immediacy, whereas desire is ambivalent and vague (337). However, while very different, disgust and desire can be seen as part of the same visceral spectrum, particularly when disgust is the emotional product of the libidinal body. Winfried Menninghaus sees desire as belonging to the same system as disgust and utilizes the term "tedium" when referring to the subject in the state of disgust (11, 28). Tedium means here not only ennui, but also the after-effects of excessive satiety, satisfaction, and gratification. Moreover, the interplay between desire and disgust mobilizes negativity. In *Revolution in Poetic Language*, Julia Kristeva explains the manner in which negativity is bound up with desire. In order for the subject to desire, which Kristeva calls a search for unity, the subject must first negate the object's alterity: "Desire is the agent of this unity; it acts as the agent of unification by negativizing the object" (134). Rejection shatters that unity and sets up loss, which in turn engages the symbolic function through the restoration of difference in loss (147–8). "*Rejection*, the specific movement of matter, produces its various forms, including their symbolic manifestations, at the same time that it ensures, by its repetition a *threshold of constancy: a boundary*, a restraint around which difference will be set up – the path toward symbolization" (160; emphasis in orig.). Rejection should be read here as the physical movement that occurs in reaction to disgust, as a turning away from that which disgusts.

Ngai further considers desire in terms of its application to literature. Desire is "associated with images of fluidity, slippage, and semantic multiplicity ... which has become technical shorthand for virtually any perceived transgression of the symbolic status quo" (*Ugly* 337–8). In its literary and cultural representation, desire is multiple; the language and imagery of desire is polymorphous. Contrasted to this, the "language of repulsion" is more "restricted" and often confined to the moral (338).[10] A poetics of disgust produces a textual symbolization that is enacted in the push and pull of desire and rejection. "As the rejection of symbolic and neurotic negation, [poetic negativity] recalls, spatially and musically, the dialectical moment of the generating of significance" (Kristeva, *Revolution* 164). Poetic language understood in this way calls up the processes "prior to language and definitive subject-object splitting, when *significance* was first engendered within the body and its pleasures" (Coole 215; emphasis in orig.). Because these poetics are also corporeal, the body and its pleasures produce significance that is itself coded negatively, particularly with regard to the depiction of intimate acts and experience.

In Brinkmann's short stories, sexual desire is the object of disgust and is ultimately replaced by disgust. Disgust does not negate desire in refusal, but instead desire's components are integrated into disgust.[11] Disgust takes on the polymorphous qualities of desire, and for this reason it ultimately becomes more threatening to, or to use Ngai's formulation above, more demanding of, the narrative subject. The short stories build their poetic language out of disgust that has a narrative origin within the body of the protagonist as he remembers past repressive experiences with genital sexuality. Ngai identifies what she calls the "grammar of disgust" to build a poetics of disgust. This grammar is broken down into six parts that follow on one another. The subject (1) utters negative sounds in response to the object, (2) points at the object, (3) shows fascination for the object, (4) turns away from the object, (5) includes the other in fascination and in turning away, and (6) creates an absence when turning away from the object ("Raw" 168). For the following stories, pointing to the object and fascination with that object (2 and 3) each occurs in the narrative act of remembering: The protagonist repeatedly returns in memory to the foundational moment of disgust in desire. The negative sound is uttered in the moment of turning away from the object (1 and 5), and can be described as the internally experienced and outwardly reproduced corporeal poetics, in which the reader as other is included. The narrative itself is the product of that negative sound or utterance. In this manner, the reader experiences the text as internal to the subject. The process begins again as the resulting loss of the object (6) is compensated for in a return again to memory. While Ngai claims that a poetics of disgust takes the form of "radical externality, based on outwardness and excess," Brinkmann's poetics of disgust as negative corporeal realism takes the form of radical internality, based on intimacy and excess ("Raw" 164).

The Short Story "In der Grube"

Mapping Intimate Spaces

In the 1962 short story "In der Grube" disgust takes numerous forms: It is related to the reader's experience of the narrative, it comments on the subjective perspective of the experience of self (private) within culture (public), and it has a linguistic and poetic dimension. The story tells of a young man arriving by train in his home town, and thus metaphorically landing in the lap of his family, after four years of absence. The text is structured in mirror-like fashion: The protagonist walks away from and returns to the lavatory in the train station, the two halves linked by the consumption of a midday meal. As he walks, the protagonist remembers with physical revulsion his adolescent experience with sexuality and his frustration with the middle-class family and oppressive atmosphere of his home town. Langston has said that the protagonist's movement both away from and back towards home describes the "ineradicable crisis of masculinity after fascism," the difficult relationship the protagonist displays towards the adolescent sexual male body referencing the "impossible constitution of a post-fascist male body" (*Visions* 116, 122, 124). The story "tags the male body as a contested and contradictory form of embodiment precisely because of its incontrovertible implication in Germany's violent past," this past and an "indifferent present" both communicated through the male body (124–5). The violent and polluted past, the protagonist's and West Germany's, is re-shaped here as narrative scatology. Part of the protagonist's past is his intimate past, familial and sexual, which has textual and contextual implications for the literary representation of family politics and the politicization of intimacy in 1960s West Germany. The narrative, produced in disgust in the act of remembering sexually formative moments, displays the protagonist's struggle with the process of developing a cultural identity formed out of his uneasy physical relationship to his restrictive, repressive, and at moments violent intimate and familial past.[12]

The movement of the protagonist's body organizes the text in space and time. This body wanders from private spaces (toilet, shed, home) to public spaces (train station, café, cafeteria, streets) and in this manner charts a path from disgust experienced towards processes internal to the subject to the subject's aversion towards external or social processes. The "kinetic" movement of the body through these spaces – physically accessible (tangible spaces), perceptually accessible (viewed or heard spaces), and imaginatively accessible (in memory, fantasy, and projection) – influences the arc of the plot (Punday 129–33). To these spaces I also add a fourth, contextual space, which, in a twist on Daniel Punday's "social imaginary," is the space found beyond the edges of the pages imagined to be experienced by author and reader alike (136).

Self-Disgust – The Toilet

The short story opens with the protagonist's anaesthetized physical state. He is overtired from his interrupted train ride to Hamburg, the skin on his face is sore, and his mouth and tongue are coated and heavy (7). These feelings are contrasted with a remembered image that was his impulse for prematurely alighting from the train on its stop in his home town, an image he describes as "die Vorstellung von einem Apfelblütenweißen" (the idea of an apple blossom white), which is light and fragile (7). The white of the apple blossom holds competing connotations of purity of desire and defiled sexuality, for the apple tree is a symbol of both fertility as well as sin. This image is produced from within his numbed body, as that which "in ihm aufgestiegen war" (had ascended within him), and it repeatedly resurfaces throughout the short story as a type of corporeal-literary fugue, each time slightly altered (7). The protagonist's intimate past and memory is therefore located within his body.[13] The symbolic marker for this past, however, is not pure as the colour white might suggest, but is instead defiled; a few pages later the protagonist describes the apple tree as located "neben dem faulenden Haufen Mist, hell, weiß gegen den Nachmittagshimmel" (next to the rotting heap of dung, light, white against the afternoon sky), and again more concretely as "der blühende Apfelbaum, die Mistbeete ... Das verstand mein Vater" (the blossoming apple tree, the hotbeds ... This my father understood; 12, 31). The contrast between the memories of the white blossoms and the pile of dung underscores the duality of the image as pure/defiled. In addition, the connection of the apple blossoms to his father's garden anchors the image in the protagonist's family. The appearance of the image, in its reference of both pollution and the family, sets the stage for the ensuing narrative.

The apple blossom image is the "Inbegriff sündhafter Geschlechtlichkeit" (epitome of sinful sexuality), which changes to disgust towards sexuality as the story continues (Schwalfenberg 74). The repression of "Geschlechtlichkeit" that ultimately causes "Geschlechtsekel" (genital or sexual disgust) is the moment, according to Sigmund Freud, when the subject enters culture.[14] The entry into culture is also the subject's access to the symbolic order and language. The importance of the image's duality and its relation to the production of waste, the erogenous zones, and the entry into culture becomes clear when, after the first mention of the apple blossom, the reader discovers the protagonist to have been remembering this while urinating. The description sets the whiteness of the lavatory tiles against the urine, mixing with water in the urinal while the protagonist zips up his pants (8). The imagery reinforces the connotations of cleanliness and pollution contained in the apple blossom image. The white of the blossom contrasted with the pile of dung morphs into the white of the tile contrasted with the suggestion of defecation as toilets behind him flush. The purity of the sentimental thought or memory mixes with the corporeal reality of yellow urine in the present. The production of language becomes similar to the production of waste; the narrative/language begins as the protagonist controls his waste, which because of the relationship between waste and sexuality that is developed as the story unfolds, is also the management or repression of sexuality. The apple blossom on the story's first page marks the subject's return to his personal culture-founding moment rooted in his intimate past.[15]

While the lavatory contains multiple images of defiled cleanliness – damp stains cover the white ceiling and the continual sound of running water suggests constant urination – these images have their roots in familial memory. The elderly female lavatory attendant reminds him of his mother's face, which he sees behind his reflection in the mirror (9). Like the lavatory attendant's regulation of space, thoughts of his mother prompt him to regulate his body: "Er sah, daß der Binder ordentlich saß, der Kragenrand seines Hemdes war kaum merklich angeschmutzt" (He saw that the tie sat properly, that his shirt collar was barely soiled; 9). The apparition of his mother promotes his self-inspection, this action intimately connected to the sounds of flushing toilets that are the aural reminder of his own waste regulation in elimination. The fact that he identifies his self in the mirror – "sein Gesicht war das" (that was his face; 9) – while remembering his mother functions as portal to those identity-formative moments (in the sense of the Lacanian mirror stage) in the past that make up the story. The conjunction between entry into culture/language and the regulation of waste/sexuality marks the beginning of the narrative but also allows for the destabilization of identity as disgust accompanies the return of his intimate, familial, and sexual past.

This opening locates the development of individual subjectivity that constructs the narrative in the memory of childhood and the space of the family. Because that memory is founded on disgust, the body and its wastes produce the narrative. The urine at the outset of the story opens the floodgates, as it were, to this internally experienced and corporeally constructed memory. As the protagonist leaves the lavatory to walk towards the city with the initial intention of visiting his parents, the smell of urine gives way to the internal experience of "es" (it) that "wieder aufgebrochen und wieder hochgespült worden [war]" (had been broken open and washed up again; 10), the "it" unidentified. Like Ngai's gesture of pointing as part of the grammar of disgust, this "it" functions like an index, pointing to the formless memory that is physical and visceral as well as unruly ("Raw" 168). "It" is located inside his body but is expelled outward, which becomes clear as the long, run-on sentence continues. He identifies

> eine Wucherung, die in ihm anzusetzen schien, die fraß sich ein, eine Flechte, das Bitterkraut, das fortwuchs, die heimliche Wucherung von Chlor, der Katzensprung innen, Uringeflecht, die Ranke Geruch, die wieder bewegt worden war, die aufblühte, eine Bewegung war es eher, die auf ihn zulief, die auf einen Strand

ihn aufschwemmte, die ihn eingeschlossen hatte, die Hose vorne offen, da es aus-
gelaufen war ... die kleine Welle, die ihn aufgespült hatte, zurückgeworfen auf die
Sandfläche in die Unsicherheit, wo er Kind gewesen war, hier, in dieser Stadt. (10)

[a growth that seemed to take hold within him, that burrowed into him, a li-
chen, the ox-tongue that kept growing, the lurking tumour of chlorine, the stone's
throw within, urine web, the tendril of smell that had been disturbed again,
that blossomed, instead it was a movement that came towards him, that washed
him ashore, that enclosed him, pants unbuttoned in front, because it had leaked
out ..., the small wave that had washed him ashore, thrown back onto the sands
into uncertainty, where he had been a child, here, in this city.]

By urinating, the protagonist unleashes the internal memory that externally
washes him ashore in the town and onto the sandbank of childhood. The language of the text connects the memory of childhood to a space in his body. The
return of the maternal in the lavatory mirror paves the way for the protagonist
to cross over into the space of familial and adolescent memory, which is also
a turn inward to the role of the body in the production and experience of that
memory.

Body wastes determine the kinetic movement, as Punday calls it, of the narrative body: Urine and, at the end, faeces mark the train station as the space for
the origination and termination of the body in text, while the middle is marked
by eating that facilitates this urination and defecation. Langston argues that in
waste elimination, the protagonist "make[s] obvious his body's actual status as
non-object, the abject" by destabilizing the subject-object dichotomy (*Visions*
119). The body's possible status as the abject in the text as well as the destabilization of the absolute split or dichotomous relation between subject and object
through waste elimination are also rooted in the subject's relationship to family
and in his development of self and subjectivity. In *Powers of Horror*, Kristeva
claims that the body's borders are set in relation to the maternal body (3). The
protagonist's memory of the mother (and the apple blossom white beside the
dung heap in his father's garden) appears at the moment of waste elimination
that signals a breach of the body's borders. But while the appearance of the
mother in the mirror threatens the protagonist's body, the feeling of disgust appearing soon thereafter strengthens the boundary between subject and object
(Ngai, *Ugly* 335). Disgust is a reaction to the potentially abject body of the self
and is bound up with the family.

Further, in keeping with the Freudian understanding that the repression of
genital disgust precipitates the subject's entry into culture, in order for the protagonist to become a speaking subject he must repress the fluid of the maternal
(here also the implied paternal) body. The appearance of the subject's bodily

waste in tandem with the memory of family represents a destabilization of the symbolic order and the subject's command of language (Kristeva, *Powers* 70). In *Revolution in Poetic Language*, Kristeva explains that the mother's body "mediates the symbolic law organizing social relations and becomes the ordering principle of the semiotic *chora*" (27). The semiotic *chora* is where the subject is constituted and negated. Drives articulate the semiotic and are organized by the family and other social structures (25). The protagonist's experience with his return to his childhood home is therefore dictated by the confrontation with the multilayered relationship among familial/maternal memory, the subject's controlled body wastes and uncontrolled sexual fluids, and linguistic production. Because as Kristeva explains the semiotic is negativity introduced into the symbolic order, the corporeal memories, in turn, dictate the negative aesthetics of the text. The disgust physically experienced by the protagonist is located at the prelingual level of the semiotic (69). The story's chaotic run-on sentences, the multiple repetitions, the confusion of subject and object, and the changing narrative perspective from the first to the third person would all suggest a non-linear approach to narrative production that is located at a primal, prelingual level just before subject constitution.

The wave of urine and memory follows the protagonist as he negotiates his way through the train station out into the city. In an effective rebirth he emerges from the "Urinhöhle, der Krypta" (urine cave, the crypt; 12), passes through the temporary space of the train station, to arrive on the "Vorplatz, gegen elf, was es war, Straßenbahnen, die Stadt, wo er war, wieder war" (square, around eleven, which it was, street cars, the city, where he was, was again; 13). The wave of urine washes him ashore on the edge of town and the edge of memory, but in a very specific spatial and temporal quadrant. The protagonist automatically thinks of the time four years prior when he had crawled out of the city (14). The past is immediate and visceral, whereas the present is strange and distanced (15). He finds himself in the "Zwischenraum" (in-between space) between then and now, at which thought he yawns, the in-between space flowing into his mouth (16). Tellingly, the first real moment of recognition the protagonist experiences occurs in the form of a man selling newspapers, the most immediate representation of the present, in front of the train station (16). The man is physically grotesque, sparking the protagonist's following associations: "Knorpel, Wasserbalg, großer Furunkel, und ich nahm mir vor, keine Zeitung zu kaufen, hatte es auch nie damals getan" (Cartilage, water sack, large furuncle, and I decided not to buy a newspaper, had not done it back then either; 17). This vocabulary appears again in the protagonist's description of his own sexualized body and connects his negative libidinal experience to his refusal to participate in the present.

The descriptions of this arrival identify physical space in terms of location and time. Further, these first few pages emphasize an internal and external spatiality that marks the remainder of the story. The protagonist clearly situates himself in demarcated spaces. As a constant observer, he remains separate from what the space contains and instead lingers in the space of memory. Kristeva outlines the spatial experience of the person who experiences the abject: "Instead of sounding himself as to his 'being,' he does so concerning his place: '*Where* am I?' instead of '*Who* am I?'" (*Powers* 8; emphasis in orig.). The glance in the lavatory mirror at the outset of the story shows not who the protagonist is, but instead destabilizes his identity as familial memory returns. Therefore, when the protagonist admits his confusion in the lavatory – "er war verwirrt" (he was confused; 9) – his unspoken question is: Where am I? And, in addition to this, when am I? In searching for an answer to both questions, the protagonist externally traverses the different spaces of his home town and internally meanders through the memory of his childhood.

Sexual Disgust – The Bicycle Shed

After leaving the train station, the narrator arrives in a café, which is an enclosed public space that allows him to sink into the flood of private sexual memories. The outside, the present, is flattened like a movie screen as shadows of passersby cross the window and recede into the background (19–20). The elements in the café function as a bridge between the narrator's surroundings and the specific memory of the sex act with the girl Manon. The cigarette he smokes becomes the cigarette he shared with her that evening, and the purse, or the "Geldkatze" (literally: money cat), the waitress wears becomes the cry of cats outside the bicycle shed where the two sat (20, 23–4). The bicycle shed is the primary space in these sexual memories, which are marked by those elements introduced already in the opening pages of the story: bodily wastes, external spaces and internal cavities, and family.

Before recounting any specific sexual experience with Manon, the protagonist remembers only sexual frustration. This frustration is communicated in memory through the imagined act of defilement, which carries on imagery of the apple blossom and toilet: "Er hatte sie manchmal nur anzusehen gebraucht, um diese Ohnmacht, der es ähnlich war, augenblicklich wie Krätze zu spüren, um sie anrotzen zu können, Schleim, mit Rotze zu besudeln, welches Verlangen er dann hatte" (Sometimes, he merely had to look at her to immediately feel this impotence, which it resembled, like scabies, to be able to spit on her, phlegm, befoul her with snot, which was a desire he felt back then; 19–20). The frustration and ultimately disgust he feels towards desire manifests itself in his wish to pollute the girl with his body fluids, a wish that represents the fantasy of misplaced ejaculate from his repressed sexual desire.[16] Further, the language of the text equates his masculinity with disgust towards the sexual object, for Manon's smile is described as able to emasculate his disgust (21). In emasculating or castrating his disgust, Manon also defuses sexual arousal.

Because the narrator's entry into culture, that is, his subjectivity and command of language, is determined by controlling his body fluids and wastes, desire as defilement represents a return to the moment before subject formation. This and all other memories related to sexuality are visceral, sticky, and negatively corporeal. The remembered evening of sitting with Manon in the bicycle shed is described as "ein stiller Abszeß" (a silent abscess), an "Ekzem" (eczema), and "die Blutung" (the haemorrhage; 24). His genitals are uncontrollable and primal, described in arousal as a "Wasserpflanze" (hydrophyte) or a "Wucherung" (growth; 27–8), or later as the "Furunkel im Unterleib" (abdominal furuncle), wet and sweaty (37). The collected images describing male genitalia, erotic desire, and sexual excitement all suggest a polymorphous quality to the male body most often reduced to the phallus.[17] The protagonist locates sexual excitement on his body as a furuncle in the abdomen, sexualizing, in turn, the description of the hunchback selling newspapers in front of the train station, injecting the present with the sexual disgust of the past. He also makes reference to his genitals as the "große, schmerzhafte Gesetz" (great, painful law), thus placing linguistic possibility (the Lacanian Law of the Father) opposite the prelingual maternal (38). In the act of genital stimulation the protagonist moves between the ability to use language as a subject and the breakdown of this language in the face of his sexual desire experienced as disgust. The breakdown of language is confirmed as the experience of orgasm itself is communicated as a series of negative words, including, "schwarz und zähflüssig, Fett, Teer, Tran, Schlamm, Öl, Talg" (black and thick, fat, tar, blubber, mud, oil, tallow; 38). The protagonist describes genital fluid negatively as a polluted, oily, and sticky waste.

This appearance of law and language as the protagonist grapples with the collapse of his desire into disgust makes appropriate his linkage between the memory of the sex act with Manon and the memory of family. The bicycle shed is the space of sexual excitement and defloration (24). The shed is starkly contrasted with the middle-class apartment blocks he looks at opposite the shed, which are "voll gelblichem Eidotterlicht, Küchen, Wohnzimmer, Toiletten, wie erleuchtete Waben" (full of yellowish yolk-light, kitchens, living rooms, lavatories, like illuminated honeycombs; 24). As in the passage of arrival in front of the train station described above, the narration moves here from what the protagonist sees – the row of apartment buildings – to an imagined close-up of or zoom into the apartments themselves, pulling the focus back into the shed, and eventually returning to his body. This very filmic pan of the narrative characterizes the nature of the protagonist's memory. As he returns or circles again and again to specific images, in correspondence with Ngai's grammar of disgust, he displays fascination for that which disgusts by repeatedly "pointing" at the disgusting ("Raw" 168). Here, pointing and fascination are seen in the narrative-descriptive return.

This filmic pan becomes more intimate as the passage continues. As he remembers placing his arm around Manon, he simultaneously remembers envisioning his home, which he describes as "muffig" (stuffy; 25). The house fronts and the rising up of body fluids prompt him to think of his parents at home, sitting in their living room after the evening meal, "verdauten, Verdauung" (digesting, digestion) and listening to opera, tangos, and waltzes (25). The cries of cats outside the bicycle shed, moreover, he associates with the remembered cries of his baby brother, whom he describes as the "Fleischhaufen, der sich beständig eingeschissen hatte ... die Mundöffnung verschleimt, Seiber, eine breiige Masse, naß" (mound of flesh that constantly shit itself ... the mouth-opening slimy, dribble, a mushy lump, wet; 34). The stuffy atmosphere of the familial home, multiplied to an entire colony of such familial homes in the beehive of small-town apartments, is coloured by the sticky disgust experienced in sexual arousal. This relationship forges the disgusted connection between his sexualized body and the memory of his perceived entrapment in the middle-class family.

Such thoughts about his family that are associated within the space of the bicycle shed cause him, in the moment of orgasm, to relate in free association the sticky and negative words of sexual arousal to larger life processes and structures:

Lebensrad, Glücksrad, unverbindlich, Duft einer großen, weiten Welt, gleichgül-tig, Welt, Weltreich, Stadtrandidylle, in der Zwangsjacke leben, der kleine Garten, das Paradiesgärtlein, Altersversorgungen, all das, Qualle, Sauger, voll mit Blut, Blutpumpe, Spender. (29)

[wheel of life, wheel of fortune, non-committal, smell of a big, wide world, indif-ferent, world, kingdom, suburban idyll, living in a straightjacket, the little garden, little garden of paradise, old-age pension, all of it, jellyfish, leech, full of blood, blood pump, host.]

In orgasm, the protagonist moves from the individual experience of his body to thoughts of life, these sparked by the apartment buildings across the way and the recollection of his family home. The images speak of a stuffy, suburban

Bürgertum by referencing the postwar ideals of owning a single-family home or apartment propagated by Family Minister Wuermeling as "familienpolitische Grundforderung" (basic demands of family politics; "Wohnungsbau" 142) that the protagonist considers to be a future straightjacket and the root of his *körperliche Starre*.[18] This future prognosis ends back in his body as a parasite, his own body becoming a host. The sex act, or the inception of the heterosexual relationship, represents for the protagonist his surrender to the ambivalence of middle-class, West German society, of which his family is the prime example, and which in his return home threatens to re-engulf him.

The connection between the sexual body and the family makes it appropriate that this section of the story comes to a close with the renewed memory of the lavatory attendant's face earlier in the morning. The surroundings of his home town are foreign but familiar, like the "Uringeruch, das Gesicht der Aufwartefrau" (smell of urine, the face of the lavatory attendant; 39). With the reappearance of the maternal the protagonist expresses the regulatory wish to shave and wash his face (40). The memory of disgust lingers as the first half of the story ends with a "zu süßer Bonbon" (too sweet candy), which hints in its excess ("zu") at the tedium towards life that dominates the second half of the story.

Ennui – The Street

Ennui, tedium, or *Lebensekel* (disgust towards life) is central to the second half of the story, during which the protagonist, after having eaten lunch, returns to the train station. The narrative continues to meld the functions of the body with sexual memories, but the disgust changes to violent boredom towards life processes as the physical space of the narrative moves from the indoors (café/shed) to the street. The street – and with it the temporal present – becomes part of the *mise-en-scène* of disgust. The protagonist describes the impending darkness of the coming evening, which in an expressionistic turn causes the shadows to lengthen and the town to grow around him (48). The "Geröll" (debris) creeps into the streets: "Aus den Gullilöchern stieg es auf, kroch hervor, Rauch, es stieg aus den Hinterhöfen auf" (It rose from the manholes, crept forth, smoke, it rose from the rear courtyards; 48). Here, the vaguely personified *Geröll* of the town, ominous and formless, represents his experience of the present. This formless present inspires the memory of the equally formless atmosphere of the day before he left the town four years prior. He describes that day as foggy, with a "dicke, urinhafte Feuchtigkeit" (thick, urine-like dampness; 51) that "fett und schwerfällig herangekrochen [war], unförmig-plump, aufgebläht, vollgefressen, ölig-fett, Tran, war trächtig, aufgedunsen" (had crept forth fat and heavy, unshapely plump, bloated, gorged, oily fat, blubber, pregnant, puffy; 53), the fog described as sour milk (55). The protagonist transfers the oozing and fluid quality of the sexual experience in the shed from the first half of the story to the external setting of the city streets here, these similar in both present and past. In his own notes to the short story, Brinkmann writes of the protagonist that he is in a state of waking unconsciousness caused both by the indifference of the city and by the constant stream of memories ("Nachweis" 408). The protagonist is unable to assert his identity against the movement of the past experienced in the street and the strange anonymity of what was once so familiar. The protagonist therefore walks dazed through the city in a tempo set by the rhythms of his body, a disgusted *flâneur* strolling through his past.

This disgust manifests itself in ennui, which while located in the past, returns to him in the present. Using the same vocabulary as above, he remembers feeling "Überdruß am Leben, der zu der Zeit immer häufiger hervorgekrochen war, grinsend, unförmig, der Gnom, Rumpf" (tedium, which increasingly kept creeping forth back then, a grinning, deformed, gnome; 52). *Überdruss*, which in the word itself contains an element of disgust's excess, creeps forth, just like the *Geröll* of the city. This disgust takes the form of a grinning gnome and is therefore again reminiscent of the hunchbacked man selling newspapers outside the train station. The kinetic narrative movement further collapses the spatial and temporal, as he remembers walking through streets described as filled with gutters and outhouses, each populated by faces and bodies through which he wades, "durch das Flüssige, die Feuchtigkeit, das Sandland hier" (through the fluid, the damp, the sand land here; 53). The temporal insecurity of the remembered movement is indicated by the last word of the sentence, "here"; the wave of memory in the beginning of the story has left him on this damp sandbank of the past, which he continues to experience in the present.

The viscous quality of these city streets comes from the city's equation with the symbol of the ditch, the title image of the story, described as filled with faecal liquid in which he drowns (60). The trench that represents the town and his childhood in that town contains his disgust towards life processes, for it is this trench that shows him that every act is one of ambivalence (62). The trench opens like an abyss inside his body.[19] This disgust towards life, too, relates to the family, as he turns to specific banal details of his last evening home: the weak tea, cheese and bread, and his father's horn-rimmed glasses and worn wedding ring (54). This familial scene, which is similar to the memory of the familial home in the first half of the story, also contains a sense of repressive sexual promise. The protagonist remembers leaving the house to meet Manon and casting a glance at the painting hanging above his parents' bed, an image of the Madonna sitting under an apple tree, the apples golden-pink and "mit einem Hauch Geilheit darüber" (covered with a hint of horniness; 55). In pursuing the girl Manon, he pursues the image of the apple blossom introduced at the outset of the story, which originates in the parental bedroom.

He therefore recognizes that the impulse to return to his home town was prompted by the hope of escaping ambivalence in the present by returning to the womb (57). Of course, this desire remains unfulfilled, or even resisted against, as he does not visit his family as planned. For this reason, ambivalence overtakes his memories of the past. The protagonist remembers his sudden adolescent realization, that

> jeder Mensch war gleich, jede Herrschaft gleich, jeder Tod, verrecken, wie sanft, das hatte sich ihm aufgedrängt, war eingedrungen, die Fallgrube hatte sich damals schon geöffnet, war unter ihm aufgeklafft, Rotze, Kot, Würmer, Schaben, Blähungen, Fernsehen, Hämorrhoiden, Altersschwäche, Verbrennungen, Gehaltserhöhung, Raketen, Weltraum, Zerstörung, Mikroben, Krebs, Sand, Wasser, Nebel, Erektionen, Blutung, Sterne, das führte den Tanz auf, den großen Reigen, kroch durcheinander, alles durcheinander, der Sud. (63)

> [every person was the same, every kingdom, every death, croaking, how gentle, it had crowded in on him, penetrated him, the trap had already opened back then, gaping under him, snot, faeces, worms, cockroaches, flatulence, television, haemorrhoids, dementia, burns, pay raise, rockets, outer space, destruction, microbes, cancer, sand, water, fog, erections, haemorrhage, stars, everything performed the dance, the great circle dance, crawled in and out and up and down, the broth.]

He transfers his negative thoughts of the future during orgasm to the cosmic order of the world, to human biology, and to the present cultural markers of West Germany (television and missiles). The physical body comes to have direct relation to larger events of humanity, the movement of the stars and political authority the same as cancer, haemorrhoids, or erections, leading the protagonist to conclude that the entire world is an "After, Loch" (anus, hole; 63).[20] All of the single thoughts come together in a broth of words that mix in disgusted uncontrollability. The apple tree or apple blossom, the erotic promise that is located in the family, had been a "Stinklicht gewesen ... sein Bauch hatte sich geöffnet, hatte den Darm entleert" (stinking light ... his stomach had opened, had emptied his bowels; 63). By locating the origination of disgust in the image of the polluted apple blossom as well as within his body, the protagonist points to the repressive private sphere of the middle-class, West German family as formative for his corporeal subjectivity based in libidinal disgust.

It is therefore fitting that, upon entering the train station, the protagonist thinks, "ich mußte auf die Toilette, ich mußte scheißen" (I had to use the toilet, I had to take a crap; 65). The scatological imagery of this last section of the story originates in his body's processes, just as the disgusted memories of the entire day are also internal to the body. The protagonist thus returns to the opening space of the story, the crypt of his rebirth into the town of his childhood and memory. Sitting now in the quiet of the lavatory stall, he thinks that all the faces of his past have disappeared. He looks at the wall and sees graffiti: "Fick dich selber, daneben war der Umriß eines Frauenkörper" (Go fuck yourself, next to it the shape of a woman's body; 67). Looking at the graffiti while sitting on the toilet bundles together all the images the protagonist experienced throughout the story; excrement and body fluids are visually bound to the sexualized female image. In addition, the writing on the wall turns away from shared heterosexuality, which throughout the narrative disgusts the protagonist, and towards suggested satisfaction in solitary masturbation. The linguistic command coupled with the drawing of the female body signifies the repressed sexual memory that repeatedly resurfaced throughout the text.

In *Male Matters*, Calvin Thomas claims that the process of writing allows for the excessive visibility of the male body: "The issue, in other words, becomes not writing about the body but *writing itself as a bodily function*" (3; emphasis in orig.). In this formulation, writing is produced inside the body as thought and then expelled from the body as a trace of this thought. Confirming this relationship, the short story equates the production of written and visual language with the production of faeces, the uncharacteristically simple final sentences of the story reading: "Es drängte hinaus, unter ihm floß es ab. Im Zug würde er den Kriminalroman zu Ende lesen" (It pushed out of him, flowed away under him. He would finish reading the crime novel on the train; 67). While defecating, ridding himself of the memories of the day in a controlled and clean act, he thinks of resuming the act of reading that the visit interrupted. As the protagonist leaves the semiotic private sphere, in the form of the town and the related memories, and returns to the world of organized symbols in the public sphere, he reassumes his role as a speaking (reading) subject. In tune with Freud's understanding of the control or management of faeces as a communicative act, the protagonist here, in the production of faeces, is able to forgo his past in the ultimate refusal to visit his parents and instead rejoin culture.[21] And in a twist on Punday's claim that texts illuminate the cultural importance of bodies and bodies communicate the meaning of texts, Brinkmann's poetics of disgust facilitate the appearance of bodies in texts that are themselves made up of bodily language (Punday 15).

The Collection *Die Umarmung*: There Is No Sexual Relationship

Brinkmann published *Die Umarmung* with Kiepenheuer & Witsch in 1965. The title of the collection gives voice to its thematic organization. Sibylle Späth, in her monograph on Brinkmann, writes of the volume that it covers the circle of life (20). It begins with death, moves through first love and coitus, and ends with birth. Whereas "In der Grube" was told in changing first- and third-person perspectives, these stories are told entirely in the third person. The stories build an overarching metavoice, as Christa Merkes notes, and are written from the perspective of a young, adolescent or post-adolescent male (86). The texts characterize each respective narrator's relationship to sexuality and erotic desire as frustrating and impossible. Slavoj Žižek's reading of Jacques Lacan's contestation that there is no sexual relationship, or no universal formula for realizing shared sexual desire, is very fitting here.[22] Žižek comments on this concept that "because of the lack of this universal formula, every subject has to invent a fantasy of his or her own, a 'private' formula for the sexual relationship" (*Plague* 7). According to this understanding, all romantic relationships are based not in shared intimacy, but in fantasy. It is that fantasy that in this collection is fissured.

This fissure of fantasy can be read as a breakage or scar in Brinkmann's fiction. Like the breakage in discourse found in Wellershoff's texts, the breakage here is located in the construction of the text and is worn on the body in text. Thomas Bauer identifies two terms marking Brinkmann's construction of the sexual body in the early short stories: "Riß und Schnitt" (tear and cut; 207). In these short stories, the female bodies from which the narrators turn away in disgust are marked by images of wounds, tears, rips, cuts, and ruptures that are in keeping with Ngai's understanding of negative space in the grammar of disgust, or with Iser's identification of the negative blanks in the text that allow for the text's doubling in negativity ("Raw" 168; Iser, *Akt* 348; Iser, *Act* 226). The absences marking disgust towards the sexualized female body are superimposed onto the male narrator's body, causing the feminine to be the physical template for the creation of masculine corporeal identity. In a slight inversion of Brinkmann's later collection of poetry *Godzilla*, which is made up of poems printed over images of women in bikinis, the female body here is written over the male body as fantasized text. If as Elizabeth Cowie claims, fantasy is the "support of desire" (136), then here fantasy supports disgust, which takes the place of both autoerotic and heterosexual desire.

The first story, "Der Arm" (The Arm), tells of an adolescent boy's experience of his mother's death from breast cancer and takes place in the few minutes between the moment he hears the bearers of the news on the stairs and their entrance into his room. The boy describes his mother's cancer as an animal or beast-like thing that grows with her illness, becoming more violent with each day as it presses him deeper into the "Sud von Ekel, Schleim, Röcheln" (broth of disgust, slime, rattled breathing; 23). The school lavatory is the only place the boy feels safe. He notes the stalls had been cleaned of graffiti that had been made up of "Frauenkörper mit offenen Fotzen, aus denen es tropfte, Geschlechtsteile in

Form geometrischer Figuren, Kritzeleien, Sprüche" (women's bodies with open, dripping cunts, genitals in the form of geometric shapes, doodles, quotes; 23). In this lavatory, the boy not only regulates his body through waste elimination, but he also regulates the fear and disgust he feels towards his mother's body. Moreover, the drawing has been erased, although it is still visible. The mother's pending death in this story eradicates the representation of her body, but that body leaves traces. These traces are replicated on the body of the mother in the form of the wound left by her mastectomy. The boy experiences the wound viscerally, describing the remaining breast as a "Lappen" (rag), the scar's blue colour, its flaky and festering surface covered in ointment, and its gaping edges (29–30). The wound is an unruly mark that refuses to heal and oozes liquid like the obscene drawings in the lavatory. His mother's patchwork body affects his budding sexualized experiences of the female body, for when he stares at the intact breasts of girls and women around him, he feels a crawling sensation (30).

The story "Geringes Gefälle" (Slight Slope) portrays a similar disgust for the sexual possibilities of the ruptured female body. The narrator in this story sits in a café and describes the people sitting at the tables around him. When summoning the waitress to pay his cheque, he is taken aback by the girl's acne (102). The sight of her face returns him to the memory of his fourteen-year-old face. This prompts, in turn, the shameful memory of his then budding sexual desire, for he believed excessive masturbation to be an illness he wore on his face in the form of acne (103). He equates the "Schmier, den weißlichen, klebrigen Rotz" (gunk, the whitish, sticky snot) of ejaculate with the pus that erupts from his pimples:

> Die weißliche Soße wischte er gewöhnlich an der Unterseite der Matratze oder des Kopfkeils ab ... Später hatte er gern solche dicken, eitrigen Stippen ausgedrückt, hatte sie zwischen zwei Fingernägel genommen, und es war ein gutes Gefühl, wenn der Eiterpollen herausspritzte. (103)

> [He usually wiped off the whitish goo on the underside of the mattress or on the headboard ... Later he liked to pop such fat, pussy pimples, took them between two fingernails, and it was a great feeling when the pus squirted out.]

The misplaced fluids – both under the mattress and on the narrator's face – do not inspire disgust in the narrator, but in the reader. The narrator's disgust first surfaces in his connection between his own pimples/ejaculate and the unattractive girl's pimples/vaginal fluids. He did not grow out of the habit of squeezing his pimples (103). The foregone conclusion, then, is that the man also continues to masturbate. The girl, whose face is covered in pimples, is therefore automatically sexualized, but because of his connection between her body and his own, that sexualization is shameful. As a result, the narrator cannot look at her and instead sees only her outstretched palm, a gesture that again refers to the act of masturbation. This causes the narrator's flight from the café.

While these two stories describe disgust towards the fantasy of the female body, the title piece of the collection, "Die Umarmung" (The Embrace), expands this disgust to the sex act itself. The narrator and a woman walk in a park that is covered in dead flowers, dry grass, and flies. They wade through the thick air "halb chloroformiert" (half-chloroformed) by the smell of plant decay (110). The narrator transforms the normally romantic imagery of flowers into deformed growths singed by the sun, a deformation that colours the man's experience of the woman as the smell of the rotting flowers mixes with the woman's perfume and sweat (110). The remainder of the story is devoted to various descriptions of the remembered unpleasant sex act. The woman is described as a "Tier, ein Klumpen Fleisch, weiß und geschält, enthäutet und wie leblos" (animal, a clump of flesh, white and peeled, skinned and as if lifeless; 117). Her body causes him to feel as if his entire body were a sex organ, and as if he were covered with a red horny rash (124). Violent verbs and fluid imagery, such as "erbrechen, das Seibern" (vomiting, dribble) reflect his helpless futility during intercourse (119). The "ontology of male desire" (Bataille) as the wish to defile the woman is here beyond the narrator's control, and is instead related to the decaying atmosphere of the park.[23] The result of this embrace is a fetus, described by the narrator as a "Popel" (booger; 132). Like the ejaculate/pus pairing above, the narrator here describes the fetus disgustedly as misplaced bodily fluid.[24]

The oozing and open bodies of the women in these stories – whether in the form of scars, pimples, or vaginal openings – exist only in the narrator's memory and thus represent the narrator's fantasy of the female body. The breakages or absences are created in the narrator's turn away from the woman in disgust ("Raw" 168). Because this fantasy is contained inside each respective narrator's body, in memory and in the physical sensations this memory produces, the female body is experienced as superimposed onto the male. This transcribes the female ruptures onto the male body. The disgust the narrators feel when confronted with female sexuality becomes disgust for their own bodies. Language describes not the sexualized woman, but repulsion towards the fantasy of the erotic male body.

Identifying Contextual Repression

When taken together, the bodies in these stories from 1962 and 1965 chart the possibilities for disturbance in the social order as they play out in the aesthetic order. They offer not a fictionalized image of the contextual writings on sexual repression, but at their core they engage in a similar problematic contained in those discourses contemporary to and postdating their publications. The stories, too, point to an atmosphere of repression located in social normativity and cultivated by the *bürgerliche* family that stifles the development of a healthy corporeal, or libidinal, subjectivity founded on sexuality. Punday explains that the body in narrative offers up a "natural means" of expressing "tension between public and private, between interior experience and exterior event" (102).[25] The tension or gap here is "meaningful mostly because it defines the individual body and renders it unruly to the larger perspective of the society" (102). Punday explains that the unruly body is identified in narrative as an "attraction to something that initially troubles social patterns," which, in turn, defines the plot lines of narratives (13). In these texts, the unruly body is the body of the remembered sexual self. The narrator is attracted to, or fascinated by, this memory in the sense that he repeatedly returns to his negative experience of his sexual body in memory (Ngai, "Raw" 168).

In the gap or tension between public and private – or between greater life processes and the intimate world of the narrator's familial experience – the narrative bodies become (sexually) unruly. That these bodies would appear only in their function as private bodies, that is, as bodies engaged with or entrapped in the private sphere and the family, suggests a relationship to the West German discursive context. In accordance with thinkers such as Reich, Marcuse, and Reiche, the repression of sexuality expressed in the texts through sexual disgust comments specifically on the *körperliche Starre* cultivated in the middle-class family and in small-town West Germany. This in turn can be read to apply to West Germany's contemporaneous present, as seen best in the protagonist's disgust towards life processes in "In der Grube." Reading these bodies as a key to the health of the private sphere and its public implications in 1960s West Germany, the repression carried out by the family is revealed to be part of normative social discourse.

In keeping with Ben Highmore's conception of social aesthetics and Marcuse's understanding of aesthetic ethos, the aesthetic charge – artistic and sensual – of a poetics of disgust maintains a socially and culturally specific function: "What makes disgust an important force ... is thus its negative potentiality as a figure of exclusion, the radical externalization it enacts in facilitating the subject's turn away from the object" (Ngai, "Raw" 167). Because of this, the possibility for disgust to be a "political poetics" is located in its use as a figure of resistance, or to use Kristeva's word, rejection (ibid.).[26] Ngai views disgust to be a politically useful emotion for mobilization against repressive aspects of society, particularly in "its identification of its object as intolerable" (*Ugly* 340).[27]

For the 1960s context, it is telling that Christian Enzensberger's *Größerer Versuch über den Schmutz* at times reads as a poetic match to Brinkmann's stories. For example: "Salbe Paste Schmiere Wachs Schmalz Brei Teig Talg und was immer sonst noch glischt knatscht mantscht und spratzt ... Auswüchse Einwüchse Geschwüre Schwären Pusteln Beulen Höcker Buckel Stümpfe mit ihrer Verwandtschaft" (Ointment paste goo wax lard mush dough tallow and anything else squidgy slippery mushy slushy and sloshy ... Outgrowth ingrowth ulcers furuncles blisters lumps humps hunches stumps with all their relatives; 17–18). The authoritarian implications of the pure and clean in Enzensberger's text are countered by the appearance of counter-normative, marginal dirt. Disgust in Brinkmann's short stories is a negative emotion and therefore a critically resistant figure. Sexual disgust points not at the sexual body as the intolerable object, but at society's repression of desire (here understood in its multiple form, not only as sexual desire) that causes the subject to experience disgust. Brinkmann's corporeal realism found in his fiction is also present in his non-fictional writings on literary and creative production, which are negatively and radically utopian.

Brinkmann's Aesthetic Ethos and Textual Freedom

In his introduction to the anthology *Silverscreen*, Brinkmann cites Marcuse emphatically in capital letters:

> The next generation needs to be told that the real fight is not the political fight, but to put an end to politics. From politics to metapolitics. From politics to poetry. Legislation is not politics, nor philosophy, but poetry. Poetry, art, imagination, the creator spirit is life itself; the real revolutionary power to change the world; and to change the human body. (qtd. in "Notizen 1969," 28)

The political impact or efficaciousness of creativity here lies in their equation. Marcuse's words express Brinkmann's understanding of the publicly engaged aspects of creative works. Moreover, that changing the body would follow on and be the pinnacle of changing the political world is telling for the relationship among literary processes, the body, and their shared ethical impact.

Brinkmann's early short stories establish a set of thematic interests also found in his later essays on creative production. The essays act as conclusive aesthetic process begun in his short stories. The writings on literature do not by any stretch of the word build a theoretical program, even expressly denying their own theoretical utility, but they instead display the perpetuation of and variation on those thinking patterns begun in the literary realm, providing a coda to the literary analysis. The reading of Brinkmann's non-fictional essays alongside the blueprint or working model of New Realism as a means for examining the interplay between the private sphere and literature through an attention to the body, the marginal, and everyday banalities opens up a better understanding of the social, political, or ethical impulse of Brinkmann's 1960s writings with respect to the contextual private sphere. These essays place the stories' display of the physical effects of a repressive relationship to intimacy as well as their commentary on stuffy and restrained post-economic-miracle family life into relationship with the implosion of literary and sexual categories.

Brinkmann's writings regularly emphasize the importance of the body and subjectivity in text and creative process ("1969" 14). Brinkmann sees the act of writing from and about the body to be the way in which language can be released from the restraints placed on it by society. In the essay "Der Film in Worten" (Film in Words), Brinkmann claims that authors are finally turning away from intellectual objectivity. Instead:

> Intellektuelle Spontaneität wird mit körperlicher Spontaneität gekoppelt – das Auf-flackern erneuten sinnlichen Bewußtseins (oder bewußter Sinnlichkeit) versucht, neue sinnliche Ausdrucksmuster zu schaffen – der Ausgangspunkt des Schreibens ist das Subjekt, Kopf und Körper zusammen, – eine nach innen und nach außen schwingende Tür ... Wahngebilde, Halluzinationen, verquere Sprache – Starre, die in Bewegung gerät. ("Film" 234–5)

> [Intellectual spontaneity is coupled with bodily spontaneity – the flaring up of re-newed sensual awareness (or conscious sensuality) attempts to create new sensual patterns of expression – the subject, mind and body together, is the starting point for writing, – a door that swings inwards and outwards ... phantasms, hallucina-tions, strange language – paralysis that is set into motion.]

Here, a specific corporeal subjectivity replaces objectivity, made of the subject's intellectual and physical spontaneous responses to his or her environment. Brinkmann proposes changing set patterns of thought and action by high-lighting the role of the body in writing and, following on this, the subjective experience of the body in literature. And as was the case for Wellershoff, this sub-jectivity is marked by negativity, for the narration of marginalized experiences – apparitions, insanity, hallucinations, or non-linear language patterns – should liberate society. He expands on this idea in an informal essay entitled "Notizen und Beobachtungen vor dem Schreiben eines zweiten Romans 1970/74" (Notes and Observations before Writing a Second Novel 1970/74), in which he com-ments on the central role the body plays in experience: "Der eigene Körper ist 24 Stunden am Tag vorhanden" (One's own body is present 24 hours a day; 277). Elsewhere, he notes this permanent corporal state should drive the aesthetic production of narrative, as a subjective narrative focus on the body's senses can free both writer and reader from prescribed meaning:

> Denn je konkreter in der subjektiven Verwendung der Bilder das einzelne Bild=Image, Vorstellung, Eindruck, *die sinnliche Erfahrung als Blitzlichtaufnahme* in einem literarischen Text da ist, desto leerer wird der vorgegebene Bedeutungsgehalt, und das wiederum bewirkt, wie leicht einzusehen ist, ein Ansprechen größerer Einheiten als nur die des Verstandes. ("Einübung" 154; emphasis in orig.)

> [Because the more concrete each picture=image, imagination, impression, *the sensual experience as a snapshot* is in the subjective use of pictures in a literary text, the emptier the given purpose becomes, and this, in turn, prompts the response of greater parts than only that of the mind, as can easily be understood.]

The subjective use of momentary or fleeting sensual experiences, here described as a snapshot of those experiences, to build the images of the text offers up a means for dissolving pre-existing meaning. Not only does the body rearrange how meaning is created, experienced, and communicated – moving the reader away from pure reason – but also the reader's physical experience of text organizes its presentation of reality. Just as Wellershoff understands that a literary focus on minute details and the chaos of subjective experience can work to dissolve pre-existing beliefs as to how to interpret meaning, Brinkmann sees this same possibility to be located in the senses of the body. Thomas Gross comments on what he calls Brinkmann's bodily empiricism, that the body is the "*realissimum*," or most real being (27). Gross suggests that in theory and literature alike, Brinkmann uses bodily senses like "Präzisionsinstrumente" (precision instruments) to work against generalized rationality that he sees as no longer effective for describing everyday experiences of the subject as it traverses reality (27).[28] In this reading, Brinkmann uses the instruments of the senses to capture the stimuli Wellershoff suggests should chart the chaos of experience ("Instanzen" 58).

The body is thus present in and essential to all subjective experiences. Part of this includes negative experience with the "terror" of the everyday ("1969" 11). Wellershoff notes in his eulogy following Brinkmann's death that the "imaginäre Sinnlichkeit" (imaginary sensuality) that is found in the early prose texts always arises from disconcertment and "Wehrlosigkeit" (defencelessness) of the perceiver ("Destruktion" 280). This tactic opens the readers to a foreign reality that is, however, always linked to a familiar and recognizable present. The literary focus on the negative aspects of the banal forms the subject of Brinkmann's introduction to *Silverscreen*:

Die alltäglichen Dinge werden ... aus ihrem miesen, muffigen Kontext heraus-
genommen, sie werden der gängigen Interpretation entzogen, und plötzlich sehen
wir, wie schön sie sind ... denn die alltäglichen Sachen und Ereignisse um uns
sind terrorisiert worden; dieser winzige, aber überall verteilte Terror wird zersetzt,
das konkrete Detail befreit. ("1969" 11; emphasis in orig.)

[Ordinary things are ... removed from their miserable, stuffy context, they are
stripped of the standard interpretation, and suddenly we see how beautiful they
are ... For ordinary things and events around us have been terrorized; this minus-
cule but widespread terror is corroded, *concrete detail is liberating.*]

He sees poetry to release banalities from their normative repressive frameworks through concrete description. The concrete experience of the everyday,
or the banal, in literature is used in resistance to the "Auslöschen des Einzelnen in dem alltäglichen Terror" (extinction of the individual through everyday
terror; 11). Influenced by Leslie Fiedler, Brinkmann calls this literature postmodern. In order to facilitate the removal of these everyday elements from
their context of terror, or normativity – that which causes *körperliche Starre* –
discomfiture needs to occur (19). By being unsettled, the reader sees familiar objects, even normative structures, in a new fashion. This effect is created
through the narrative use of filmic techniques to construct a new vision of reality. Brinkmann writes:

Die eigene *Optik* wird durchgesetzt, *Zooms* auf winzige, banale Gegenstände ohne
Rücksicht darauf, ob es ein "kulturell" angemessenes Verfahren ist, *Überbelichtungen,
Doppelbelichtungen* (etwa bei Biotherm), unvorhersehbare *Schwenks* (Gedanken-
Schwenks), *Schnitte*: ein image-track. (29–30; emphasis in orig.)

[The subject's own *optics* are enforced, *zoom* in on tiny, banal objects without considering whether this is a "culturally" acceptable practice, *overexposures, superim-
positions* (as by Biotherm), sudden *pans* (mind-pans), *cuts*: an image-track.]

Brinkmann generates a link between the destruction of cultural acceptabil-
ity and literary poetics that create what he calls an image-track by using ex-
perimental filmic practices. This equation makes clear that the transformation
of the subjective perspective – or as Marcuse writes, the creation of a new
sensibility – has cultural consequences.

Brinkmann continues to suggest, therefore, that such techniques do not
merely promote new literary forms, but instead dissolve the "*negative Program-
mierung der Sprache*" (*negative programing* of language) perpetuated by the

literary establishment ("1969" 30; emphasis in orig.). He continues to explain, in a parenthetical aside, that the established phrases for describing the ugly are far more nuanced than those for the beautiful, something he sees to be the result of a "Mangel-Gesellschaft, die bis *in* die Sprache rein 'männlich' orientiert ist!" (deficient society that has a "male" orientation, *all* the way down to its language!; 30; emphasis in orig.). While Brinkmann here specifically refers to the authors of New Subjectivity, his own early New Realist texts already display his interest in using the vocabulary of the ugly to undo programmatic and patriarchal language. By approaching the negative programing of language, the author presents texts to readers that are free from prescribed meaning and therefore shake off repressive normativity by clearly displaying its linguistic catches. He continues: "Das Häßliche steckt nicht im Außergewöhnlichen, vielmehr in dem Vertrauten, so wie das Schöne nicht im Außergewöhnlichen steckt, sondern im Alltäglichen" (The ugly is not in the extraordinary, but rather in the familiar, just like the beautiful is not in the extraordinary but instead in the everyday; 30). Such intimate close-ups of reality disband pre-existing meaning and ask the reader to question normative expectations that are rooted in binary categorizations.

What is clear from the above discussion is that although Brinkmann's writing is conceived as antipolitical and antitheoretical, it does contain a strong commitment to the creative act and the reader. In keeping with the Marcuse quote introducing this section, Brinkmann's call for a reconfiguration of image and word combinations that do not depict a tired portrait of reality has poetic, literary, or artistic consequences as well as a social impulse. Such a subjective creative process creates a liberated reality, which in turn helps facilitate the use of violence against the "militarisierten Standard" (militarized standard) on behalf of the "Unterdrückten, Unterprivilegierten, Ausgeschlossenen und Außenseiter" (oppressed, underprivileged, marginalized, and outsiders; "Film" 228). Literary and creative works offer a means for countering standard categories for understanding or processing experience that are perpetuated by and uphold the antilibidinal and antisensual militarized standard. He places this standard in diametric opposition to the outsiders of society, a thought that corresponds to Marcuse's "Great Refusal" at the end of *One-Dimensional Man* (257). Such creative processes would dismantle normative standards and offer new arguments for these marginalized subjects. The body and its senses, the negative experience of banalities, and the use of close-ups, repetitions, and cuts all play a part in the negative dimension to Brinkmann's understanding of literary and creative production. Because Brinkmann is highly critical of language's ability to capture real experience and portray meaning, he sees the body's language to be one primary way in which subjective experience can be textually communicated.

Brinkmann's literary commitment to the reader would suggest a social, perhaps even political, aspect to his own literary production. His interest in maintaining or preserving the individual's imaginative and sensual capacity, which he finds dwindling in the face of a rational system, is what Woolley terms Brinkmann's ethical project: "This is because he perceives existing language, logic and explanations to be upholding a stagnant society and obstructing the individual's ability to think and feel outside its structures" (8). The structures of society that merely perpetuate the militarized standard are upheld through an adherence to logical language, a language that Brinkmann sees in Germany to be cynical ("Film" 240). Because "Sprachformen" (patterns of language) dictated by genre classifications are equal to "Verhaltensformen" (patterns of behaviour), the new and subjective use of language would prompt the reader to embrace new habitual actions that ultimately liberate the reader from the repressive aspects of society (243). The physical, sensatory, and emotional processes of the body configure this language.

Brinkmann's ethical commitment is his commitment to his reader; the central issue is the reader's, and with him or her the writer's process of self-discovery, set into motion through the activation of imagination ("Einübung" 151–2). The author, or the implied author, and the reader are one and the same in this experience. Author and reader exchange perspectives and take on each other's experiences, for "das Schreiben als Spaß aufzufassen, besagt nichts anderes, als daß die kulturelle Definition 'Autor' aufgehoben ist und damit die Definition 'Leser.' – Natürlich ist das eine Utopie" (understanding writing as fun means nothing more than doing away with the cultural definition of "author" and along with it the definition of "reader." – This is of course a Utopia; 152). The author and reader are categories that belong to a tired understanding of literature that needs, according to Brinkmann, to be overhauled. By disbanding the prior meaning of literature through the use of subjective and sensual dimensions of the body and the combination of text and image, the text can approach the reader in a manner that does not speak merely to rationality. Literature should be a total body experience, and not merely regurgitate literary formulas for rational or cognitive experience. Of course Brinkmann warns that while this might sound like a theory for a new type of literature, it must not be taken as such (154). But even as he claims that literature should not be required to transmit meaning, Brinkmann's reconfiguration of literature – his aesthetic ethos or social aesthetics in relation to the author and reader – contains an ethical dimension that must be understood within the 1960s context politically and socially.

Woolley suggests that Wellershoff, though critical of society, sees society as ultimately good whereas Brinkmann, or the implied author, sees society to be the root of all negativity and foresees a reader who is critical and "anti-social"

(8). Kristeva writes of avant-garde texts that they "evolve within a system of representation that is exclusively corporeal," continuing to explain that the "moment of rejection invests that system in an a-social present and keeps it locked there" (*Revolution* 195). This negativity also indicates a critically intentional mode, as is demonstrated in Brinkmann's literary use of intimate disgust as a publicly engaged category. His essays uncover the radical implications of the negativity contained in the poetics of disgust. The suggestion that Brinkmann writes for an antisocial reader returns us to just this negativity. Ngai claims that a poetics of disgust makes room for a "reader *willing* to occupy the externalized place of radically other" ("Raw" 186). The writer-readers Brinkmann conceives of occupy the position of the other, the marginalized, the deject, and in so doing they can experience the rejection (Kristeva) contained in the emotion of disgust as a productive utopian impulse. Brinkmann's own admission above that his thinking is utopian is also an admission that negativity is utopian; the label "utopia" contains the recognition that his creative and literary processes contain ethical, moral, and cultural, if not socio-political intent – even as he denies intent: "*Ich kann ruhig zugeben, nichts damit zu meinen*" (I can easily admit that I do not mean anything by it; "1969" 14; emphasis in orig.).

Wellershoff remembers how Brinkmann, during a meeting in the Eifel, attacked New Realism's political motivation, claiming that politics are ineffective and reality can only be changed through a change in subjective feeling (Geduldig 116). Brinkmann's categorization as a New Realist has been a point for contention in literary scholarship. Moritz Baßler claims that instead of suggesting that Brinkmann belongs to New Realism, Brinkmann's early writings should be seen as inspiring Wellershoff's literary essays, something also claimed by Wellershoff (17). The relationship between the body and subjectivity, the commitment to the reader, and the focus on the private sphere, whether understood in its political form or not, are all literary interests shared by Brinkmann and Wellershoff. The above sketch of Brinkmann's essayistic thoughts on literature echoes aspects of Wellershoff's working model. And although Brinkmann's literary-theoretical musings are documented in the late 1960s and into the early 1970s, his early short stories already display issues of corporeal subjectivity, creative freedom, and an ethical relationship with the reader through negativity, issues which are also at stake at the essays' thematic core.

Regardless of Brinkmann's professed dislike of politically or socially charged literature, these early texts and the later essays reveal a commitment to the reader that must also necessarily include the reader's political and social context, the same contextual space that is traversed by the narrative bodies. The reader should not be transformed through literature, but through change in critical perspective as experienced during and after the reading act (Schäfer

71). Brinkmann's understanding of total-body writing allows the writer to re-frame momentary experience to produce a counter-normative impulse in the reader, which in turn drives the change in perspective. The corporeality of Brinkmann's "In der Grube" and the collection *Die Umarmung* resonates with socio-political debates on the political role of the body and sexuality in con-textual public discourse. However, whereas the liberation of sexuality was seen as a positive political force in most New Left writings, Brinkmann's disgusted narrators show the negative underbelly of sexual repression, *körperliche Starre*, and the effect on subjectivity. They thereby uncover the libidinally repressive aspects of the private sphere.

Chapter Three

Consumption, Vertigo, and Childhood Visions: Gisela Elsner's Grotesque Repetitions as Resistance

A glance at feuilletons of the 1960s provides the impression that a horde of beautifully horrific female authors had infiltrated the West German literary scene. Authors such as Gisela Elsner, Renate Rasp, Helga Novak, and Barbara Frischmuth were each criticized as "ungeratene Tochter deutscher Literatur" (German literature's wayward daughter; "Wir" 198).[1] Klaus Jeziorkowski's review in the *Frankfurter Allgemeine Zeitung* of Renate Rasp's 1967 novel *Ein ungeratener Sohn* (*A Family Failure*) exemplifies this:

> Was ist mit Deutschlands literarischen Frauen los? Nun, gottlob, der lesende Deutsche ist nicht mehr mit den Gretchen alleingelassen, nicht mehr nur verwiesen an die fruchtbaren Mütter mit der Last der blonden Flechten im Nacken. Jetzt sind bei uns die Biester am Zuge ... In den Verlagen schieben sich die Spezialistinnen des Bösen, im Sortiment stapeln sich die Expertinnen des Abgefeimten, die Satansbraten duften auf den Messen ... wenn die deutsche Frau – die schreibende und die beschriebene – sich wandelt, dann mit den bei uns üblichen Wonnen der Gründlichkeit, mit der Lust am Extrem. (1)

> [What is going on with Germany's literary women? Well, thank God, the German reading public is no longer left alone with Gretchen, no longer merely referred to the fertile mothers with the burden of blond braids at their necks. Now the beasts take their turn ... The female specialists of evil are pushing their way into publishing houses, the experts of slyness are packing the catalogues, the devil's brew is boiling at the book fairs ... when the German woman – the one who is writing and the one who is written about – transforms herself, then she does so with that delight in thoroughness and pleasure in the extreme customary to us.]

In the words of this reviewer, the West German reading public appears helpless against the flood of monstrous images created by equally monstrous female authors. The mention of supposedly typical Germanic qualities, noted here as thoroughness and desire for the extreme, suggests that the reviewer sees an in-born cruelty to these authors, which through the reviewer's key choice of words becomes a not-so-hidden reference to National Socialist tendencies. Both El-sner and Rasp, two of these "specialists of evil," utilize New Realist techniques of negative corporeality, extreme subjectivity, and an exacting detail of the ev-eryday to bitingly criticize what they perceive to be the double moral standard of West Germany, particularly acutely felt in the family and the private sphere. Differently however than Wellershoff's engagement of neurosis or Brinkmann's use of disgust, Elsner and Rasp clothe this critique in a hyperbolical, excessive, grotesque, and dryly humorous negativity, a feature that prompted literary his-torians to label these women's texts Black Realism.

In the preceding chapters, the private sphere was examined as the space into which society funnels unwanted and marginal behaviours or the structure in which acts deemed socially taboo were regulated. Further, the individual body in that private sphere was examined as the site at which the resulting social repression erupted. Individual subjectivity as formed in the family or private sphere, therefore, was read as depicting the problems with and display-ing the health of the public sphere, society, and the nation. In Elsner's work, a critique at once more global and localized is in play. She does not depict individual subjectivity, for individual subjectivity in her fictionalized West Germany is untenable, unstable, and, finally, impossible. Instead, she draws a bitterly critical portrait of an imaginary and collective national subjectiv-ity based in institutional hierarchy. This more generalized critique is made specific in her attacks on those institutions that are the foundation of con-temporary, postwar, middle-class society. Elsner reveals these institutions – including religion, medicine, education, and the military, and with these, national-historical identity – to be repressive, violent, and absurd. These institutions, in turn, are entangled with and dependent on the nuclear family. In a twist on the West German 1950s and early 1960s Catholic conservative government's understanding of the political, social, and national role of the family, Elsner shows the private sphere not to be merely the space for critique of the manner in which society violently regulates and represses individual desires, but also to be an organism that feeds and feeds on all other forms of institutional violence. This interest is central to her debut novel *Die Riesenzw-erge* (The Giant Dwarfs, 1964).

Negativity in this study is essential to the creation of corporeal subjectivity and the socially engaged aesthetical impulse, owing primarily to the political or ethical intentionality the literary texts display towards their readers. In El-sner's negative corporeal realism, negativity emanates not from the individual body but instead is part of the visual landscape and narrative fabric. Visuality comes together with language in *Die Riesenzwerge* to create multiple, slightly variegated, repeating reflections, which destabilize perception, reception of meaning, and representation. These repetitions form a negative affect-based aesthetics, which is best described, in Sianne Ngai's words, as a "literature of exhausting repetitions and permutations" for which she devises the word "stuplimity" (*Ugly* 9). Further, the focus of the repetitions is not only on perception, but also on bodies, body parts, meat, animals, waste, and other bits of organic minutiae. The textual landscape and fabric thus link narrative form and pattern to the critique of consumption and institutional hierarchies found in the novel's critical content and in its cultural context. The negativity in these organic repetitions is located not in the apparent effects on the individual subject in the text, but instead in the dizzying effect on the reader. Through the strangely spiralling writing style and the projection upon projection of consumptive images, the reader experiences vertigo. This is what Ngai calls "affective disorientation," which is true of many textually manufactured negative feelings (*Ugly* 17). Elsner's negativity produces a "noncathartic" emotion that brings about a "noncathartic aesthetic" as a "kind of politics" (9). This politics is one of refusal as resistance.

From New to Black Realism: Gisela Elsner and the Literary Market

Elsner made her arrival on West Germany's literary landscape through channels of the literary establishment: She read at the 1962 Gruppe 47 meeting to general applause, Hans Magnus Enzensberger published an excerpt of her work in progress in his 1962 collection *Vorzeichen* with Suhrkamp Verlag, and she received the Prix Formentor in 1964 for the publication of *Die Riesenzwerge* in that same year.[2] However, the text and the author were met with a flurry of criticisms that quickly marginalized both author and work.[3] Reviews of the time combine critique of Elsner's text with commentary on her appearance and body, a tendency that is often openly and unapologetically misogynistic. The critics regularly use language that suggests Elsner's childlike naivety is distorted by her evil feminine wiles. Günter Blöcker describes her in the *Frankfurter Allgemeine Zeitung* as a "junge Ehefrau und Mutter, kaum dem Twenalter entwachsen" (young wife and mother, barely grown out of her twenties; "Ausgeliefert" 5). *Der Spiegel* tells of the "Debütantin mit dem Kleopatra-Look" (debutante with the Cleopatra look), who, during the reading in Wannsee "vor einer teils schaudernden, teils staunenden, teils grinsenden 'Gruppe 47' als ausgewachsene Schriftstellerin entpuppte" (in the presence of a part-shuddering, part-astonished, part-grinning "Group 47" turned out to be a full-grown author; "Vom Fleisch" 118–19). These positive critiques are wrapped up in suggestive surprise that the childlike literary debutante is actually a serious author. In a different article commenting on the prize ceremony of the Prix Formentor, *Der Spiegel* provides an additional dimension to the infantilized description of the author: "Das 'sexy thing' war ... Träger des 'Prix Formentor' geworden" (The "sexy thing" was ... the recipient of the "Prix Formentor"; "Sieg" 123). The magazine's appropriation of the sexist commentary made by an English-speaking critic in the audience suggests that this prize might have been allocated with the wrong motivations.

What causes these critics to highlight her young years and attractive figure is the perceived contrast between her looks and her writing style; her texts are believed to contain a coolness and evilness that critics, in turn, seek in her person. For Walter Widmer, she is a "kalte Sphinx" (cold sphinx) who says the "unerhörtesten Dinge" (most outrageous things) with a smile (17). Blöcker names Elsner the "Kleinmeisterin des Abscheulichen" (little master of repulsion) and a "frühfertige Virtuosin des Ekelhaften, zart, aber leistungsfähig" (precocious virtuoso of the disgusting, delicate yet powerful; "Ausgeliefert" 5). Finally, a reviewer from *Der Spiegel* succinctly calls her "schwarze[] Gisela" (black Gisela; "Sieg" 123). These reviews categorize Elsner as a deviant outsider of the literary scene, a label she was never able to shed.[4] Implicit also in these reviews is the critics' understanding of Elsner's embodiment of an incongruous connection between femininity and disgust, an interest that undermines the evaluation of her prose; her body forms the object for critical analysis. Helmut Salzinger's response to Elsner's second novel in *Die Zeit* approaches this fact pointedly: "Manch einer zeigte sich schockiert, Gisela Elsner, diese noch dazu bemerkenswert gut aussehende Frau, mit einem derart offensichtlichen Vergnügen im Dreck wühlen zu sehen" (Many a person was shocked to see Gisela Elsner, this also remarkably attractive woman, rolling in dirt with such obvious pleasure; 3). This focus on the woman who writes, rather than the text she writes, is noted by Elsner herself in a later essay entitled "Autorinnen im literarischen Ghetto" (Female Authors in the Literary Ghetto), in which she takes critics to task for demanding that female authors write recognizably as women (42). Those authors who do not comply, she continues, are given "monströse Züge" (monstrous features) that suggest a danger in both their works and person (44).

This disregard for the author's texts in favour of a characterization of her appearance might also explain why Elsner has been, until recently, almost fully ignored in German scholarship.[5] Further, past scholarship fails to address adequately Elsner's aesthetics and the sociocultural framework out of which she works, wanting instead to see in her writing autobiographical tendencies or a strongly feminist stance that does not exist.[6] Her contemporary critics identify a coldness and anger in both her choice of narrative content and her aesthetic style as directly, albeit reversely, related to her feminine and costumed figure.

Although destructive for her literary import, it is this disconnect between appearance and intent that is central to her writing.

The critical reception hints at another aspect of Elsner's prose: her unique narrative aesthetics. Although the critics never discuss her style beyond the hate that they identify in the words, what they implicitly interpret as her style can be found in their own references to strange worlds belonging to fairy tales or puppet shows. Blöcker, for example, describes the imagery found in the debut novel as follows:

> Eine Welt von Automaten, die Lebewesen, von Zwergen, die Riesen zu sein vorgeben, marschiert mit marionettenhafter Präzision auf, wie auf Pappe gezogen, rückhaft am Zwirnsfaden einer eingleisigen Phantasie weiterbewegt – ein makabres Ballett von schauerlichem Gleichmaß. ("Ausgeliefert" 5)

> [A world of automatons and dwarfs that pretend to be life forms and giants, marches by with marionette-like precision, as if drawn on cardboard, jerking along the thread of a one-track imagination – a macabre ballet of frightening proportions.]

Blöcker's choice of fantasy-like words comes not from Elsner's text, but is inspired by the title of the book, a title that never appears in the text itself. Widmer claims that Elsner takes the Grimm brother's fairy tales and puts them in the contemporary everyday context of the German middle class. He continues to say that in her version, the evil witch really is pushed into the oven, and "Hänsel und Gretel hätten sachgerecht in Auschwitz aushelfen können ... Hänsel und Gretel, erfahren wir von ihr, sind lieb und harmlos, sicher auch blauäugig und blond, und sie morden!" (Hansel and Gretel could have helped out in Auschwitz ... Hansel and Gretel, she tells us, are nice and innocent, probably also blue-eyed and blond, and they are murderous!; 17). In seeing in her text a take on the Grimm brothers, Widmer diminishes the object of Elsner's criticism. Her textual focus is on social structures that she deems made the National Socialist rise to power and its crimes possible, and that continue to support the conservative Christian-democratic West Germany. Widmer circumvents a calling of the critique by name, thus making those acts part of a fairy-tale past.

While the reviewers rarely categorize Elsner's texts within any particular genre or movement, their discussion of the critical stance, the grotesqueries, and the darkness of her work corresponds to the label placed on her texts by literary historians: Black Realism, described always as an offshoot of New Realism.[7] However, it is difficult to clearly pinpoint the techniques of Black Realism as they differ from New Realism. This difficulty originates in the fact that Black Realism has rarely been used as a category of literature beyond mention in a select number of literary histories, making it a tenuous and admittedly problematic term. But Black Realism, because of the implied reference to black humour's critical and subversive potential, to the negative aesthetic implications of the colour black, but also to the word's affective charge, is ideal to describe this absurdist, grotesque, and satirical literature that is focused on the contextual everyday of the immediate present. In particular, the collision between the strange emotional detachment of these texts, their non-cathartic nature, and their narration of contemporary and recognizable concerns suggest both "black" and "realism" to be appropriate descriptors. Further, an analysis of the literary texts reveals a connection between New and Black Realism with regards to aesthetics, critical content, and implied relationship to the reader. Black Realism begins in New Realism, but essentially exacerbates all aspects of New Realism hyperbolically.[8]

As gleaned from Wellershoff's writings and Brinkmann's early practice, the important features of New Realism – or the corporeal and intimate aspects of this realism – can be consolidated and summarized as follows: the use of a subjective gaze that describes the details of the everyday world in an unfamiliar manner; the unease in the reader that disbands accepted patterns and models for the creation of literary meaning; the emphasis on the body and its negative physical reactions as a directive force for the narrative and its poetics; and the insistence on the private sphere as the prime setting for critically engaged social aesthetics. The reader's affective relationship to the negativity produced by this corporeal realism is what opens a literary portal to the connection between the private and the politically charged public sphere of the 1960s.

Like New Realism, Black Realism takes as its point of departure the present contextual context and uses the camera-like techniques of minutely examining everyday objects, turns of phrases, or actions. In the case of Black Realism, this reality is made grotesquely strange. In the first literary-historical description of Black Realism and New Realism, Heinrich Vormweg devotes an entire chapter to the literary texts analysed in these chapters. In his sketch of postwar prose for a 1973 edition of *Kindlers Literaturlexikon* (Kindler's Literary Lexicon), entitled "Zwischen Realismus und Groteske" (Between Realism and the Grotesque), Vormweg identifies a relationship among Walter Höllerer's discussion of the strange appearance of everyday detail in contemporary prose in the 1964 edition of the literary journal *Akzente*, Wellershoff's own literary debut in that journal, and Elsner's first novel (Vormweg 309). Vormweg references Höllerer in order to note the shared characteristics of Wellershoff's novels, Brinkmann's literary writings, and texts by those authors who quickly transcended their hyper-realistic descriptions (Vormweg 313). He singles out Elsner in particular, noting that her grotesques come directly from real experience, that is, from a contextually recognizable reality also experienced by the reader (314).

Elsner repeats the minutiae of this contextual reality until that selfsame reality is revealed to be absurd. In a second literary-historical categorization of New and Black Realism, Karl Esselborn, who was the first to use the exact label *Schwarzer Realismus*, deciphers the difference between these two forms of realism for Fischer's 1986 edition of *Literatur in der Bundesrepublik Deutschland bis 1967* (Literature in the Federal Republic to 1967). He sees the difference to lie in Black Realism's use of a "verzerrenden und grotesk überzeichnenden" (distorting and grotesquely overdrawn) detailed realism to create an "entstelltes Bild" (disfigured image) of middle-class life (468). H.M. Enzensberger's foreword to *Vorzeichen* supplies a formula for analysing Elsner's writing: He introduces her to the reading public as a humorist of the monstrous, a monstrous that rears its head in the everyday (15). Elfriede Jelinek confirms this formulation, seeing normality and monstrosity as coming together in Elsner's writings (27). Humour, monstrosity, and normality collide in Elsner's textual world in a manner akin to Wolfgang Kayser's description of the grotesque: "Die groteske Welt ist unsere Welt – und ist es nicht" (*Groteske* 27) (The grotesque world is – and is not – our own world; *Grotesque* 37).[9] Peter Fuß's formulation of the grotesque in modernity is also appropriate here: "Das Abnorme wird Normalität und das Normale zur Abnormität par excellence" (The abnormal becomes normality and the normal becomes abnormality par excellence; 338). Alternatively, in Gerhard Armanski's words on Elsner's writing: "Nicht der Ausnahmezustand ist die Katastrophe, sondern die Normalität selbst" (It is not the state of emergency that is catastrophic, but rather normality itself; 42). Each of these phrases is akin to Brinkmann's formulation of the ugly and the beautiful found in the familiar banalities of daily life ("1969" 30). Even in their negative portrayal of the corporeal reactions to repression of the marginalized individual, the images of Wellershoff's *Ein schöner Tag* and Brinkmann's short stories were each recognizable as part of the narrative subject's experience of a reality similar to the reader's own. In Elsner's case, however, while the details are still recognizable as based in the reader's contextual environment of 1960s West Germany, the removal of intact individual narrative subjectivity makes that world entirely strange.

Moreover, like New Realism, the Black Realist texts produce unease in the reader in order that the reader critically examines his or her own reality. The texts do so not by disbanding pre-existing meaning or images, but instead by foregrounding these to their critical advantage. Existing patterns of meaning are distorted, exaggerated, emptied, or turned on their head with a dizzying effect. The grotesquing gaze of the narrative subject in Black Realism heightens the discomfiture Wellershoff proposed should inspire the reader to rethink his or her private life. Here, the possibility of relaying a social or political message through literature can either be intensified, as in the case of Rasp, or become disorientingly ambivalent and non-cathartic, as in the case of Elsner.

If New and Black Realism share critical affinities, these are also communicated through congruous interests in the body's marginalized, negative, and subversive functions. By allowing bodily processes to dictate the narrative, this literature becomes critically productive because the integral relationship between the public and private sphere politically charges these processes. Ralf Schnell summarizes this in a third literary-historical look at these realisms in the 2003 edition of the *Geschichte der deutschsprachigen Literatur seit 1945* (History of German-Language Literature since 1945). He claims that both New and Black Realism wish to make reality tangible, but do so through two different styles (333). He says of the difference that New Realism listens closely to reality to turn that reality into language, while Black Realism gives poetological expression to distrust towards reality (333). He continues to explain that Black Realism uses alienation, distortion, and surrealism to destroy the surface of reality in order that "aus der Banalität der Erscheinungsformen die bürgerliche Realität des alltäglichen Schreckens und Erschreckens hervortritt" (the bourgeois reality of everyday horror and fright emerges from the banality of representation; 333). The marginalized body in these Black Realist narratives communicates this contextual horror and fright, for corporeal negativity is, as is true of New Realism, central to the textual critique of 1960s social structures.

In this sense, the distinction between "black" and "new" in these 1960s realisms is less categorical than the labels imply, and more a question of the "feeling tone" (Ngai, *Ugly*) of the critical voice found in or guiding the narrative. Moreover, while negative aesthetics, corporeality, and contextual linkage to the politicized private sphere are shared by both modes of realism, the difference is the belief in literature's power to transform the reader's experience of the world. While New Realism sees literature to have an ethical and transformative effect on the reader in that the reading act questions or offers freedom from normativity, both Elsner's and Rasp's texts do not hold such a promise. Instead, their texts ask the reader to resist normativity through refusal, as is the case with Elsner's novel, or passivity, in Rasp's text. The former enacts this aesthetically by allowing the narrative to "go limp" and with it, the reader (*Ugly* 297).

The Novel – *Die Riesenzwerge*

The blackness in the tone of Elsner's *Die Riesenzwerge* has its roots in two aspects of the text's use of exaggeration, excess, and hyperbole. These, in turn, are essential for understanding the political or social intent of the depiction of the private sphere in Elsner's writing. The first relates to Ngai's term "stuplimity," which describes "thick" language created of modal differences that are compounded in ever-repeating, and only slightly varying, words and sentences, images and visual artefacts (*Ugly* 250). The layering in the presentation of language or minutiae destroys all notions of progress, and instead stupefies – has a directly negative effect on – the reader. The reader's resulting paralysis comes out of the tedium that occurs in the confrontation with congealed masses of banal objects and scraps of information. The negative affect emerges from both the linguistic and the visual fields, for the "accumulation of visual 'data' induces a similar strain on the observer's capacities for conceptually synthesizing or metabolizing information," resulting in the "fatigue of the viewer's responsivity" (263). Ngai's concept of "metabolizing" visual information in literary writing is particularly apt with regard to Elsner's novel, for here, gastric, consumptive, and metabolic processes dominate the repetitions. Further, the paralysis or fatigue experienced by the reader of *Die Riesenzwerge* is brought on by the feeling of vertigo resulting from the towering distance at which the reader must view the quickly spiralling nature of the repetitions.

The world of *Die Riesenzwerge* is composed of minutiae repeated and permutated so that they coalesce into an at once simple and confusingly complex landscape. The second aspect making up Elsner's black tone relates to the grotesque nature of these minutiae. The objects of this landscape that create the narrative's textual fabric are comprised of organic matter including bodies and parts, meat, animals, waste, and parasites. Appropriately, stuplimity – different than the sublime – belongs "more properly to the dirtier environments" that are also the arena of the grotesque (*Ugly* 271). Further, other objects of the early 1960s context familiar to the reader are described with a detail-oriented obsession, in what Carsten Mindt calls a simulation of authenticity (16). It is through the grotesque that the strangeness and discomfiture produced in the reader's confrontation with the unfamiliar in the familiar occurs. Because the grotesque is part of cultural order and is a distortion of that order, transgressions that determine the grotesque's appearance must be read for their critical potential.[10] In his exhaustive study of the grotesque, Fuß claims that grotesques appear following historical, psychological, or social upheavals, because these spur on the disintegration of social structures and the breakdown of the relationship between society's elements, including its institutions and norms (93). Fuß identifies three culturally instituted symbolic ordering structures (or hierarchies) that are integral to the production of the grotesque and that are destroyed or transgressed in that production. The first, the *Verhaltensordnung* (rule of behaviour), connects morals and laws to culturally accepted ways of fulfilling desire and drives (174). The second, the *Sprachordnung* (rule of language), determines the manner in which the subject and culture are formed (174). Language is managed by the family, as a miniature of society, and inserts the child into the cultural order, thereby directing how it should act as a subject (175). The transgression of this order therefore also affects the family. The third, the *Erkenntnisordnung* (rule of recognition or understanding), structures the ascription of meaning to experiences (184). When the grotesque destroys this structuring capability, the meaningful identification of experience breaks down into unnamed chaos, causing a sensory overload. All three ordering structures are symbolic, culturally instated, and collectively constructed, and as such they are dissolved, reformed, permutated, or modified in the reformation of cultural or social structures and institutions as grotesque (192). Each of these orders is transgressed in Elsner's novel. The rule of behaviour is questioned through the emphasis on consumption and animal-like drives. The rule of language is undone as language repeats itself in endless patterns, the familial hierarchy is questioned, and individual subjectivity is eradicated. Finally, the rule of understanding is destabilized in the loss of meaning of all institutional or social experience. Because stuplimity is that which both "dulls" and unsettles, producing simultaneously "sharp, sudden excitation and prolonged desensitization, exhaustion, or fatigue," the grotesque transgressions of the novel are not actively engaged in by the reader, but are limply, dully, or even stupidly experienced (Ngai, *Ugly* 271). Elsner's text ultimately offers this experience to the reader as a mode of institutional or societal (and thus political) resistance.

Die Riesenzwerge is made up of ten chapters, entitled *Beiträge* (reports), which with their references to journalism insert realism into the novel's subtitle (*Ein Beitrag*). These *Beiträge* are narrated by a young boy of about five-years-old, named Lothar Leinlein, the double diminutive an absurd match to the already grotesque title of the novel. He watches the adult world around him with precision and vocabulary beyond his age; however, his cognitive ability to interpret what he sees remains that of a child.[11] The visual landscape of Elsner's text, the layers of representations that are reflected in the repetitive language of the text and in their grotesque content, represents Lothar's perception of his world. Further, the grotesque content of these repetitions, the text's taxonomy of the organic, underscores the quiet and consumptive violence found in Lothar's middle-class nuclear family. Finally, the critique of the family is extended to the family as one social institution among many in the cultural context that moulds, but here eradicates, individual subjectivity. As a result, the individual is no longer the space for political, social, or ethical critique, but instead is a reflective surface for the projection of the reader's own dizzying experience of the loss of subjectivity through violent institutional absurdity.

Consumptive Visuality: Repeating the Organic and Destabilizing the Real

The architecture of *Die Riesenzwerge* is one of embodiment. The repeated and collected items that craft the landscape, and thus the setting or atmosphere, of the text present us with a taxonomy of organic matter made up of bodies, body parts, waste, meat, animals, and parasites. Because the reader engages in a metabolizing, to use Ngai's term, of the repetitions, the text's fabric and landscape are consumptively visual. The final *Beitrag* of *Die Riesenzwerge*, entitled "Die Hochzeit" (The Wedding), is indicative of the visuality of the novel as a whole. The chapter contains reflections, layers, and glass, all of which highlight, impede, or obscure the act of looking and representation. In it, Lothar, the child narrator, describes a feast in celebration of his uncle's wedding that takes place in a banquet hall. The chapter begins with the wedding party sitting at the banquet table under a large painting that also depicts a wedding party at a banquet table. Opposite the painting is a wall made up of alternating windows and mirrors. An apartment block is visible through the windows. The action of the chapter is minimal: First the wedding party holds still for a photograph, then they begin to eat, and finally the bride and groom dance. Although at the novel's end, the chapter functions well to introduce the visual landscape of the novel as a whole because it highlights the problematic aspects of looking and representation and clearly identifies how these aspects affect the construction of the narrative voice itself. Visuality (what is being depicted) and language (how it is being depicted) are interconnected in their repetitiveness.

Lothar's descriptions are carried out with attention to minute visual detail with a matter of fact, dulled, or stupefied tone. "Von der Mitte der Decke hängt ein Lüster herab. Der Saal ist hell erleuchtet. Die Tische sind zu einer langen Tafel zusammengerückt" (A chandelier hangs from the middle of the ceiling. The room is brightly lit. The tables are pushed together in one long dining table; 249). This description is linguistically simple and bare of any evaluation or stylization. In keeping with Wellershoff's and Brinkmann's interest in filmic techniques in literature, the narrative functions much like the lens of a camera, for it records the environment in a close-up as it moves over the scene. Further, the carefully placed vases, plates, cups, and other items measure out the table (249). The people at the table, too, are ordered, facing forward and with no person blocking another (251). The reason behind the stiff and organized manner in which the wedding guests sit at the table becomes much clearer midway through the chapter, as the narrator describes what can only be a photographer emerging from under a black blanket (258). The use of an outmoded camera places vision in this scene in an unclear temporality, further disorienting the reader.

The fact that the wedding party's still-life pose is reflected in the room itself reinforces the pictorial nature of the scene and thus highlights the gaze and the act of looking. Above their heads hangs a painting of a wedding party eating at a long table, and the opposite wall, in the direction of the wedding party's gazes, is made up of a long row of windows and mirrors (249–50). Throughout the long description of the photography session, therefore, the wedding guests stare at themselves and at the painting above their heads reflected in the mirror. They also stare through the windows at the windows of the apartments across the way, through which others are staring back into the room. This mixture of looking is described in the following, the "sie" (they) here being the wedding party and the "Zuschauer" (audience) the onlookers:

> Sie blicken in die vom Fußboden bis zur Decke reichenden Spiegel, sie blicken durch die vom Fußboden bis zur Decke reichenden Fenster auf die in den Fenstern liegenden Zuschauer des gegenüberliegenden Hauses oder in die hell erleuchteten Zimmer hinter den Rücken der Zuschauer, sie blicken einen Augs in einen Spiegel, anderen Augs zum Fenster hinaus. (253)

> [They look into the mirrors that reach from the floor to ceiling, they look through the windows that reach from floor to ceiling at the audience in the windows of the house opposite or in the brightly lit rooms behind the backs of the audience, they look with one eye in the mirror, one eye through the windows.]

That the narrator calls the onlookers an audience adds performativity to this static scene. And appropriately, this strange moment of examination is brought to life in a grotesque manner when the guests at the table smile unsteadily at their own reflections, their faces stretching to wide grimaces, baring their teeth as if ready to bite (252). In seeing their faces in the mirrors, the people become contorted images of themselves. Through this distorted representation of the visual experience, representation as a mode of communicating meaning is placed under attack. Moreover, Elsner "denaturalizes identity by emphasizing at every conceivable juncture its imaginary bases" through the use of windows, mirrors, and paintings (Silverman 133).[12] If the act of being photographed is a performed act as suggested by the wedding party's unnatural pose for the camera, but this act is viewed through painting and mirrors, then the differences between reality and its representation, including that of identity, become blurred; the truth in representation is here found in its distortion.

The representations, and thus the text, throw their own projections and the reader is caught in the vertigo of the experience. Ngai discusses projection in the film *Vertigo* by Alfred Hitchcock (1958), claiming that the women and the man become multiple projections of each other, cast by the anxiety of the protagonist. Ngai implements the concept of "thrownness" to capture the quality of these projections (*Ugly* 216), a word apt for the quality of Elsner's text. In *Die Riesenzwerge*, "thrownness" is enacted not on the protagonist but on the reader. In a sense, the text "throws" itself repeatedly in order to place distance between the reader and the narrative. This is particularly clear in the position from which the narrator gazes on the scene. He describes seeing the faces of the wedding party not directly, but instead "zwischen ihren abgewendeten Köpfen hindurch und über ihre Schultern hinweg" (between their averted heads and over their shoulders), his position behind the wedding party locatable in the prepositions (252). His narrative gaze is given layered depth as a result of the objects and people in the immediate foreground that partially block his view of the mirror. It is this obstructed image in the mirror that the narrator describes throughout the *Beitrag*. Through the narrator's destabilizing gaze, the text illustrates for the reader not the immediate experience of the "real" image, but the image's reflection or thrown projection. This causes the bottom to effectively drop out of the "real" and the reader's sensation of vertigo to set in.

Unlike the static wedding party below it, the painting depicts a feast with the people around the table animated by food and drink. The painted people are turned towards each other, away from each other, reaching for food or holding their bellies, and springing up from their seats. Wine and meat are laid out on the table in various states of consumption and spilled or scattered across table and ground (253, 255). Just as the table of the wedding party is measured and ordered, the table in the painting is chaotic. However, the complete view of people continues to be obscured, as wine jugs or pieces of meat partially cover their faces (253–4). Again, it is important to note the mirror in this narrative description, for throughout the scene the reader has no direct view of the painting. Further, the painting also displays in its subject matter the obstruction of the visual. The items blocking the full view of the people suggest that the bodies, painted or not, are layered behind the objects in the foreground.

The presence of the painting, the mirrors, the gaze of the cameraman through the aperture, and the gaze of the audience across the way through the two sets of windows tessellate the narrative fabric of this visually complex final *Beitrag*. The scene thereby questions perception and representation through the mode of framing. In *Framing Attention*, a study of windows in modern German culture, Lutz Koepnick notes that the window connects dissimilar spaces while at the same time reinforcing the boundaries between those spaces (1). The frame "reorders spatial arrangements and demarcates competing zones of distance and proximity" (2). In so doing, the window frame helps to define the nature of the visible while teasing out "different habits of looking and perception" along with our place or role as onlookers, or "viewing subjects" (3). Koepnick reminds us that perspective always comes in the plural (38), which is here shown in the many positions of the gaze. In the scene at hand, the windows are not so much portals to be looked out of, allowing the seer to connect to the temporal and spatial difference of the landscape outside, but are instead windows for looking inside, into the private and intimate space of the party. Because of the presence of the painting in the room and the immobile state of the party, the windows and mirrors act no differently than a painting. The audience members of onlookers, moreover, remain out of sight and the majority of them cannot see what is actually taking place. Instead, they call to their neighbours above and below for visual information. Even in its obstruction, vision is central.

The frames, too, underscore vision. Koepnick notes that the picture and window frame never recede from view (5). This is also true of this final *Beitrag*. If images are blocked in the painting itself, the framing of the painting by the windows and mirrors exacerbates this obstruction, as in the following example:

> An den Rändern der gespiegelten Bildteile beugen sich kopflose Rümpfe weit zu irgend wem hinüber ... An den Rändern der gespiegelten Bildteile beugen sich rumpflose Köpfe einem zwar teilweise durch Gegenstände oder andere Teilnehmer verdeckten, doch verdeckt im Spiegel Sichtbaren zu. (256)

> [At the edges of the painting's reflected parts, headless bodies lean toward someone ... At the edges of the paintings reflected parts, bodiless heads lean towards something that, while partially hidden by objects or other participants, is nevertheless visible hidden in the mirror.]

This complex play with words, perception, and representation shifts the focus to the obscured and missing item as the visible object. The description becomes even more convoluted as the audience of neighbouring onlookers outside the windows joins in, here looking in at the room seeing the reverse of the above:

> Die rumpflosen Köpfe sowie wem sie sich zubeugen, müßten die zwischen zwei Spiegeln durch die Fenster aus den Fenstern des gegenüberliegenden Hauses blickenden Zuschauer erkennen ... Die kopflosen Rümpfe müßten die zwischen zwei Spiegeln durch die Fenster aus den Fenstern des gegenüberliegenden Hauses blickenden Zuschauer erkennen. (256)

> [The audience between two mirrors through the windows looking out of the windows of the opposite house should be able to make out the bodiless heads and the people they are leaning toward ... The audience between two mirrors through the windows looking out of the windows of the opposite house should be able to make out the headless bodies.]

The thick language created through the use of the participle construction and the repetitive subjects and objects grammatically mirrors the complex image presented here. The wedding party, framed by the windows, replaces the painting for the onlookers. From the wedding party's perspective, they see themselves as a painting, the mirrors framing and reflecting their faces along with the painted faces above them.

These complex forms of perception offer a visual translation of Elsner's understanding of the relationship between the real and its representation. Through the multitudes of reflective surfaces, the real itself becomes a problem. Jean Baudrillard's characterization of the orders of the simulacra, particularly the third order in which simulation "threatens the difference between the 'true' and the 'false,' the 'real' and the 'imaginary,'" supports Elsner's play with the concept of the real by making the real always already a simulation (*Simulacra* 3). Instead of separating the real object from its reflection or displaying the possibility of the real to reproduce itself in a series, Elsner presents readers with models that repeat with modulated differences (*Simulacra* 3).[13] The visual is central here, but its ability communicate meaning is rendered uncertain. The heaviness of the stuplimitous text focuses solely on minute details, the "finite and small," repeating these to the infinite and the eradication of the original (Ngai, *Ugly* 278). This minute repetition is true of both the visual and linguistic fields.

The relationship between the objects represented and the real objects in this scene is presented as a relationship of layers and obscurity. The "real" wedding party not only looks at a representation of a representation, but they, too, cover items in the painting as if they were part of the painting itself (249). In the mirrored reflection, the heads of those standing below the painting are superimposed onto the dirty floor of the painting, which is covered in pieces of meat and pools of wine (257). This creates a connection between the pictorial debauchery of the feast and the ordered cleanliness of the wedding party's table below. Inspired by the painted table, the wedding party begins to eat their chicken drumsticks with their hands, thereby obscuring their faces with the meat just as in the painting (264). The painting as a representation precedes the real.

Moreover, the reflective surfaces in this scene make it appropriate that speech acts are crafted out of repetitive nonsense, creating a linguistic chain that folds back on itself endlessly, as in the following example: "'Man irrt sich eben,' sagt der, der gesagt hat: 'So ist das also,' und dann: 'Wer hätte das gedacht'" ("Well, people can be wrong," says the one who said: "Well, it's just like that," and then: "Who would have thought"; 273). These empty phrases, which function as identity markers, are those used in everyday speech and do not communicate meaning. One figure breaks down with: "Kann einer von euch vielleicht sagen, was ich meine?" (Can one of you maybe tell me what I mean?; 265). In answer, the other guests stuff their mouths with the drumsticks in their hands, consumption replacing the act of communication. Language has no content-based meaning and is merely representative, even as these representations are thrown projections.

But in Baudrillard's thinking, the era of simulation is very much ingrained in a digital age, a mode in which genetic repetition is also one of digital copying. Elsner's visual world belongs not to a digital age but instead to an organic and even what could be called a gastric age. Elsner's simulations are after all of the body and are specifically made up of the body's acts of consumption; the simulations function as the waste of the lost "real." For this reason, they are not binary, but multiple – Ngai's heaps – and are entirely made of organic matter. Gilles Deleuze's characterization of the baroque in *The Fold* provides additional understanding of Elsner's repetitions. He writes: "The Baroque trait twists and turns its folds, pushing them to infinity, fold over fold, one upon the other. The Baroque fold unfurls all the way to infinity" (3). Like Baudrillard's simulation that is a series with no true original, "every fold originates from a fold," which becomes an infinite process (11). The folding and pleating of the baroque trait relates to the inorganic as well as the organic. In the case of the inorganic there is a repetition with "difference of proximate dimension," whereas the organic "envelops an interior site that contains necessarily *other* species of organisms" (10; emphasis in orig.). Both inorganic and organic folds are at work in the final *Beitrag*. While the visual landscape is created out of inorganic folds of language, each minutely different from the other, the content of these folds is corporeal and organic.

The second chapter of *Die Riesenzwerge* introduces a key image for further understanding how Elsner's language augments the aesthetic construction of the visual landscape of the text with organic matter. The second *Beitrag* of *Die Riesenzwerge* sees the narrator, Lothar, accompanied by his mother to the doctor because she fears he houses, or hosts as the title of the chapter "Der Wirt" (The Host) suggests, a tapeworm. The parasite is a prime symbol for Deleuze's discussion of the organic fold, for it is an organism within an organism, which multiplies endlessly. However, as a symbol, the parasite is also distinctly related to language. In a study of parasitic theory entitled *Die Logik des Parasitären* (Parasitic Logic), Claudia Jost notes that the parasite is someone who eats with the other, or eats/uses the other (4). She explains that language creates a tension in the parasitic act that simultaneously portrays the act of violence and the release of that violence. Both movements are part monstrous, part enjoyable, an enjoyment that reaches destructive excess in the absolute eradication of the other (6). The worm can be read as a marker for the language of the text that is created out of worm-like segments, as Mindt argues in a reading of *Die*

Riesenzwerge in comparison with the *nouveau roman*.[14] The doctor explains to Lothar and his mother the biology of the tapeworm as a "Kette von Gliedern, sonst nichts" (chain of segments, nothing else; 49). In addition, the doctor elucidates that the worm, as a parasite, needs no organs of sense because his host has these (49). The reader also takes up the position of the parasite, reliant on Lothar's vision as host to create the text. For this reason, the visual landscape is Lothar's external projection of the internal sensory experience of the parasite and its destructive metabolism.

Like the parasitic worm, Elsner's individual sentences are simple and minute, made up of repeated small segments that create a thick and complex whole (Mindt 51). Illustrative of this quality, the novel's openings lines are constructed of simple subjects, verbs, and objects: "Mein Vater ist ein guter Esser. Er läßt sich nicht nötigen. Er setzt sich an den Tisch" (My father is a good eater. He does not need cajoling. He sits down at the table; 7). At the end of the first *Beitrag*, this simplicity has become a long run-on sentence continuing over seven lines of text, only to be stopped by the short sentence "Meine Mutter ist eine gute Köchin" (My mother is a good cook; 31). Not only do the individual segments of language grow like the tapeworm, but also the chapter is closed by a slightly upended version of the opening sentence. The mother cooks for the father, placing the two poles of the normative, nuclear family at each end of the first *Beitrag*.

The opening and closing sentences of the first chapter underscore a second feature of language in the text: relationality. Just as the worm's segments follow on one another, words and phrases are repeated in a way that they mirror, reflect, or somehow alter that which came before. In the wedding scene, the textual descriptions of the difficulties surrounding representation and vision are directly connected to a skewed repetition of linguistic phrases that become meaningless. The repetition occurs each time out of the slightly different order of the repeating phrases and sentence elements. The only way in which sense can be made of these passages is in the relationship of the elements to one another. Lothar grotesquely orders his visual world, which in turn works as an effect of or as affecting the language of the text, again through grotesque transgression. This segmented and relational quality of language becomes central to multiple aspects of visual representation throughout the ten *Beiträge*. Further, the endless repetition renders the content nonsensical and destabilizes the *Erkenntnisordnung* that orders meaning-making capabilities.[15] The sleuthing that the reader must engage in places the text at a further vertigo-inducing distance.

Elsner's characterization of language and the visual in these chapters suggests that subjects and objects alike obscure reality's representation. That the minutiae of the repeated descriptions would both be of language and about language adds language itself to those representations that throw their own projections. The clear link between language and the tapeworm also allows for language to take on an organic quality by proximity. The final feature of the tapeworm is that it continues to grow; the segments can replace themselves ad infinitum. Throughout *Die Riesenzwerge*, Lothar asks his father what number comes after ten, a question to which he never receives a reply. In the final chapter, Lothar counts ten people who leave the ballroom. The text closes with the exchange: "'Welche Zahl,' frage ich einen Kellner vor dem Saaleingang, 'kommt nach zehn?' 'Elf,' sagt der Kellner" ("Which number," I ask a waiter outside the entrance to the hall, "comes after ten?" "Eleven," says the waiter; 281). Lothar is his own answer as he is the eleventh person to leave the ballroom. The child's acquisition of meaningful knowledge here in the form of representable language is the first step down the path to acquiring subjectivity. However, like the worm, whose wriggling tail continues to grow, this path is endless: after 11 comes 12.

Familial Permutations: Consumption, Excess, and Parasitic Order

The tapeworm cannot be read only in terms of the language of the text, but must also be seen in terms of the organic content, or the corporeality, of the repetitions. The sole function of the tapeworm is to feed off the body of its host, having gotten there, as the doctor explains, through the host's consumption of raw meat. Fittingly, the doctor hopes that the tapeworm lodged in Lothar's intestines is the "Schwarzen" (black one; 48). Like the Black Realism of Elsner's prose, the worm that is the metaphor for the language of the text is black. The content of the repetitions, series, folds, and permutations that describe the prose are marked by the grotesque in the form of bodies, meat, organics, and waste, all in states of violent consumption or being consumed. If the above discussion hinted at the linguistically transgressive aspect of the grotesque as well as its ability to undermine meaning making, here this comes together with the transgression of the rule of behaviour. Elsner's Black Realism critiques the private sphere and the nuclear family, and all other middle-class institutions upholding Christian conservative West German society of the 1960s, as violent and destructive, in particular for the development of individual subjectivity.

The narrative construction of the text mimics the segments of the worm that grows as it consumes its host. It is therefore none too surprising that the primary thematic focus of the novel remains centred on bodies found in acts of consumption. Like the grammatical structures and visual imagery, the figures as well as constellations of families multiply before the reader's eyes, though these are often mirrored in fun-house-like fashion. Elsner's critique is not based in individual subjectivity, but in the structures and institutions that form individual subjectivity. That this is rooted in the act of consumption – be consumption the eating of food, the buying of goods, or, more broadly, the intake of that which is fed to the subject (religion, education, military or national history) or that which capitalist society makes the subject desire – would suggest a metabolic, organic, and grotesque quality to Elsner's social aesthetics.

The clearest connection between consumption and the familial institution is found in the opening image of the text. As already noted above, the novel opens with a meticulous description of the family midday meal:

> Mein Vater ist ein guter Esser. Er läßt sich nicht nötigen. Er setzt sich an den Tisch. Er zwängt sich den Serviettenzipfel hinter den Kragen. Er stützt die Handflächen auf den Tisch, rechts und links neben den Teller, rechts und links neben Messer und Gabel. Er hebt das Gesäß ein wenig vom Sitz. Er beugt sich über den Tisch, daß seine Serviette herabhängt auf den leeren Teller, und übersieht so den Inhalt der Schüsseln. Dann senkt er das Gesäß auf den Sitz. Dann greift er zu. (7)

> [My father is a good eater. He does not need to be cajoled. He sits down at the table. He wedges the corner of the napkin behind the collar. He places his palms on top of the table, right and left of the plate, right and left of knife and fork. He raises his buttocks off the chair slightly. He leans over the table so that the napkin hangs down onto the empty plate and surveys the contents of the bowls. Then he lowers his buttocks onto the chair. Then he digs in.]

The nuclear family, made of father, mother, and son, sit down to their midday meal and therefore set the critical, gastric, and black-humorous tone for the entire text. The repetitive surface tension created by the visual imagery in the final *Beitrag* is already present at the start of the text: The grammatical forms, the relationship between the sentences, and the ordering of movements so that one follows another all create a narrative fabric of unending reflection organized around the feast.

The narrator's precise description of the father introduces the family figurehead and sets up the familial structure and relations of power, to be repeated in differing configurations throughout the text. Künzel writes that consumption, as a social and cultural concern, is the central theme of the text, particularly when it comes to the display of power and violence ("Gisela" 98). Consumption is connected to the family and the private sphere. Power relations and violence in the family are already clear in this first depiction of the meal, and each of its members is determined by consumption. The first sentence not only claims that the father is a good eater, but also introduces the narrative voice, his child Lothar, who describes his own meal as one that would fit into the father's many times over (7). The difference between the son's and the father's meals is relational and hierarchical. The mother's position within the family is introduced through the intake of food. The father chews while staring at the mother's head, which is lowered as she dishes up her own, smallest portion (7). The mother's meal, even smaller than that of her son, reflects her lowly status within the familial configuration. She bows her head throughout the meal, and her disgust towards food reveals itself in the fact that she can only choke down a few small bites (8). Moreover, the fits and starts in which she eats her food are related to the manner in which she speaks in half-finished sentences, such as "ich weiß wirklich nicht wie ich mich" or "ich komme mir vor wie" (I really don't know how I, ... I feel as if; 62, 66). Both food and language disgust her.

The familial hierarchies and configurations of power as suggestive in this meal are made threatening in the figure of the father. The narrator places the accent on the father's excessively large corporeality: "Sein Bauch berührt die Tischkante. Seine Schenkel klaffen so weit auseinander, daß ein Kopf Platz hätte zwischen ihnen" (His belly touches the edge of the table. His thighs are spread so far apart that a head could easily fit between them; 7). The father, the well-nourished head-of-house, rests his belly against the table and spreads his legs in a self-assured and sexualized image. The threatening aspect of the father's consuming body becomes clear in Lothar's description of his father's mouth, filled with teeth, including gold-capped incisors, that snap shut over the fork like a dog gnawing on a bone (9). The gold incisors, along with the large belly, are an indication of the successful West German economic miracle. The father's closing words for the meal, after wiping his face with a napkin and pushing his chair demonstratively away from the table, are therefore intended as entirely ironic: "Ich bin kein Vielfraß" (I am not a hog; 10).

If the opening scene characterizes the family as a deeply hierarchical, threatening, and fundamentally parasitic institution and does so through the theme of consumption and middle-class ritual, then the closing scene of the wedding party shows how these structural aspects of the family are not specifically gendered, as the opening might indicate. The wedding party scene closing the book also describes a family feast. This time, the woman is the threatening and corporeally dominant figure, while the man is diminutive and submissive. The bride eats with excessive enjoyment, while the groom eats small bites, which he washes down disgustedly with water (264). Upon finishing the meal, she, like the father in the opening scene, wipes her face with a napkin, pushes her chair back from the table and comments: "Ich bin kein Vielfraß" (I am not a hog; 266). The groom resembles the mother of the opening scene, for he is small and pale (261). Further, the painting that hangs above their heads augments this visual pairing of the opening and closing feasts of the novel. The bride below the portrait exclaims that she is sitting under the bride, to which the other guests remark that the groom is sitting under the groom (260–1). The bride and groom in the portrait match in figure the husband and wife in the opening of the novel, the painted bride pale and worried, the painted groom wearing a "prahlerischer Miene" (boastful expression) and pointing with a fat finger at the painted bride (260, 261). This complex reverse mirroring of familial portraits underscores a secondary dimension to these distorted *Doppelgänger*. The painted groom's pointing finger as well as the bride's recognition of the painted bride suggests misrecognition of self and other and therefore a destabilization of individual subjectivity in the face of institutional, here familial, hierarchy and violence.

Fulfilling the threatening nature of the feast as a theme in the novel, the wedding party turns violent. As the bride and groom are called to the dance floor, the bride's hunger follows. She lowers her face over the groom's head and bites his hair: "die Braut, spuckt das Haar auf den Boden, beugt das Gesicht, als habe sie Heißhunger auf Haar" (the bride spits the hair onto the floor, lowers her face, as if she were craving hair; 271). The ritualistic aspects of love, celebration, and feasting are transformed into the ingestion of the loved one. This scene of cannibalism also has its counterpart in the opening chapter. As the first *Beitrag* continues, the reader discovers that the father presented in the first few pages is Lothar's stepfather, who has, at least according to the narrator, killed and eaten Lothar's biological father. The first chapter breaks to recount an event that occurred in the past. The family, now made up of Lothar, his mother, and his "smaller" father, or the biological father, goes to a hotel restaurant to eat because the mother has burnt the roast. As Lothar wanders through the restaurant, he describes the hungry guests as they become restless, waiting for their food. In the main dining room, Lothar encounters the man who will become his stepfather, identified as the Herr Oberlehrer (Mr Schoolmaster): "Sein Bauch berührte die Tischkante. Seine Schenkel klafften so weit auseinander, daß ein Kopf zwischen ihnen Platz gefunden hätte" (His belly touches the edge of the table. His thighs are spread so far apart that a head could easily fit between them; 21). The appearance of the Herr Oberlehrer introduces the importance of institutional hierarchy in the already hierarchical configuration of the family, and it does so by repeating in exact words the image from the novel's opening. His entrance causes Lothar's family to panic; Lothar's biological father is a schoolteacher and the Herr Oberlehrer his supervisor. Lothar's biological father worries that the Herr Oberlehrer has noticed him before he has had a chance to initiate greetings (25). This fear of having breeched the hierarchically determined code causes the mother's and father's oblivion to the increasing chaos around them in the restaurant. By using the excessively large body of the Herr Oberlehrer to represent institutionalized as well as familial power and by comically highlighting the family's panic at the breech of etiquette in light of the absence of food and hungering masses, the text questions the importance of such hierarchies through absurd exaggeration.

The breach of hierarchical propriety, a transgression of the rule of behaviour, allows for the cannibalistic act to take place. When the Herr Oberlehrer notices the lesser teacher, he rhetorically questions in a manner appropriate to his pedagogical role: "Was tun zwei, die sich kennen?" (What do two people who know each other do?; 27). As if using the weaker man as a scapegoat, the Herr Oberlehrer suggests, with the anxious and hungry crowd gathered around him, that it was perhaps the transgressor who had eaten all the food (28). The assignment of guilt paired with the suggestively physical prod of the fork into the man's side sets the mob in motion. They attack the father, turning into a "großes knurrendes Knäuel aus Armen, Beinen, Rümpfen" (large, growling ball of arms, legs, torsos), out of which appears the occasional arm raised overhead with fork in hand (28). When the mob scatters, the guests drag pieces of the father away to hide under the restaurant tables. The breech of the first rule of behaviour in the hierarchical misstep gives way to another breech as the mob satisfies their hunger (primary drive) in an animal-like manner not condoned by culture. As this occurs, the mother excuses herself to the bathroom, refusing to stop the violent act from occurring but also unable to watch. By refusing to see, or rather refusing knowledge of the event, she is able to retain the moral high ground and opt out of participating in what becomes the collective guilt of the restaurant patrons. The satisfied patrons leave money on the table before exiting the restaurant, paying for the guilt of eating human flesh.

Franziska Meyer, in her contribution to the collection *Post-War Women's Writing in German*, correctly reads this opening chapter as a critique of the West German economic miracle, particularly the "wave of gluttony that had been conjured up was now to wash away the evil spirits of the German past and give large parts of the West German population a false new sense of self value" (50).[16] The power relations contained within the constellation of the family as it mirrors other social institutions sparks this violence of "unrestrained gluttony" (50). Meyer's analysis engenders a useful connection between the context of consumption in the late 1950s and early 1960s and the devouring of the father's body. The scene challenges the harmlessness of the successful economic miracle and links prosperity to an unresolved question of guilt, uncovering the violence at the root of West German economic recovery that has been channelled into consumption.

In keeping with contemporary realities, Elsner's critique finds consumption originating in the private sphere. Throughout the boom of the 1950s and early 1960s, economic growth and modernization of consumer society occurred in West German households. Volker R. Berghahn argues in his essay in *The Miracle Years*, "Recasting Bourgeois Germany," that the *Bürgertum*, or middle-class society, had been reconfigured by the end of the 1950s to include mass culture, and with it mass production à la Fordism (338). The integration of mass culture into the *Bürgertum* sparked, in turn, the development of mass consumerism in the private households of West Germany. Arnold Sywottek argues in the same collection that Economics Minister Ludwig Erhard's slogan "Prosperity for All!" was by 1957 applicable to most West Germans, their private living standards of the prewar years reached or surpassed (341). This increase in standards was related to the rise in homeownership, or "living space," by the end of the 1950s (348). The home allowed for the addition of modernized living features, bathroom facilities, central heating, and entertainment devices such as televisions.

The discussion of increased consumption within the familial or private living space corresponds to Family Minister Franz-Josef Wuermeling's writings on the economic support of families, the necessity of living space for the family, and the emphasis on single-family homeownership. One of the primary protective concerns of his family policy was economic. He writes in 1960 that economic family politics aim to create equal opportunities for all families with children, "also soziale Gerechtigkeit" (that is, social justice; "Schutz" 88). For Wuermeling, this economic support was primarily intended to ensure that mothers remained true to their roles within the family and did not seek employment outside the home. He explains in a second essay from 1960 that "Familienlastenausgleich" (family burden sharing) means "Kaufkraftausgleich innerhalb jeder sozialen Schicht zugunsten der Familienväter" (balance of purchase power within each social class in favour of fathers), which should change a society he perceives to have become hostile towards families and children ("Gefahr?" 102). Hans Harro Bühler's 1961 study of these policies claims at the outset that since its inception, family politics has two primary motivations, these centred around socio-political issues and the market (9). Bühler closes with the claim that family politics through property politics should be the focus of the family ministry's policies (99).

While subsidies for the financial assistance of families with children were central to Wuermeling's family policy, his primary concern was the promotion of private property through single-family homeownership (Wuermeling, "Acht" 159). Homeownership had both financial and moral implications. In his 1961 retrospective look at eight years of family politics, Wuermeling cites as one of the primary economic successes of his family policies the "*Förderung der Eigentumsbildung* unserer Familien" (*promotion* of our families' *property development*), the focus being homeownership ("Acht" 168; emphasis in orig.). This support of homeownership was intended to build a new German society, a rebuilding which began within the private walls of the home.[17] In a 1963 essay "Wohnungsbau als angewandte Familienpolitik" (Apartment Building as Applied Family Politics), he writes that the task of family politics is to secure for families "Lebensraum ..., den sie brauchen, um in sittlicher Ordnung gesund leben und sich natürlich entfalten zu können" (living space ..., which they need in order to live in healthy moral order and to develop naturally; 142). In order to achieve this goal, the state must support "familiengerechte Wohnungen" (family-friendly apartments) and "wo nur möglich Eigenheime" (wherever possible single-family homes; 142). The single-family home in particular acts as the family's economic support system and as the "Grundlage ihrer politischen Freiheit und Unabhängigkeit" (foundation of its political freedom and independence; 151). Wuermeling therefore sees homeownership not only as financial security for the family, but also as protective space for the family's freedom and as such, necessary for a "wohlfundierter Staat" (well-established state; 152). Homeownership solidifies the economic and moral bonds of the family and, by extension, strengthens the nation.

Dietrich Haensch criticizes this policy in 1969. He quotes Wuermeling as citing the single-family home as offering the family space for true development, and goes on to explain that development meant for Wuermeling "Kinderreichtum" (large numbers of children; 82). In turn, many children and property ownership complicate divorce, and family property makes it difficult for youth to leave their parental home in due time (82). It is this repressive home, one of Wuermeling's family-friendly apartments, that dominates the protagonist's thoughts in Brinkmann's "In der Grube," while the attempt to prove lost single-family homeownership by the father causes the son in Wellershoff's novel psychic distress. Elsewhere, Haensch continues, "Familieneigentum bindet die Kinder an die Familie und sichert damit einen langandauernden Erziehungseinfluß der Eltern auf die Kinder" (family property ties children to their family and thus secures the parents' long-term educational influence on the children; 136). According to Haensch, this makes it more difficult for the child to become independent, binding the child more closely to the parents. In the 1950s and early 1960s national imaginary of the economic and political foundations of the West German private sphere, private homeownership and familial consumption was seen to empower the family economically, morally, and politically and thus to solidify society's fundaments. By the end of the 1960s, it represented the entrapment of the child and the repression of individual and societal growth. Elsner's 1964 text prefigures this late-1960s critique of consumption and consumerism.

Wuermeling's early 1960s praise of his financial support of the family leading to the spread of ownership specifically of single-family homes and Haensch's analysis of this view from 1969 suggest that Elsner's first novel slips neatly into the postwar discourse on the role that familial consumption played in promoting the moral health of the nation.[18] Elsner transfers her depiction of consumption almost solely to food, a central "wave" of 1950s economic-miracle West Germany (Sywottek 349–50). If Elsner's texts are bent on dismantling the "Spießbürger" (philistines; Salzinger 3) as most reviews of her subsequent novels imply, then the family is the space in which the *spießige* (philistine-like) attitude is learned and cultivated through consumption. By focusing on the consumption of food as a violent metaphor for the past and locating this consumption in the family, Elsner has taken Fordism to the organic level. As with the mass production of automobiles, the subject is mass-produced (as is the visual landscape) and therefore is devoid of individualism. Moreover, the private sphere that creates the consuming public is unreflective about the violent atrocities of the past, continuing to spout empty phrases of discipline such as "wie man ißt, so ist man!" (you are what you eat), without being a model for that behaviour (*Riesenzwerge* 9).

Such empty phrases return to the rule of behaviour that is transgressed in the feast scenes. The transgression occurs when family hierarchies and learned social propriety are each exposed as artificial and rooted in violence. Moreover, the masses' willing participation in the murder and their devouring of the smaller father all indicate the brutality of the inheritance of the fascist past and are a critique of its masked perpetuation in 1960s West German society through the topos of consumption (Cremer 55). As seen in the discussion of cultural context above, the family and the private sphere are essential to this connection. Elsner allows the nuclear family to be violently reconfigured through consumption. The father's murder by his double suggests his self-consumption, meaning not an upheaval of the social and a reorganization of law in terms of the Freudian murder of the father, but a continuation of violence condoned by the original father and thus of a violence condoned by society overall.[19] *Die Riesenzwerge* corresponds to Wellershoff's understanding that New Realism's larger social and political critique should address specifically the private realm.

The narrative authority places the inception of the violently reconfigured family in the destruction of individual subjectivity through a reference to the Freudian primal scene, which is the identity-forming moment the infant or young child sees or hears his parents engaged in the sex act.[20] The restaurant scene of cannibalism is told within the narrative structure of the first *Beitrag* as a flashback or memory occurring on the day the family has visited the biological father's grave. This memory is textually framed by orality. Fleeing his parents' fighting voices, Lothar locks himself in his room to take refuge under his bedcovers and suck on a bag of candy given to him at the graveyard (18).[21] At the end of the recounted cannibalism scene, the bag of candy is empty and he emerges from under the bedcovers (28). The movement of time, from present to past to present, is inscribed by the full and then empty bag of candy as well as the entrance into and exit from the bed. Because the parents fight over the death of Lothar's biological father, their fight catapults the child back to the moment of his death, which becomes the primal scene, and allows for its retelling in the text. A key component to the primal scene is the child's experience of his parents engaged in sexual intercourse as a violent and transgressive act instigated by the father on the mother. Read as Lothar's primal scene, the cannibal scene pairs familial violence with consumption and locates the transgressive act not between mother and father, but between father and father. The family dynamics are configured by sexualized and violent transgression. Künzel suggests that a reading of this moment as a primal scene makes clear that the cannibal scene is merely an imaginary; that the cannibal scene is introduced from Lothar's bed connotes a dream-state that paves the way for the imagined memory of the father's death ("Gisela" 103). Whether fantasized or remembered, the text presents the child-narrator's interpretation of this moment as a true experience. Therefore, the effects on the child – and thus on the reader – are part of the text's constructed reality. Further, the second time Lothar listens to his parents fighting, they fight over who is to blame for the tapeworm in Lothar's intestines. The mother's words "weil er es noch weiß" (because he still remembers it) from the original fight are here replaced by "weil du das Fleisch halbroh willst" (because you want the meat nearly raw; 17, 32–3). The visual and linguistic repetitions as marked by the symbol of the worm as discussed above thus have their origin in the subject's identity-foundational, primal experience of the family as violently consumptive.

Through her manipulation of this and other Freudian moments, Elsner's transfer of sex to food comments upon familial configuration. From the boy-narrator's point of view, the mother marries and cares for the man who consumed her first husband. In so doing, she perpetuates that consumption. Both sexes are culpable for the postwar perpetuation of violence as located in the private sphere. The day after the visit to the gravesite the mother prepares the midday meal, and the reader is reminded of the cannibal scene. "Sie kniet nieder vor dem Kühlschrank, zieht einen großen Klumpen roten rohen Fleischs aus dem Eisfach, trägt das Fleisch behutsam in beiden Händen vor sich her zum Abguß" (She kneels in front of the refrigerator, pulls out a lump of red, raw meat from the freezer, carries the meat carefully in front of her with both hands to the sink), the passage and chapter ending with: "Meine Mutter ist eine gute Köchin" (My mother is a good cook; 30–1). The mother facilitates the step-father's consumption of meat/the father through her assumption of the role of the good wife. The conclusion of the first *Beitrag* containing the cannibal scene with the preparation of the bloody clump of meat reminds us of the father's bloody flesh and illustrates a cycle of cannibalism. The son and mother eat the father symbolically in the form of meat, thus placing the origin of the violent cycle of social hierarchy in the home and family.

Further, the raw meat lodges the worm in the child. Because the worm is a visual and linguistic narrative device, even writing itself and the creative act are not free from this familial violence (32). The common usage of the term parasite to refer to someone who takes advantage of another also sustains the broader critique of consumption. The parasite lodged in Lothar's intestines eat-ing and eating with Lothar, therefore, is symbolic of the textual characterization of problematic familial intimacy. Elsner characterizes consumption in a folding of organic bodies that is an intimate and violent act of pleasure ending in de-struction. The cycle of death and rebirth of the fathers continues; because Lo-thar effectively receives the worm from his stepfather through the stepfather's preference for raw meat (read human flesh), the worm references the parasitic enjoyment of eating the flesh of the biological father. As Mikhail Bakhtin writes of the grotesque body: "From one body a new body always emerges in some form or another" (26). Like the worm that continues to add more segments as it grows, the bodies in *Die Riesenzwerge* multiply.

The Destruction of Subjectivity and Institutional Absurdity

The sexualized violence of the meal conjoins the 1960s critique of fascism and the critique of 1950s gluttony to the image of the grotesque male body and fatherhood as well as complicit motherhood in the text. However, this critique of violent consumption is not reserved for the family. In the sixth *Beitrag* of *Die Riesenzwerge*, "Die Ruderer" (The Rowers), the mother disappears, noted by stepfather and son only through the missing midday meal. During their search among the women of the town, Lothar and his stepfather come across a family, the woman identical to his mother with a young boy and small father in tow (150). The information that they are going out to eat because the woman has burnt the roast compounds the eerie constellation of the look-alike mother, dead father, and son. This reminder of the starting point that ushers in the can-nibalism gives way to a different type of meat orgy: The search by father and son leads them to a butcher's shop that is surrounded by a mob of "schmatzenden" (lip smacking) people, cheering at intervals (150). This mass of people resemble the cannibals, and the streets are teeming with pieces of meat akin to a scene of slaughter, blood replaced by pools of oil and fat (150). As if wounded in battle, people lay among the pieces of meat with pants unbuttoned and clutching half eaten sausages (150–1). The earlier depiction of hunger is now one of absolute gluttony.

The masses inform stepfather and son that the butcher is celebrating his twenty-fifth anniversary by inviting his customers to eat as much as they can. The narrator describes the butcher, his red and sweaty head turned towards the crowd, his mouth wide open and his eyes squeezed shut as he throws sausages to the waiting people (152). This image conjures up the figure of a grotesque carnival barker, drawing the masses to his sideshow, the association compounded by the people jumping up to catch the falling sausages with their mouths like trained animals (152). The offer of unending consumption of free meat causes their immediate eradication of human subjectivity. Moreover, Meyer suggests that the butcher's twenty-fifth anniversary would put him opening his shop around 1939 (55). The sausages therefore also symbolize the dead bodies of the war. The social commentary on the excesses of 1950s and 1960s capitalism connects these excesses to the elation of the beginning of the war, aligning the feasting masses feeding on the war dead with the text's cannibals. Further, the text monstrously sexualizes the image of grotesque consumption, describing in minute and excessive detail how the butcher licks then presses the sausage slowly into his mouth, deep enough to bring tears to his eyes, and pulls it slowly back out again (153–4). This portrait reinforces the sexual element of consumption in Elsner's prose as the butcher mimics an act of deep-throat fellatio. The bursting skin of the sausage implies the rupture of male flesh and the ensuing devouring of the sausage returns the reader to the consumption of the father. This image teeters on the pornographic as the customers voyeuristically watch the butcher, eyeing the sausage jutting from his mouth with the saliva and juices running down his cheek like ejaculate.[22] Lothar's spectatorship of the butcher, moreover, links this scene with the boy's primal scene. As in other sexualized images of consumption, the image of the butcher possesses an undercurrent of violence, adding an excessively threatening aspect to the nature of both production and consumption. The consumption of the suggestive sausage represents the gluttony of economic-miracle production that was built upon the dead of the war. This shows on the butcher's body, which also oozes like the ruptured sausage in an overdrawn caricature of economic success.

Elsner portrays these bloated cannibal-like bodies as markers of socially accepted immorality, such as killing to retain institutional hierarchy or gluttonous waste in the face of suffering. She locates the origination of this social commentary in the family as a social institution that fails to uphold the tenuous border between acceptable satisfaction of desire and its transgression. Returning to

Fuß's grotesque orders, in these scenes of gluttony, the rule of behaviour and rule of language break down in grotesque permutations. Because each of these ordering structures is culturally bound and dictated by normative, acceptable, or social-historically constructed understandings, then reading their grotesque reformation unlocks their contextual critique.

The scenes of consumption also coincide with a destabilization of individual identity of the family members: the twinned father and the multiple mother.[23] The sixth *Beitrag* ends with Lothar becoming the *Doppelgänger* child. Lothar notices a boy on the other riverbank (156–7). Lothar begins to gesticulate and the figures mime each other until Lothar has difficulty deciphering who moves first, the boy or himself. The scene ends with a definitive answer, as Lothar stretches out his arm and the boy does the same: "Ich meine ihn, er meint mich. Diesmal ist kein Irrtum möglich" (I mean him, he means me. This time there is no error; 163). Like the pointed finger in the wedding-party scene, this moment for potential self-definition is mere misrecognition. Lothar attempts to separate his understanding of self from the image of the *Doppelgänger* across the way. The language of the text makes this act of self-definition impossibly absurd; contrary to Lothar's claim, this moment holds nothing but error and confusion. When later Lothar walks back to the town centre, he is mistaken for another boy and called to supper (167). When asked by the family who he is, Lothar cannot answer (169).

While this loss of subjectivity destabilizes the narrative authority even further, it also refers to the overall critique of the institutional eradication of the subject found in *Die Riesenzwerge*. The family, and with it the private sphere, is the foundation and backbone for multiple institutions implicated in Elsner's critique of capitalist and consumerist society, including the military, religion, and the medical profession. The critique of the education system warrants a closer examination here because of its immediate relationship to the Leinlein family and its formative role with regard to children and the private sphere. In the third *Beitrag*, "Der Knopf" (The Button), the education system is shown not to mould new subjectivities, but to eradicate subjectivity all together.[24] The Oberlehrer as the family patriarch also represents the institution of the school, which is located across from Lothar's home. Lothar watches him teach from the vantage point of his bedroom window. Each school morning begins with strife at home: "'Jeden Morgen das gleiche!' ruft mein Vater jeden Morgen" ("Every morning the same thing!" yells my father every morning; 59). This strife begins with a button missing from the father's shirt. No matter how hard she tries, each day the mother cannot sew on the button and must ask a neighbour for help. Lothar watches from the window as the appalled father goes to the school and drills the room full of boys on how they would go about sewing on a button in an over-detailed lesson in procedure. Simultaneously, back in the home, the mother manically practises sewing buttons onto the tablecloth. The father's lesson parodies pedagogical techniques. Using one of the students, Jaul, as the example for the entire class, the father takes the students step-by-step through the process by asking them questions that guide them through the task in an absurd manner (73). The father punishes the students by forcing them to stand and hold their books above their heads. The lesson ends in the students' loss of self: "'Was tut ihr?' ruft mein Vater. 'Alle!' 'Nähen,' rufen alle Schüler ... 'Und wie heißt ihr?' ruft mein Vater. 'Jaul,' rufen alle Schüler" ("What are you doing?" shouts my father. "All together!" "Sewing," the students shout ... "And what are your names?" my father shouts. "Jaul," the students all shout; 84). Not only do the students mistake holding their books for sewing, they also lose their identities and become the example student Jaul. Lothar cannot identify individual students, because all he can see from his vantage point at the bedroom window are arms raising books overhead.

The father teaches a traditionally female task to his all-male class, a task that his wife cannot accomplish. Concurrently, Lothar hears a grammar lesson wafting from the windows of another classroom in which the students chant noun declinations of *der Vater* (father), *die Mutter* (mother), and *das Kind* (child). The lesson reinforces the hierarchal nature of the family and the school as an institution and grounds this hierarchy in language, the subject's acceptable mode of self-expression. The sound of the children's voices declining nouns accompanies the lesson of the button, thus the declination of family members underscores the social and gendered order of the family. In addition, from within the home Lothar hears his mother breaking dishes as she pulls the tablecloth closer with each button (84–5). The scene equates familial and gendered tasks with institutional tasks, exposing them all as bizarre and meaningless through strangely empty repetition. School represents the training ground for familial hierarchy made absurd. When coupled with the violent institutional importance of hierarchy from the cannibal scene, this scene undermines the power of the institution that the violence above instated.

What this critical vignette shows is the manner in which Elsner deconstructs the "Alltagsmythen der Adenauerzeit" (everyday myths of the Adenauer era) in order to uncover the institutional structure behind West German society as threatening and violent (Cremer 42). This violence is grounded in a historicity that has been covered up by consumerism, be this of food and goods, or of teachings and belief rituals. Elsner exposes this violence by using absurdist or transgressive imagery. The text reorganizes the acceptable manner for the individual satisfaction of drives and, in so doing, reconfigures the recognition of the meaning of that institution in society. The institutional critique is founded on a critique of the private sphere. Elsner deconstructs the everyday myth of the morally intact nuclear middle-class family as having the utmost social, political, and national importance by exploring all the absurd possibilities of power, violence, and hierarchy built into the family. To do so, she uses a realism founded on everyday and banal experiences recognizable to the reader as part of early 1960s West Germany, these taken to an extreme hyperbole through stuplimity. In accordance with Brinkmann's formulation, "das Häßliche steckt nicht im Außergewöhnlichen, vielmehr in dem Vertrauten" (the ugly is not in the extraordinary, but rather in the familiar), we find Elsner's negative critique of an absurdly structured society to be in the ugliness of the familiar and the intimate ("1969" 30).

Elsner claims in an essay published in 1989 entitled, appropriately, "Bandwürmer im Leib des Literaturbetriebs" (Tapeworms in the Body of the Literary Market): "Ich schreibe seit langem realistisch" (I have been writing realistically for some time now; 250). In the same year as this essay she writes with characteristic black humour in a letter, "ich bin eine schmutzige Satirikerin" (I am a dirty satirist; qtd. in Künzel, "Schriftsteller" 346). Her interest in realism is present throughout *Die Riesenzwerge*, as is her biting self-aware humour. Elsner's characterization of consumption as housed in the family and the private sphere is largely a critique of the institutional eradication of individual subjectivity in West Germany. In keeping with satire's political stance, the family's negative depiction gains political, even national importance; Elsner's critique of the family is also a critique of all those institutions at the base of West German society. The text, depicting the family as a network of permutated bodies – the doubled father, the replicated mother, the multiplied family, the brides and grooms, and the proliferating children – destabilizes the family as a socially based and culturally defined institution. Like the visual landscape exemplified in the final *Beitrag* in which the "real" is no longer identifiable or even available, the outwardly and inwardly multiplying bodies eradicate all original individual subjectivity. This understanding takes the one-dimensional, progress-oriented, consumer-capitalist society that Marcuse critiques, also in 1964, the same year as the novel's publication, and multiplies that one-dimensionality to a grotesque monstrosity. Elsner's text makes the claim that in 1960s West Germany, only institutionally manufactured individuals exist, their subjectivities and therefore the private institutions on which the subjectivities are based rendered absurd, animal, and violently transgressive.

Nowhere does this have more implications for the reader than in the doubling of the narrative authority in the sixth *Beitrag*, which in turn creates a "vertigo of doubling" in the text for the reader (Baudrillard, "Order" 70). Because of the use of the first person as well as our reliance on his gaze for the visual landscape and the text's narrative fabric, or linguistic architecture, Lothar's position is also the reader's position. His and our inability to lock onto one original, not even with regards to the narrative self or authority, causes a negative disorienting and dizzying feeling. The reader's uneasy vertigo brought on by this corporeal and organic stuplimity insists on the reader's critical recognition of the parasitic nature of intimate and familial institutions and their role in perpetuating historical violence in the reader's own experience. The contextual political implication of this negative corporeal realism returns us to the non-cathartic effect found in negative affects. Elsner harbours an "aversion to the fictions which make psychic and social existence tolerable," and therefore her aversion is not solely class-based, gender-based, or even historically based (Silverman 126).[25] Instead, like her narrative permutations, the source of her criticism has not one original but multiple institutional forms. As a result, the only impulse communicated by the text is resistance to all institutions of power in the form of refusal. Ngai writes: "The negative affect of stuplimity might be said to produce another affective state in its wake, a secondary feeling that seems strangely neutral, unqualified, 'open,'" which in turn makes possible the "resistance" of the subject within a larger system (*Ugly* 284, 294). The reader of Elsner's *Die Riesenzwerge* is asked to, in confrontation with these institutional systems, resist by "going limp or falling down, among the bits and scraps of linguistic matter" (297). Because the text does away with the individual body, the heap of bodies should be read as a parable for the national body, for as Punday writes, "society ... is comprised and defined precisely by the multiplicity of the 'body'" (160). The body politic cannot be singularly embodied, but instead is a multiplied body that becomes the "imaginary position from which the whole of the nation can be narrated" (160). In Elsner's text, the nation is a monstrous collection of bodies and organic matter. The infinite aspect of these permutations is negatively portrayed to inspire a loop of continual critical resistance, for as Helmut Salzinger notes: "Die Spießer sterben niemals aus" (The philistines will never die out; 3).

Chapter Four

Discipline, Love, and Authoritative Child-Rearing: Renate Rasp's Satire as Pedagogical Tool

Die staunenden Zuschauer im Panoptikum der ausgepichten *femmes de lettres* recken gern weiterhin die Hälse nach jeder Neuen, um so lieber, wenn man uns kommt wie Renate Rasp. (Jeziorkowski 1)

[The marvelling spectators in the panopticon of the cunning *femmes de lettres* like to crane their necks for every novice, especially if that novice is one like Renate Rasp.]

Like Elsner, Renate Rasp was one of the "Spezialistinnen des Bösen" (female specialists of evil), gracing the literary market with her darkly humorous texts.[1] Rasp made her debut in 1967 with a reading of her poetry at the Gruppe 47 meeting at which Günter Grass reportedly exclaimed: "Sie drücken uns nicht, sie *schreiben* uns an die Wand, die Frauen" (These women are not pushing us, they are *writing* us against the wall; qtd. in Bender 180, emphasis in orig.). In that same year, Wellershoff commissioned a short story of Rasp that was published in the follow-up volume to *Ein Tag in der Stadt*, entitled *Wochenende*. Also in 1967, Kiepenheuer & Witsch published her novel *Ein ungeratener Sohn* (*A Family Failure*).[2] The novel received a flurry of primarily positive reviews that were nevertheless what Birgit Kneip has termed "gönnerhaft lobend" (patronizingly praising; 222). Elsner and Rasp have the literary market's misogynistic response to their debut novels in common, a response couched in critical approval. Indicative of this, at the Gruppe 47 meeting, the audience asked Rasp to read a second time because, as critic Hans Bender reports, the audience members made up of mostly men wanted to be sure they had heard correctly what Rasp read with cool calculation (180). In Bender's assessment, it is the female author's lack of emotion and the directness with which she presents her social critique that remains both surprising and beguiling to the male-dominated literary market. However, like the critical response to Elsner's writing, the appraisal of Rasp's texts takes a back seat to the fact that the author is surprisingly "auch noch fotogen" (on top of it all photogenic), the critics transforming her readers into spectators craning their necks in the quote above, more interested in the female author as an image than the texts she produces ("Wir, Zöglinge" 198; Jeziorkowski 1; Krüger 4).

But Rasp herself engenders a connection between her body and the literary marketplace: She appeared topless at a 1968 reading of her poetry at the Frankfurt Book Fair. This performance was reported on as a scandal and outlined within the context of a surging popular interest in sexuality and the sexualized body by such media outlets as *Der Spiegel*.[3] It is clear that Rasp intended the move to be a political statement that should be read within the context of the burgeoning feminist movement in West Germany and the critique of cultural consumption determined by a patriarchal literary establishment. What Rasp's book fair stunt displays is the increasing public face of all aspects of literature (author, text, market) that works in tandem with the undeniable politicization of literature by 1968. These two aspects come together with the author's increasing interest in controlling that marketing and politicization.

Rasp's debut novel is also blatantly political. *Ein ungeratener Sohn* confronts the family's authoritarian and violent capabilities in the disciplining of its children. The nuclear family, again configured by the realities of the postwar period as a mother and stepfather, attempt to cultivate their son, Kuno, into a tree. In the previous chapters the political aspects of literature were always tied to the repression or distortion of social, psychological, and institutional subjectivity recognizable to its readers as formed in the private sphere and family. Rasp's literary-political interests are directly communicated through the text form itself in her use of satire, a mode of writing in line with New and Black Realism's critical interests.[4] This direct communication is the result of satire's demand not only for very specific contextual references in the text, but also for an author-reader critical consensus on that context, a consensus that demands politicized negativity.

As was the case in the previous texts, in Rasp's novel, corporeal subjectivity is central to the text's communication of critique. Kuno is both subject and object of the text's parable-like satirical critique of discipline and authoritative child-rearing practices. He relays the experience in a subjective yet non-critical manner to the reader and is the bodily object around which the parable turns. Here, the subjective voice is collapsed entirely into the corporeal, which is ultimately also where the negativity of the text form is communicated to the reader; the non-mediated and non-evaluative first-person stance of this highly embodied narrative voice is the voice of satire. A closer look at subjectivity, embodiment, and the familial configuration reveals that it is not "holy hate" that guides this satirical impulse (Lukács), but rather "unholy" love; love, instead of hate, drives the satire by creating the familial nexus and thus forging the negativity of the social aesthetics. The novel is a parable for the contextual discourse on discipline, education, and children in the reshaping of historically-bound national identity in the postwar period. The contextual discourse about child-rearing forms a critical consensus on anti-authoritarian pedagogy for the novel. *Ein ungeratener Sohn* shows very clearly how the private sphere jumps from the literary page and becomes political in practice in late 1960s West Germany.

Realism and the Satirical Impulse

Rasp's first publication, the short story "Der Spaziergang nach St. Heinrich" (The Walk to St Heinrich), was published and received as an exemplary New Realist text. As was the case with Brinkmann's "In der Grube," Wellershoff commissioned this short story with specific outcomes in mind. In the introduction to the volume he discusses his choice of its topic, the weekend, because of its strong connotations of the private sphere and individual experience (10). However, of the texts included in the volume, he comments that from under a seemingly harmonious surface, hidden aggressions and violence bubble up, which are often expressed as "betuliches Um-einander-besorgt-Sein" (fussy concern-for-one-another) in mimesis of private experience (11). Further, Wellershoff writes in this introduction that he has often heard the outcry that this or that text is too private. He calls this an all-too-common argument that seems superfluous in a time that is characterized by the "Privatheit des Lebens" (privacy of life; 11). This privacy includes the increasing subjectivity, intimacy, and psychology of daily life in the face of dissolving norms and values, all of which have become the focus of literature. Here, Wellershoff formulates similar concerns as in his essay "Zu privat: Über eine Kategorie der Verdrängung." These thoughts about the private sphere that are key to Wellershoff's new-realist blueprint are sparked, in part, by soon-to-be black-realist Rasp's contribution to the volume (*Wochenende* 12). Rasp's novel also confirms Wellershoff's assessment of the short stories, for the non-evaluative, non-critical, and highly satirical subjective voice creates for the reader a surface under which familial violence and aggression bubbles.

In his review of the novel, Bender says that it should be called a satire, "die das Lachen verbietet" (that prohibits laughter), and continues to note that the novel's reality is obviously contemporary reality (180). With a sharp gaze and darkly humorous or satirical voice, Rasp's narrator describes the surroundings of the home in a manner recognizable to 1960s readers. Bender confirms that the setting for the novel is one that is new-realistic, for the novel's expressed interest in capturing the slightest changes and impressions correspond precisely to what

Bender sees as the agenda of New Realism (180). Other critics also comment on the close relationship between Rasp's writing and West German reality, paying particular attention, however, to its dark tone. K.H. Kramberg comments ecstatically, "Welch grausamer Einfall!" (What a horrific thought!), and continues to claim that the story is not fictional, but instead "innerlich wahr" (internally true), the core of the disciplinary program surely one that many parents would like to follow (26). The words "horrific" and "true" merge here in an affective synonym for Black Realism. Jeziorkowski takes the identification of a specific reality behind the parable further. Instead of merely claiming the parable's internal truth-value at its core, he sees its direct contemporary references:

> Wir kennen solche totalitären Strukturen in der Familie, die der schiere Hohn sind auf jenes Bild einer deutschen Ludwig-Richter-Hausidylle, wie es Familienministerien noch immer als Buntdruck verbreiten. (1)

> [We know of such totalitarian family structures that are a downright mockery of the image of the German Ludwig-Richter idyll of the home as it continues to be spread in Technicolor by the family ministries.]

Here, the mention of the West German family ministry points to specific contextual political structures built up around the private sphere as resonating in the story. Contemporary critics therefore were keyed into the fact that Rasp's short novel is to be read with the 1960s West German reality of the family and the private sphere in mind. This recognizable reality is essential if satire is to be politically effective. However, also because of satire, the literary re-rendering of this reality is dark. Black Realism, as indicated by the two parts of the term, utilizes the affective charge of the emotive word "black" to describe and critique contemporary, everyday reality. Words such as distortion, strangeness, and the exacerbation of unease are essential to Rasp's writing. However, the result does not have the same dizzying effect on the reader as was the case in Elsner's *Die Riesenzwerge*. Instead, an excessively sober tone emanating from the embodied subjective voice collides with the utter lack of distance between the reader and text in the satirical perspective.

The thinking about satire in the twentieth and twenty-first centuries generally goes hand-in-hand with the discussion of a specific set of tangentially related aesthetic features and shared content-based intents. Satire is most often seen in relationship to, though not as synonymous with, humour, comedy, farce, irony, the grotesque, or the absurd, and is primarily ascribed critical – sometimes revolutionary – socio-political functions. In his examination of twentieth-century German satire, Ludger Claßen calls satire not a genre, but a form of expression most often founded upon an idealistic, utopian image (8–9). Because of this, the satirical impulse is more or less understood as the "Negation des dargestellten Negativen als Utopie" (negation of the portrayed negative as utopia; 9). Negativity is essential to satire, for it provides satire with its weaponry (Arntzen 6). In the section "Juvenals Irrtum" ("Juvenal's Error") contained in *Minima Moralia*, Theodor Adorno points out that irony, which he calls the voice of satire, highlights the negative by taking the object at face value, that is, by taking the object to mean the positive thing that it claims to be based on (239; "Juvenal's" 210).[5] But this negativity can be properly understood as such only when the conditions for satire are found in the text's context, or rather, the reader's immediate reality (Claßen 9). The negativity with which that context is approached builds a negative utopia that functions as a provocation. The recognizable relationship between text, audience, and context is essential for satire to be read as such and not merely as a fantastic, or more worrisome, mimetic, representation of reality.

Georg Lukács explains in the essay "Zur Frage der Satire" (On the Question of Satire, 1932) that literary satire is a fiercely political form of expression (87). Its primary purpose is to uncover the direct contrast between *wesen* (being, or reality as it is) and *Erscheinung* (appearance, or reality as it appears to be) in society (90). This contrast must be obvious to the reader; the reader must agree that what is being portrayed is truly possible in that society, system, or class for the satirical effect to succeed (93). However, the satirical content must be seen as related to reality, but entirely separate from reality, thereby producing an obvious contrast between the real (*wesen*) and its representation (*Erscheinung*). Fifteen years later, Adorno seems to agree with this assessment, even as he claims that in postwar Germany there can be no more satire, not because there are no more norms, but because in post–Second World War society, ideology and reality are one and the same ("Juvenals" 241; "Juvenal's" 211). Adorno argues that for satire to functionally exist, a portion of society must recognize the difference between reality and ideology and form a critical consensus about that gap (241; "Juvenal's" 211–12). If reality itself tends towards the satirical, any possibility of its satirical negation through critical consciousness has been eliminated.[6] Claßen summarizes Lukács and Adorno by writing that both understand consensus to be a part of society "der zur gesellschaftlichen Wirklichkeit in Widerspruch steht" (that stands in contrast to societal reality), continuing to explain that "die Kritikwürdigkeit des in der Satire Dargestellten ist nur aufgrund des gesellschaftlichen Konsenses evident" (that which is critique-worthy in satire is only evident through societal consensus; 16). Essential to the effectiveness of satire according to this reading is the critical consensus existing beyond the narrative. The intentional critique of the text is not formulated within the text, but it is only recognizable in text because of extraliterary consensus (Claßen 16).

The narrative strategy of satire is driven by negative emotion. Lukács sees socially critical literature becoming satirical when it is written with passionate and clairvoyant hate that sees in the symptoms of a social system its illness and "Todeswürdigkeit" (death-worthiness; 100). He calls this passionate and negative impulse holy hate, which sees through all possible representations to get to the core of society's despotism. Hate is the primary affective form of satire. Arntzen calls this emotion indignation and sees it not to come from the author, but from within the text itself (14). This emotion results in its aggressive potential that sometimes overtakes the reception of its aesthetic form (Künzel, "Schriftsteller" 348). Powered by hate that plays an artistic role in shaping creative potential, satire must fight the central crimes of a specific normative or social order and form the vehicle for radical revolution (Lukács 99–100, 103). How this is done formally in terms of textual aesthetics is indivisible from *wer-wen*, or who criticizes whom (99). Claßen reminds us that satirical novels leave us with no figures for identification and forgo plausible plot, but instead they build on their own constructedness by incorporating fragmentary typologies into their texts instead of true characters (158). Straddling realism and avant-garde strategies, the satirical novel oversteps boundaries, breaks rules, and combines forms, in a sense as aesthetically radical as its intended effect.

Satire's features correspond to those of Black Realism, for literary satire is strikingly dependent on realism to formulate its recognizable context and on darkly humorous negativity that originates from within the text. That the focus of satire functions only when that which is criticized is part of normative culture corresponds with Wellershoff's understanding that literature should critique normative aspects of society to allow the reader to question that normativity in his or her reality. Lukács sees this critique in satire always to be directed at a certain social class, and in keeping with this understanding, the critical attack on reality in New and Black Realism has been directed at the postwar West German middle class. The question raised by these texts, though, is not one of economics or social inequity, but of learned behaviour patterns modelled by society's institutions. The satirical aspect to the contextual reality of Rasp's *Ein ungeratener Sohn* is found in the exacerbated gap between reality and ideology, or *wesen* and *Erscheinung*, found in postwar discourse surrounding the historical-national import of child-rearing and education. The true revolutionary potential of this satire comes through in its clear linkage to the political role of the private sphere in the 1960s family. Moreover, throughout this study the corporeal aspects of aesthetic narrativity provide the reader with a window onto contextual reality. This corporeality is markedly negative, including affective emotions of neurosis, disgust, and "stuplimity" (Ngai) in the respective chapters. In Rasp's novel, negative corporeality forms satire's skeleton; the embodied narrative authority at the centre of the narrative is both subject and object – *wer-wen* – of the satire. This satirical *wer-wen* is empowered not by hate, but by love that is horrifically violent.

The Novel *Ein ungeratener Sohn*

Rasp utilizes satirical strategies in order to provoke a critical reflection on individual conformity. Her portrayal of the authoritarian family Merz plays on the critical consensus on child-rearing, discipline, and education found in public and political pedagogical discourse of the novel's context. The short novel charts Kuno's attempts to please his stepfather by agreeing to a regimen of torturous discipline, the goal of which is Kuno's metamorphosis into a tree. The plan fails when the stepfather prunes the child: The graphic description of the severed hands returns the boy to human form, for he bleeds instead of oozing sap. After the plan fails, the son is left to languish, becoming an obese and immobile figure with pincers for hands. The plan to turn the child into a tree is to be read as a satire on the effects of authoritative child-rearing that is told through a highly subjective narrative voice. The novel itself is constructed in dual-flashback form, as the middle-aged Kuno tells the story from the perspective of two different time periods: the duration of the discipline and the period following its failure. Because of this remembering subjective voice, the reader is given no distance to the events in the text, but instead experiences them along with the subject and object of the satire, Kuno.

Discipline is central to the interplay between text and context, and thus to the extraliterary critical consensus in *Ein ungeratener Sohn*. In *Discipline and Punish* (1975), Michel Foucault defines discipline in the following manner: "Discipline increases the forces of the body (in economic terms of utility) and diminishes these same forces (in political terms of obedience)" (138). The disciplined body is both productive in the sense that it performs or becomes that which discipline requires of it and political in that it submits to the power working behind discipline. He locates disciplinary practice, as an "'anatomy' of power," within society and its institutions, including penitentiaries or the army (215). He notes that special attention should be paid to how the family has absorbed the practices of these institutions, "which have made the family the privileged locus of emergence for the disciplinary question of the normal and the abnormal" (215–16). The family, as a disciplinary institution that has itself been disciplined through its internalization of other courses of discipline, determines normativity for the individual subject in the private sphere as he or she moves into the public sphere. Disciplinary practice makes up the primary plot of the parable. The satire uses the family Merz as a private disciplinary institution to access national discipline. The topic of discipline connects the private sphere with the public and political spheres in late-postwar West Germany and with the emergence of leftist critical consensus that disciplinary practices must be radically overhauled. The child mutilated by the family stands in for the individual mutilated by the state.

Love is the negative affective emotion behind this satirical impulse. Like neurosis in Wellershoff's novel and disgust in Brinkmann's short stories, a violent appearance of love configures the familial nexus that allows for the deformation of corporeal subjectivity, thereby producing a negativity that is to be read in political terms. And like the stuplimity of Elsner's novel, this "unholy" love is produced solely from within the narrative fabric of the text, and as such it is neither evaluated nor condemned by the author or by the narrative authority. But because satire demands that the reader actively engage with the resulting negativity, lest the satire be misrecognized as fantasy or mimetic representation, this love inspires in the 1960s reader radically intimate change.

Disciplining the Family Tree: The Parable

Two images offer us a visual entry point to the topic of discipline central to the novel's parabolic form. The cover of the first edition of *Ein ungeratener Sohn* sports a drawing reminiscent of medical textbooks of the early modern era.[7] It pictures a nude male figure with the muscle tissue exposed, showing the grain of the arms and breast with its bald head turned slightly to the side as it looks off into the distance. The arms are opened to the viewer, palms turned outward in an inviting gesture. At the genitals, which are white and stand out against the darkened grainy tissue, the legs are joined in a tree trunk. The figure resembles an arboreal merman as the legs open only at the feet to give the impression of roots. A second image provides an interesting topical turn on the dust jacket, this image found in a reprint of a 1744 French medical textbook by Nicolas Andry on children's orthopaedics.[8] The text catalogues deformities of the child's body and contains images that explain how to correct these. All but one of the images depict human forms; the image accompanying the article entitled "Ungestalten der Schenkel und Füsse: krumme Schenkel" (Deformities of the thighs and feet: bent thighs) pictures a bent sapling roped to a pole.[9] The text instructs the parent or guardian to straighten the child's misshapen thighs as one would straighten a young tree by binding a metal pipe to the child's legs (Andry 277).

The cover of *Ein ungeratener Sohn* places the object and issue of corporeal discipline at the absolute centre of the text, while the second image suggests that the difference in disciplining the child's body like a tree or to become a tree is minimal. The novel's parable-like depiction of discipline is made up of different layers: the discipline of the body, the discipline of the senses, and the discipline of language. Each layer is intended to eradicate all aspects of the child's humanity, bringing him closer to the disciplinarian's goal: the transformation of the child into a tree. Throughout Rasp utilizes familiar and intimate objects of the postwar West German household to create the recognizable link to the contextual private sphere. At the same time, the novel itself – in keeping with the concept of the parable – is timeless, for it is never quite clear when the story takes place. At the outset of the disciplinary process, the narrator is ten years old and at the end of the book, fifty, placing the entire course of discipline in unclear temporality. The novel is to be read as a contextually driven satire that doubles as an immutable parable.

The stepfather, whom Kuno calls "der Onkel" (Uncle) or "Onkel Felix" meticulously orders the discipline of Kuno's body, beginning with the careful planning and regulation of the task. The stepfather has considered every detail of the project of discipline, creating his tactic and measuring the movement of the shadows of other trees in the garden at the place set aside for Kuno's planting. This measurement takes place daily over years (18). He minutely records every change of the garden in a logbook in preparation for the beginning of the course of discipline. This fastidiousness continues in the stepfather's written outline for completion as well as his detailed record of the daily process as it proceeds.

> Er hatte vierhundert linierte Blätter in Leinen binden lassen und in der Bibliothek eine Ecke für weitere Bände und Leitzordner ausgeräumt. Auf dem Etikett am Rücken des Buches las ich meinen Namen: "Kuno I," und kleingedruckt: "Gymnastische Übungen." Ich sah an Onkel Felix' grünem Lodenarm vorbei auf die leeren Seiten mit dem Wort "Beobachtungen." (20)

> [He had four hundred lined pages bound in linen and made space in the corner of the library for more volumes and binders. On the label of the spine of the book I read my name: "Kuno I," and in small print: "Gymnastic exercises." I looked past Uncle Felix's arm clothed in green loden cloth at the empty pages with the word "observations."]

Aside from leaving empty pages for notes on the observation of the development of the boy's body, the stepfather has filled the book with sketches of gymnastic stick figures taking up a variety of positions. The book, therefore, contains a corporeal codex the boy must follow. The book, once bound, becomes family law.

The stepfather as disciplinarian breaks down the boy's body into a controllable anatomy, which he will then monitor, measure, and chart. Foucault explains that discipline of the body is achieved through its meticulous structuring by controlling the use of its time and gestures. Each body part is economically ordered to support the act required by discipline (152). This exhaustive scheduling of the body has four features: "It is cellular (by the play of spatial distribution), it is organic (by the coding of activities), it is genetic (by the accumulation of time), it is combinatory (by the composition of forces)" (167). These four features, moreover, are matched with four techniques. Discipline "draws up tables; it prescribes movements; it imposes exercises; lastly, in order to obtain the combination of forces, it arranges 'tactics'" (167). These features and techniques together display an organized and rational strategy for the discipline of the body that is based in power. This strategy describes the stepfather's own. The spatial distribution of the discipline moves the body from rooms within the house and to the garden as it increases its affectivity, the coding of activities is seen in the organization of exercises or food intake, and the accumulation of time is clear not only in the planning phase but also in his growth from age ten to seventeen at the time of planting, and beyond. That these forces work together is clear in the library of volumes, where the combination of all features and techniques are mapped and archived. For not only does the disciplinarian order each of the body's modes according to plan, from biology to movement, but he also extensively charts the process. Specific to the exercise of discipline is the means of observation that watches the effects power has on the disciplined body. These effects are formative: "Discipline 'makes' individuals; it is the specific technique of a power that regards individuals both as objects and as instruments of its exercise" (170). The individual body constructs itself – as subject – by carrying out the discipline of which it is the object (*wer-wen* or who-whom of satire).

It is among the volumes in the library that we find the first layer of discipline: corporeal discipline. The task of transforming the human boy into a tree brings with it first and foremost the physical changes his body will undergo. This begins already in the planning, or tactical, stage. When the stepfather turns his interest to Kuno's feet, for example, he pulls out his collected volume on roots. The stepfather explains that plants with a strongly developed root must be cut back, using the books to illustrate his point. The root book portrays every kind of root possible, from the healthy roots of flowers and plants, to grey and rotting roots (94). On its final pages, the root book establishes a connection between the human body and plant-life.

Für die vorletzte Tafel hatte er ein medizinisches Sachbuch verbrannt, nur eine Abbildung des menschlichen Mundes übriggelassen. Ein Gebiß zum Aufklappen. Onkel Felix ließ uns die roten gemalten Lippen, das bräunlich getönte Pappkinn beiseite biegen. Zweiunddreißig Zähne bleckten auf dem Papier. Ein Griff unter das Zahnfleisch legte Wurzeln bloß, die weiß und spitz im Kiefer steckten, wie in einem roten Beet. Den Abschluß bildete ein Farbphoto von meinen Füßen, rosa und sorgfältig pedikürt, wie sie damals waren. (94)

[For the second to last chart he had burnt a medical textbook and left nothing but a picture of the human mouth. A jaw to flip open. Uncle Felix had us fold aside the red painted lips, the brownish tinted cardboard chin. The paper bore thirty-two teeth. A grasp at the gums exposed roots that jutted out of the jaw as if in a red flowerbed. A colour photo of my feet, pink and meticulously pedicured as they had been back then, concluded the book.]

The book visually compares the roots of teeth with the preceding roots of plants, making both essential to the transformation of the boy's naked and pink feet. It thus draws preliminary parallels between organic human matter and organic plant matter. This menacing image doubles also as the primary goal of the course of discipline, for the plan survives or fails with Kuno's ability to grow roots.

The stepfather begins externally moulding the boy's body by changing his diet, commanding the child to eat only vegetables and water (19). Kuno feels the effects of this starvation about halfway into the text, when he begins to steal rye flour, holding the wet clump in his mouth for hours, slowly swallowing it to prolong relief from hunger (53). In starving the boy, the stepfather trains the boy's physical appearance to remain bony, with the intent of resembling wood. The hunger also forces the boy's increasing dependence on his parents, as all food is kept under lock and key. Moreover, the child must follow the gymnastic assignments written in the book of exercises, carrying these out in his mother's sunroom. In one of the few glimpses the reader receives into the book of exercises, we learn of their menacing names that hark back to torture devices, "das Körbchen, den Stiefel, die Waage, das Rad" (the little basket, the boot, the scale, the wheel; 43). This list of items anticipates the torture to come, as benign objects are used to describe rigorous figures of physical discipline. As in the case of the control of the child's food intake, these figures are used to control the child, the difficult exercises used by the stepfather as punishment (42). The text correlates discipline as educative cultivation and discipline as punishment, each of the disciplinary tactics originating in a place of power, domination, and authority.

By starving him and guiding his body's movements, the parents gain control over the child's human bodily functions, the culmination of which is the absolute immobilization of his body. Kuno's mother awakens him early one morning and tells him to hurry down to the kitchen, where the boy finds it

transformed into an operating room, with a folding cot, enamel bowls filled
with water, and a pile of towels monogrammed with the stepfather's initials
in red at the ready (64). The kitchen, the space for sculpting the boy's physical
appearance through controlled food intake, becomes the space for transforming the human body into a tree. Familiar things of the home turned unfamiliar
through their new utilitarian value populate the room. This also applies to his
parents. Both stepfather and mother have dressed for the occasion in white,
becoming doctor and nurse (64). The hospital atmosphere quickly changes to
that of a mad scientist's laboratory when the parents strap the boy to the cot.
The stepfather winds iron wire around his knees that are stabilized by a block
of wood, while the mother wraps his feet together (65). With his legs bound in
this manner, Kuno resembles the corrective image from the medical textbook
mentioned above and comes closer to resembling the image on the cover of the
novel itself.

In her groundbreaking study *The Body in Pain*, Elaine Scarry explains that
the act of physical torture is most often contained in a single room and all
objects within the room become possible weapons, often perverting their familiar, everyday function (40). In the familiar kitchen, the public and private
also become blurred in the disciplinary process. Scarry writes: "This dissolu-
tion of the boundary between inside and outside gives rise to ... an almost
obscene conflation of private and public. It brings with it all the solitude of
absolute privacy with none of its safety, all the self-exposure of the utterly public with none of its possibility for camaraderie or shared experience" (51). The
tortured person is isolated from the outside world and the private body is laid
open to the torturer's gaze (the public) as if flayed. Throughout Kuno's operation, the windows are darkened with heavy sacks that earlier held the flour the
boy stole to keep from hungering, and the sills are stuffed with towels to block
out all sensory input from the outside. The sphere of the home has become
utterly, and horrifically, private. At the same time, Kuno's body is no longer
private, but is made public as the parents, and later a neighbour, share in its
moulding.

The transformation of Kuno's body does not stop with wires and wooden
blocks; in the kitchen the parents also eradicate his human senses, which is
the second layer of discipline. While ultimately related to the disciplining of
the outer corporeal shell, the control of the senses brings isolation and the
humanity-eradicating aspects of institutional discipline to the fore. His parents obstruct the boy's sight by placing over his eyes crosses of bandage tape
normally reserved for the closure of wounds and dampen the boy's hearing
with wax (67–8). The stepfather attempts to remove the boy's human senses
in preparation for life as a tree. The boy is then placed alone in his mother's

sunroom where he previously practised his exercises. He is therefore returned to the space of physical practice in order to begin the phase marked by his newly acquired sapling-status.

There are two senses that cannot be eradicated, which speaks to the perseverance of humanity or the individual despite torturous disciplinary practices: touch and smell. Kuno is able to feel air movement and decipher the feeling of different hands on his skin. Moreover, the boy uses his sense of smell not only to distinguish his parents from one another, but also to continue taking part in family affairs, deciphering "wann der Onkel aus der Küche, vom Holzplatz, aus dem Garten kam" (when uncle came from the kitchen, wood shed, or garden) and realizing that they had returned to their former eating patterns through the smell of food (70). Left with his remaining senses, Kuno continues to join in family life, which in turn roots the violent course of discipline ever more firmly in the private sphere.

The disciplining of language makes up the third layer. The development of the linguistic aspects of discipline begins already with the library of texts, which describes the development of a discourse specifically tailored to this course of discipline. The volumes in the library are constructed of pictures and descriptions the stepfather has cut from rare medical and botanical texts gathered painstakingly from antique bookstores, which together formulate a discourse of power in a collage of written words from across centuries. What the stepfather cannot use, he burns (93). The stepfather reconfigures texts to create an appropriate guidebook for his disciplinary quest. The connection between the volumes and Kuno's body makes it fitting that when the experiment fails, the stepfather orders the mother to shred them with the kitchen scissors and throw the scraps into the fire (120). The new books eventually meet the same fate as their sources. The failure of the child's body also signifies a failure of the new discourse created solely for Kuno's course of discipline.

In addition, the stepfather monitors the influx of any competing discourses. One day he announces to Kuno that the boy no longer will attend school (44). The stepfather thus not only takes him out of circulation with the outside world, but also removes the boy from any rival institutions of discipline and structures for the acquisition of knowledge. Kuno intends to make one last trip to school to return his books, which are symbolic of these other institutions. When the time comes, the boy cannot find them, and further, his jacket has disappeared. The removal from school as a public disciplinary institution leads to an increase of the private disciplinary tactics: "Der Onkel ließ mich an diesem Tag zwei neue Übungen machen" (Uncle had me do two new exercises on this day; 47). The disappearance of Kuno's books and jacket is the prologue to his absolute separation from the outside world and the ultimate eradication of his subjectivity. The boy's body has become a purely private entity meant not to communicate or to receive communication. The towels in the kitchen scene described above remind us of the child's slow loss of language; the towels embroidered with the stepfather's initials extend the language of discipline from the books to the kitchen, the discourse marked ominously in blood red (64).

The dampening of senses, the relegation of the immobile body to a separate room, as well as the wrapping of the boy's body in wire that constantly threatens to cut open the flesh trains the body through physical torture. All of this paves the way for the boy's loss of language, which in turn marks the boy as an absolutely private body devoid of a communicative function and unable to circulate in the public sphere. Scarry characterizes the language and world-destroying nature of pain specifically as experienced in torture with the following: "Torture inflicts bodily pain that is itself language-destroying, but torture also mimes (objectifies in the external environment) this language-destroying capacity in its interrogation, the purpose of which is not to elicit needed information but visibly to deconstruct the prisoner's voice" (19–20). While Kuno is not interrogated, the volumes of discipline contain rigid instructions that fulfil this objectifying function. Scarry explains her word choice: She uses "deconstruct" here instead of "destroy" because torture follows a path backwards to where language comes into being and uncreates that process, thus uncreating being or identity. The system of torture thus deconstructs the self and the individual's world (35). This discussion is in keeping with Slavoj Žižek's connection between language and violence: "Language simplifies the designated thing, reducing it to a single feature. It dismembers the thing, destroying its organic unity, treating its parts and properties as autonomous" (*Violence* 52). The language of discipline created in the library of books anatomizes the process of the boy's corporeal torture by reducing the boy as a thing into its single, dismembered parts. Already here we see the uncreation of Kuno as a human subject.

The deconstruction of language and, in turn, identity, through torture and violence is a clear focus of this phase of discipline. Scarry explains that the final step in the structure of torture, ultimate domination, transforms the prisoner into a "colossal body with no voice" (57). The torturer, in turn, becomes all voice and no body, that is, merely identified by his torturous commands. Torture turns Kuno into a colossal body and cuts off his ties to the world by eradicating his senses. The colossal body is best described in the moment Kuno discovers his entire body has been shaven. "Ich war nackt. Meine Mutter fegte unter mir die Haare zusammen" (I was naked. My mother swept up the hair below me; 86). The pile of hair, including his armpit and pubic hair, represents the traces of

The Political Economy of the Child's Body

The colossal body created in torture here contains political implications. In keeping with Foucault's suggestion that systems of punishment must be understood in terms of what he calls a "political economy of the body" (25), or how the body and its forces are dominated by and distributed in society, an examination of those forces behind the disciplining and torture of Kuno unlocks the context necessary for the critical consensus of satire. In the above, the stepfather and mother discipline the child in a manner that retains all aspects of the process within the family. However, because the family is understood as a microcosm of society, the parable of familial discipline should not be read only within the context of discourse on child-rearing in the postwar family, but also within the larger discourse related to the political economy of the child's body. This discourse has multiple public facets, including education, the role of authority, and the regulation of gender dynamics, each of which is linked to identity-political private aspects of negotiating West Germany's recent past in the 1960s.

In his exhaustive study of discipline and youth in the immediate postwar period, Jaimey Fisher makes the very concrete connection between issues of discipline and education, or re-education, and overcoming the recent past, by claiming that "discourse about youth and reeducation became an essential means by which (adult) Germany narrated its transition from its own, abruptly dubious history" (4). Fisher's study traces the connection between the final days of the war and the immediate postwar period's discussion of re-education and youth, and the late 1940s and 1950s debates about youth that would come to shape German identity (6). Those debates about youth, children, and education in the 1950s that wish to establish a new German identity located in the normative family lay the groundwork for later debates about the identity politics of child-rearing in the 1960s and 1970s.

In the immediate postwar period, this begins with re-education, which is specifically linked to reformulating German identity in the wake of the war. But in diverting the issue of re-education from the nation to its youth, postwar Germans trained their focus on selecting those aspects of traditional German culture that would determine the construction of national identity through the education of that youth (Fisher 16). The Germans could, as Fisher claims, look "back as well as forward" at their cultural history and to the future in a selective manner, and in so doing, "mastering the German past became in large part a disciplining of the 'German young'" (16). That education and discipline of youth were very much intertwined with notions of a historicized German identity remains true well into the late 1960s and early 1970s. Dagmar Herzog explains how in writings on leftist child-rearing practices from 1968 onward, the National Socialist past was most often "invoked" to demonstrate the public and political applicability of New Leftist child-rearing theories (171). Rasp's text, published a good decade later than those texts presented in Fisher's study, plays on this historical and identity-political relevance of discipline within the postwar family following on the heels of the discourse on re-education. Rasp's literary reaction to this foundation is produced at a time when, as Herzog notes, persisting connections between youth, discipline, and the historical past were beginning to form in leftist debates on the child.

References to the historical past in the form of the war and the Holocaust are more than hinted at in the torture of Kuno. The shaving of the boy's body is very reminiscent of the preparation of the prisoners for the showers in the concentration camps. The use of wire and wooden blocks directs reader's thoughts to the violent manipulation of bodies behind the barbed wire. The bony frame of the starved body evokes emaciated prisoners. The text also draws direct parallels to National Socialist book burnings and the creation of a new, authoritarian discourse. This relationship to the recent past is picked up on by critics at the time of the novel's debut. Jeziorkowski goes so far as to see the experience of those interned in concentration camps written within the story's figures, and, further, the stepfather as of the same ilk as those "die in den Mordlagern Häftlinge zum Stück Holz dressierten, zum Experiment abrichteten, um sie schließlich zu zertreten" (who trained the inmates in the murder camps into a piece of wood, into an experiment, in order to squash them; 1). In critic Jeziorkowski's words, the stepfather is patterned after members of the SS.

The text also allows for very brief glimpses of the historical past in the outside world that exists beyond the realm of the family. Midway through the disciplinary process, Kuno's absolute isolation from the world does not go unnoticed; the neighbours begin to suspect a crime has been committed after hearing screams. "Rauch sei vom Schornstein aufgestiegen, ein merkwürdiger, strenger Geruch" (Smoke was reported to have risen from the chimney, a strange, strong smell; 73). The missing body of the boy presumably going up in the odd-smelling smoke refers unavoidably to concentration camp crematoriums. Even the nosy neighbours, here in a positive twist, reference the denunciations of the prewar and war periods. The boy is produced and paraded in front of the investigating official. Although his wire-bound legs are hidden from view, Kuno's inadvertent grimaces prompt the visitor to ask: "Sind Sie körperlich behindert?" (Are you bodily impaired?; 77). A second instance of the outside world penetrating the family displays not denunciation but support of the plan: Their neighbour Herr Schorscht, who ironically has done work in their garden before, helps transfer the boy in his pot to the terrace (100). The neighbour's complicity references again the recent past. These brief allusions to the Holocaust insert the violent legacy of the National Socialist period into the family. Moreover, the satire functions as such because the belief in the success of the plan is not shared by family members alone. If this were the case, the family Merz would be merely a singular instance of deformed child-rearing. The satirical suggestion is that deformed child-rearing is rampant.

The child and the education of the child in the broadest sense become a site at which postwar Germany could inject its "anxiety about the stability of the patriarchal family, the security of society, and the continuation of culture" (Herzog 64). Herzog confirms that the leftist literature on child-rearing was "very much about the parents as well," and, moreover, "West German radicals saw their childrearing efforts in national terms" (170, 165). Discourse on children, then, should be seen as directed at parents, who in turn represent the state. That this moves both ways – that is, that the understanding that the family is a microcosm for the state, and that the state and its interests are perpetuated in the family – is clear in the novel and in the contemporaneous discourse. In "Die Aufgabe der Familie" (The Family's Task, 1954), Family Minister Franz-Josef Wuermeling reminds readers that the family holds three roles in relation to state and society: It is a "Schule für Charakter und Leben" (school for character and life), it works as a "Träger und Übermittler unserer Kultur" (bearer and transmitter of our culture) – of which he reminds us that culture is not only arts and science, but also "die Form, in der wir leben" (the way we live) –, and the family is the "natürliche Lebensquell des Volkes" (people's natural source of life) in very concrete form (11–13). These roles underscore the validity of Fisher's connection between education, discipline, and nation in postwar Germany's discussions of youth and family. Education and discipline, in terms of character and culture, are not only institutional matters, but also very much familial matters, which in turn makes them national matters. Moreover, education and discipline within the family invoke the failure of these building blocks for national identity, in keeping with the New Leftist belief that the "nuclear family was a diseased and pernicious institution" (Herzog 170). Rasp's text satirically reconfigures these understandings.

This failure of the family in terms of discipline and the rethinking of child-rearing practices is grounded in the 1960s catch-all word "anti-authoritarian." While the anti-authoritarian family and pedagogy become central to discourse on youth, education, and child-rearing in the latter half of the 1960s and early 1970s, discussion of authority in the family begins already in the prewar period, most notably with the 1936 writings on the subject by members of the Frankfurter *Institut für Sozialforschung* (Institute for Social Research). However, these discussions continue to unfold rapidly in the immediate postwar period, particularly with regard to the shaky configuration of normative family relations after the war and with reference to youth in re-education policies. Fisher cites a 1946 report commissioned by the US occupying forces that looks at aspects of educational reform. In their contradictory findings, they see German youth to be in crisis due in part to the loss of authority in families in the aftermath of war. However, they also see youth to be affected by the "most undemocratic trait of the Germans, their tendency toward authoritarianism" (Fisher 71).[10] The US reporting body sees German youth as becoming confused when that authority is removed or lost.[11]

Despite the conflicting analysis from the US report, the issue of authority is central to postwar West German discourse on the importance of the health of the family for the nation. Wuermeling comes to the defence of authority in the essay "Zur inneren Ordnung der Familie" (On the Inner Order of the Family, 1954), adapted from a speech given before the Bundestag. He sees individualism, on the one hand, and state-sanctioned socialism, on the other, each to be the downfall of the family. Instead, he supports authority as the characteristic feature of the family (16). He continues to claim that any fears that authority in the family is necessarily connected to the state authority of 1933 to 1945 are unfounded, for authority is prevalent equally in democracy and totalitarianism (16). Most likely referencing the 1936 Frankfurt School studies, Wuermeling writes: "Nach dem ersten Weltkrieg wurde die Ansicht vertreten, daß die Autorität in der Familie, insbesondere in der Erziehung der Kinder, die Ursache für spätere politisch-autoritäre Haltung sei. Das hat sich als falsch erwiesen" (After the First World War people held the opinion that the family's authority, particularly the education of children, was a reason for the future political-authoritarian attitude. This has proved to be wrong; 16). He claims that this misunderstanding comes from a misunderstanding of the nature of familial authority in general. When it comes to families, the "Sinn der Autorität ist Sorge und Verantwortung für das Familienwohl und sicher mehr eine Pflicht als ein Recht" (reason for authority is care and responsibility for the family's well-being and is surely more a duty than a right; 16). Wuermeling states that this type of authority does not demand blind commitment but trust. He warns that although abuses of authority should not be sanctioned, the "Wohl der Familie [verlangt] eben in schwierigen Situationen auch ein Opfer des einzelnen" (family's well-being does also require individual sacrifices in difficult situations; 17). Rasp's text references this concept of the sacrifice individual family members should make in the face of authority for the good of the whole institution through the figure of Kuno.

The above discussion of education and discipline of the child with relation to familial authority, in text and context, clearly shows the importance of the topic for the national imaginary. What Rasp brings into the discussion, in keeping with 1960s discourses on the private sphere, is the violence enacted on the individual in the act of sacrifice. The plan ultimately fails when the stepfather prunes the child using his gardening shears, which is also the climax of the satire. As if guessing that the pruning might not work, the stepfather prepares the boy by injecting his arms with anaesthetic for three days in a row until his arms are numbed (108). The stepfather, as doctor-cum-gardener, has difficulties cutting through the flesh and bone of the child and must attempt the procedure twice, these attempts described graphically in the text (108–9). As a result of the injections, the boy's appendages are numb, almost as if he has turned into a tree, were it not for the blood and torn flesh. This moment marks the end of the experiment: the boy spouts blood, not sap. The narrator sees this as his own failure, for he describes his pruning as the moment "in dem der Onkel mein Versagen klar erkannt hatte" (that Uncle clearly recognized my failure; 109). True to Wuermeling's belief that the welfare of the family lies in the difficult sacrifice of its individuals, the son gives himself up in sacrifice to the authoritarian family.

Authority and discipline continue to play a major role in the literature on family politics, psychology, and sociology well into the 1960s and early 1970s. Alexander Mitscherlich's groundbreaking psychological and pedagogical study *Auf dem Weg zur Vaterlosengesellschaft* (*Society without the Father*, 1963) identifies a necessary change in the authoritarian practices of the family. He writes: "*Erziehung* ist unendlich öfter Terror als Führung zur Selbständigkeit" (27) (Infinitely more often education takes the form of terrorism rather than guidance toward independence; *Society* 15).[12] He identifies the failure of the allied post-war re-education plans to be the reason why the old forms of discipline and authoritarianism meant to be re-educated out of the Germans are re-emerging in the early 1960s, for now "blüht die alte Identität buchstäblich aus den Ruinen" (86) (the old identity has sprung up again from the ruins; *Society* 64). Rasp satirizes the persistence of this old identity in the figure of the authoritarian father and willingly complicit mother.

Congruently with Mitscherlich's thoughts, sociologist Friedhelm Neidhardt defines the structure of the family in 1966 as the "Verteilung und Ausübung der sozialen Herrschaft innerhalb der Familie" (division and execution of social authority within the family), of which he sees the primary feature to be the subordination of the children (10). Neidhardt examines a 1965 poll of West German citizens with regard to the most important qualities in children, comparing these with other Western countries. Here, he sees what he terms in English as a "cultural lag" in the "relativ totalitären Erziehungsverhalten mancher Eltern" (relatively totalitarian education style of some parents) in West Germany (50). One in five citizens believe "Gehorsam und Unterordnung seien die obersten Erziehungsziele" (obedience and subordination are the main educational goals; 51). While this is down from the numbers in 1957, where one in four believed in the same, Neidhardt is nevertheless concerned that such a point of view will hinder the development in children of independence and individuality, those characteristics necessary for the building of a free society, the cultivation of which he sees as an important function of modern families (51).

The West German understanding of the family as a politically relevant institution combined with Foucault's political economy of the body suggests the discipline of the children within this institution codes children's bodies as political. For Wuermeling, the authority of the family and in the family is "wesentlich" (crucial) and this true nature of the family is essential for society and the culture of all people ("Ordnung" 19). In his understanding, familial authority, society, and the culture of a people are intertwined. In 1969, Dietrich Haensch writes that the bourgeois family is structured similarly to bourgeois society, claiming of the authoritative parent–child relationship: "Die Herrschaftsstruktur der bürgerlichen Gesellschaft manifestiert sich in der Familie als ökonomisch begründete Herrschaft der Eltern über die Kinder" (The authoritarian structure of bourgeois society manifests itself in the family as an economically justified domination of the parents over the children; 42). Although Haensch's interest is in the controlled suppression of sexual freedom passed on through the family, the reflection of the bourgeois society in the family also reflects the political economy of the disciplined body, whether this disciplining is sexual in nature or otherwise behavioural. In terms of society's formation, Haensch continues to explain that the man, who within the family is the dominating father, is dominated outside of the family: "So entsteht die spezifische Dialektik von Herrschen und Beherrschtwerden der autoritären Gesellschaft" (Thus arise the dialectics of domination and being dominated specific to the authoritarian society; 44). This statement identifies the establishment of the hierarchal authority of the family as originating in the disciplinary and hierarchically authoritarian nature of society and vice versa. In the 1968 report prepared by the family ministry for the federal government on the state of the family in West Germany, family and education continue to go hand-in-hand well into the school years (Wingen 15). The authority of the parents within the family in terms of the child's discipline and character cultivation reaches into all forms of public and institutional education. Therefore, the authority of the family clearly shapes society. In keeping with this understanding, the disciplining of Kuno's body in the text results from and resonates within not only the family, but society as well.

Fisher's study displays how those challenges to national identity faced by postwar Germans were displaced onto discourse about youth and education. This displacement does not just disappear in the following decades, but is instead sublimated into a concern for a new type of national identity. If, as Fisher claims, the "negatively coded young person" and the discourse surrounding his or her discipline formed a way of managing "modern adult subjects" after the war, in the later 1960s this was only partially flipped on its head (261, 268). While the negatively coded young person remains central to representations of the private sphere and its public-political import, the negativity no longer merely manages adult subjects, but directly reflects the repression, violence, and authority perpetuated by adult subjects, as well as on adult subjects perpetuated by the state. Management is no longer the goal. Instead, the problems with youth created by adult subjects in the private sphere are left as blemishes to be interpreted in the public realm.

In the immediate postwar period, youth and education became a place in which to "reinscribe" bourgeois discourse after National Socialism and reconstruct German national identity on the "ruins of tainted cultural categories" (Fisher 63). It is this reinscription that critical and radical pedagogues fought against in the late 1960s and into the 1970s, all the while continuing to see youth and education as a matter of national identity.[13] The Berlin-based *Kinderläden* (storefront day-care centres) were begun by the women's action committee with intentions of counteracting the shortage of childcare centres and the authoritarian nature of those existing facilities that were perceived to mirror repressive family structures.[14] In the 1970 introduction to the theories and documents behind the *Kinderläden* movement, translated in 1973 for an English-speaking readership, the authors suggest that the centres provide a "practical alternative" to those methods currently used in West Germany, which placed preschool education in a "State of Emergency" (Sedoun, Schmidt, and Schultz xi, xviii). In a familiar rhetoric, they point to the politicization of the family and the child as the primary goal of the movement, for the *Kinderläden* activists did not want to raise well-behaved robots for children, but instead revolutionaries: "This meant permissiveness to free the children from those 'normal' family pressures which breed people resigned to the system, trapped in passivity, exploitativeness, or ineffectual rebellion" (xvii). The essential link between the well-being of, here leftist, society, through providing the revolution with well-trained offspring, and the experience of the child within the family (read state) has essentially the same purpose as the politicization of the family and child in the 1950s and early 1960s, if to different ultimate ends: the good of the future of the German nation. In the words of the authors to the book's introduction, the so-called experiment arose not from questions of improving child-rearing, but from the questions:

"'How can we ourselves do more political work?' and 'How can we do revolutionary work in education to mobilize people'" (xvii). This formulation is found again in the documentation on the establishment of the Schöneberg Centre in Berlin: "Founding nonrepressive kindergartens is practical action upon our political beliefs" (Authors' Collective 21). Change in public politics and the private care of children are indivisible.

The goal of the non-repressive childcare centre is the reformulation of discipline, child-rearing, and long-term education in anti-authoritarian manners so that education no longer equals "blind submission to the status quo" (Authors' Collective 20). In the beliefs of the organizers, the children, through self-guided experimentation with such adult issues as sexuality, property, cleanliness, violence, and authority, learn to decipher the manner in which their behaviour affects and has consequences for others and to value the importance of independent thought and action. More specifically, the *Kinderläden* organizers saw the realization of their goals in the reconfiguration of the nuclear family, for as the collective authors of the 1971 text *Kinderläden: Revolution der Erziehung oder Erziehung zur Revolution?* (Kinderläden: Revolution in Education or Education for Revolution?) write: "Im sicheren Gehege der Familie, kollektiver Kontrolle entzogen, werden die Fundamente der autoritären Persönlichkeit gelegt" (Free from collective control the fundaments for the authoritarian personality are set within the safety of the family compound; Breiteneicher et al. 9). The *bürgerliche* family reflects the structural characteristics of society, particularly through the gendered hierarchy of the division of work, economic dependency, and the distribution of power, of which the child is the recipient (ibid. 11). The authors continue to explain that the family can work against such characteristics, for it is potentially the "sanfteste, gewaltloseste Instrument" (gentlest, non-violent instrument) for the reproduction of bourgeois society (12). By couching these *Kinderläden* in national terms and citing the relationship between a non-repressive education and the creation of freethinking and independent adults, the writers invoke recent memories of National Socialism, suggesting that the existing form of education, repressive and authoritarian, led to the creation of a nation of followers, but also a nation of aggressive and authoritarian cynics (16).

This description of the expectations placed on the political economy of the child's body in postwar West Germany, whether in its conservative or radicalized form, prompts the final question as to whether it is necessary for the child in Rasp's parabolic text to be male. Ultimately, the role authority plays within the family and society in the above discourse is highly paternal, as seen in Haensch's discussion of the family father in 1969. Haensch's formulation is part of a longer postwar trajectory. When approaching the "Wesen" (being) of the family, Wuermeling defends authority most specifically in terms of the gendered order of family, as a community made up of husband and wife, and the children entrusted to them ("Ordnung" 15). That he would place the education or discipline of children, the goal of which is the cultivation of a specific "Verhaltensmuster" (behaviour pattern; Schroedter 19), at the centre of his definition of family has its roots in his understanding of authority as patriarchal: "Nach wie vor liegt die Autorität der Familie beim Manne" (The family's authority continues to be in the man's hands; Wuermeling "Ordnung" 19). In 1966, Neidhardt comments at length on the patriarchal structure of the family and its political meaning:

> Ergibt sich zudem aus spezifischen politischen Bedingungen, daß die Herrschafts-struktur der Gesellschaft ausgesprochen männerbestimmt ist, so wird der "pri-vate" Patriarchalismus in der Familie durch einen "öffentlichen" Patriarchalismus im Staatswesen zusätzlich gestützt. Dabei kann sich der Vater um so autoritärer verhalten, je mehr das Staatswesen selbst ... autoritär bestimmt ist. (46)

> [If the specific political conditions lay the ground for a distinctly male dominated governing structure, the family's "private" patriarchy is additionally supported by the state's "public" patriarchy. With this, the father is allowed to behave more au-thoritatively all the more the state itself ... is governed authoritatively.]

This line of thought is very akin to Haensch's claim above. The family reflects political order, which is patriarchal. The authoritarian family is publicly ac-knowledged as a "politisch relevantes Erziehungsinstitut" (politically relevant educational institute; Neidhardt 46). The father can be the dominant authority only when the state is organized along masculine authority principles. The 1968 report on the state of the family sees changing authority in the family to be re-lated to increasing equality among partners in marriage. This new, degendered partnership does not eradicate the question of authority, but instead begs the question as to how to make education and discipline effective through bind-ing authority (Wingen 11). Whether in the patriarchal structure of the post-war family or in increasing interest in gendered equity within the family, the role of authority in child-rearing and education remains central to questions of discipline and therefore to the political economy of the child's body in West Germany.

While the discipline and respect for authority expected of a young child even in the mid-to-late 1960s applies to both sexes, the recognition of the order of the family and the state along patriarchal lines makes it appropriate that the satiri-cal critique of discipline and education within the authoritarian family would be placed in the body of the son. The future family patriarch in *Ein unger-atener Sohn* acquires not learned authoritarian but docile behaviour. "A body is docile that may be subjected, used, transformed and improved" (Foucault 136). By creating Kuno as malleable and blindly trusting all forms of authority, Rasp ultimately criticizes what she sees as the continued individual-eradicating fascist authority that runs through 1960s family and state, which she identifies as patriarchal. Moreover, the patriarchal organization of the family also calls the disciplining of the male soldier to mind. Thomas Schroedter reminds us of the other side to this: "Antiautoritäre Erziehung ist ... nur denkbar als antimili-taristische, pazifistische Erziehung" (Anti-authoritarian education is ... imagin-able only as antimilitaristic, pacifist education; 145). The militaristic nature of Kuno's discipline is referenced through his body, deformed by patriarchal vio-lence. At the outset of the novel Kuno and his mother prepare to greet a sales-man who peddles prosthetics that could replace the metal pincers on the end of Kuno's arms (9). The prosthetics inevitably ground Kuno's mis-disciplined body in the aftermath of war, the prosthesis a symbolic reference to mechanized and rationalized capitalist society (Hille 146).[15] The stepfather denies Kuno the prosthetics that would return to the boy his human form and reinsert him into the machinery of the state. The docility of the authoritatively disciplined son is further underscored by Kuno's obesity at the outset of the novel (5). The step-father lectures: "Fettleibigkeit bedeutet Trägheit. Ein dicker Mensch bringt es zu nichts" (Obesity means lethargy. A fat person will never get anywhere; 6). He closes this diatribe with the statement that people can do as they please, for "der Mensch ist frei geschaffen" (man is created free), to which the narrator comments: "Nur die ihn näher kennen, wissen, was er mit Freiheit meint" (Only those who know him well know what he means by freedom; 6). For the reader, this introduction to the stepfather's conception of discipline, which precedes the experiment in the text, references the continuation of the National Social-ist perversion of the ideal that a healthy body reflects a healthy mind and soul.

Throughout the text, Kuno's body has been disciplined within the familial network, which reflects the political network. This reading of the parable is possible only when the extraliterary discourses are read alongside their satirical re-rendering and when a clear critical consensus about those discourses exists. A critical consensus on the dangers of the authoritarian family and the child's political import developed in the 1960s and early 1970s. Rasp's text works within the critical consensus surrounding the gap between the ideology (*Erscheinung*) of the normative discourse on the discipline of youth and the reality (*wesen*) of that discourse in praxis as understood by counter-normative discussions, even if this consensus crystallizes into political action after the date of her text's pub-lication. The moral evaluation contained in the satirical critique remains locat-able outside the text in the reader's reality. Rasp's novel is very much a product of its time; without the debates surrounding the national import and evils of authoritarian child-rearing practices, education, discipline, and youth in private and public spheres, the text would miss its critical mark. But Rasp's satire cannot function solely on the basis of a parabolic approach to that extraliterary consensus, that is, it cannot function solely on the basis of its content. It is also dependent on negativity produced from within the text. The narrative aesthetic is crafted through violent love, which dominates the construction of a negative corporeal subjectivity.

Embodied Subjectivity and the Negativity of Love

In Rasp's first collection of poetry, published under the title *Eine Rennstrecke* in 1969, love and violence are presented as intertwined. The intimate relationships described in the poetry and the familial relationship described in the novel confirm Žižek's claim that love is "*the domain of pure violence*" (*Violence* 173; emphasis in orig.). The poems reflect the emotional timbre of the novel. The physical acts of intimate violence are communicated through an ironic, highly subjective, and embodied voice.[16] This is illustrated in the poem entitled simply "Liebe" (Love):

> Den
> dessen Anblick
> einen so quält
> daß man hinten
> kotzt ihm
> statt der Zunge
> Scheiße in den
> Mund preßt ...
> den
> sollte man nicht
> loslassen! (21)

> The one
> whose mere sight
> tortures you
> so much that you puke
> in the back
> instead of your tongue
> you press shit
> into his mouth ...
> this is one

you should not
let get away!

This poem approaches love as disgust, which in turn prompts a physically violent reaction from the narrative subject. Although the narrative subject is not described in the poem, the aggressive action of pressing waste into the face of the loved one provides a strong sense of narrative authorial embodiment for the reader. Much like Brinkmann's use of bodily excrement to describe the subject's experience of remembered sexual desire, here the movement towards the loved one is inscribed with waste. The poem also hints at the irony of the subjective voice, exemplified by the final lines.

This irony is even more marked in the cycle "Häschen in der Grube" (Little Rabbit in the Burrow). Rasp references the German nursery rhyme to describe the violent sexual relationship between a man, the *Häschen*, and a woman, the "I" of poem VII:

Jedes Mal
auch wenn er sich wehrt
steck ich ihm
zwanzig Mark
in sein Arschloch ...
Und jetzt wartet
er mit seinem Arsch
er liebt mich. (36)

Every time
even if he fights back
I stick
twenty marks
up his ass ...
And now he waits
with his ass
he loves me.

The poem's aggressive play on the vulgar turn of phrase joined with the title's play on a children's song turns love into menacing child's play.[17] A combination of (financial) dependency and the desire to possess the loved one describes love here and in the novel. This same poetic voice is strongly, and self-effacingly, negative, as seen in the final lines of the poem "Bildnis" (Portrait) that closes the collection:

Ich fresse
meinen eigenen Dreck.
Ich bin Dreck

...

Sage bloß
daß du mich nicht liebst, jetzt! (60)

I eat
my own dirt.
I am dirt.

...

Just say
that you don't love me, now!

The subjective voice turns violence towards the self in a demand for self-hate clothed in love. The subjective voice in these poems is purposefully naive, highly dependent on its intimate relationships, and strangely masochistically sadistic. A similar subjective voice is found in the novel. As is the case in the poems, the reader's experience of the narrative authority in *Ein ungeratener Sohn* is attached to a strong sense of the voice's embodiment; however, Kuno's (colossal) embodiment is enacted upon him. For this reason, the violent relationship in the novel is not clearly delineated between subject and object of love, but is instead collapsed into one. The subjective voice is on the receiving end of the violence that he mistakes for love, a violence that is also self-enacted. Because of this collapse, the satirical narrative authority is not a figure for identification, but instead causes discomfiture or unease in the reader. However, because of the lack of distance between text and reader engendered by the corporeal subjectivity, this unease is intended to become the reader's self-reflection.

Narrator embodiment is developed through what Punday calls "corporeal levers." He references Scarry's discussion of bodily levers as projective tools to transform corporeal experience for the reader (Scarry 310). Scarry illustrates what she means by bodily lever through a discussion of the manner in which a chair is created to relieve the weight of the body, whereby the body transfers its experience of weight onto the chair (321). Within narratives, Punday suggests, these levers express to the reader the corporeality of the narrative subject in a manner that "remake[s] the narrative situation as a site where authority is not an issue" (Punday 180). Narrative authority is not an issue because of the reader's own corporeal investment in the text. Punday utilizes Scarry's illustration to suggest that the reader uses the text like a bodily lever, transferring his or her own corporeal weight onto the text by using the narrative as a projective tool. In Rasp's text, the corporeal levers – instruments that are banal everyday objects recognizable to the reader as part of his or her own familiar context, such as wire, bandages, blocks, garden shears, and the pot – create the embodiment of the subjective voice through the way they interact with Kuno's body to transform its satirical meaning. Through these bodily levers, the reader experiences the physicality of the embodied narrative voice as his or her own.

This subjective closeness is forged not only through bodily levers, but also in the construction of the narrative form. Because the story is told as a flashback, the reader is entirely dependent on the subject's narrative decisions. Moreover, the narrator gives us no specific hint as to what will happen by commenting on the events unfolding. The reader, through the text form, is asked to evaluate the parabolic story. We meet Kuno as a ten-year-old boy on his birthday after he has eaten three pieces of cake. We are informed of the plan at the same time as he and in his child's voice. The stepfather comments that Kuno will most likely need to be put into a pot first, prompting Kuno to remark tentatively: "'Du meinst' – hoffentlich sagte ich das Richtige – 'ich könnte ein Baum werden?'" ("You mean" – hopefully I was saying the right thing – "I could become a tree?"; 19). This realization introduces the disciplinary nightmare that forms the main storyline of the short novel. The boy's worried aside allows for the author's satirical voice to shimmer through, a voice similar to that in the above poems. Like the exclamation point after "loslassen!" in the poem "Liebe," the concept of "Richtig" is meant ironically, at least in the moral sense of the word.

What is also shown in this introductory interlude is the dependent relationship between stepfather and son, as well as narrator and reader. The child, in his unending love, wishes to please the stepfather at every turn, whereas the narrator – as a grown man – winks and nods to the reader that this intimacy and love will be perverted, though he does not divulge how. In many ways, the satirical aspect of the text is not that the child is to be moulded into a tree, but rather that the child remains – even after the plan fails – intimately trusting of his stepfather's torturous love. Kuno's attachment to his stepfather is expressed corporeally. The first cue is his desire to imitate his stepfather in action and to resemble him in looks (30). The boy searches for their physical similarities, and he trains his body to move like his stepfather's, an addendum to the stepfather's physical discipline of the child. The adult narrator laments: "Hätte ich meine Hände noch, würde ich sie reiben wie er oder beim Sprechen die Fingerspitzen gegeneinanderdrücken, eine Geste, die mir manchmal fehlt" (If I still had hands, I would rub them together just like him or press the fingertips against each other while speaking, a gesture that I sometimes miss; 30). The first time Kuno manages to complete one of the gymnastic exercises for twenty minutes, the stepfather rewards him by recounting a neighbour's mistaken assumption that Kuno is the stepfather's biological son (31). While the stepfather attempts to mould the son's body into a tree, the son attempts to mould his own body to alternately match the stepfather's or to please the stepfather, thus becoming a self-disciplinarian. This love moves Kuno to take all blame for the failed plan (16). Further, the son's relationship to his mother is one of rivalry. Like duelling suitors, mother and son compete physically for their shared object of affection. Through the subjective description of the competing bodily networks – stepfather-son, son-mother – the family nexus is formed.

Just as he functions doubly as the who-whom of the satire and takes up the subject and object of love, the narrator occupies the position of both the masochist and the sadist within the structure of the family. This fact has ramifications for understanding the negativity of love as the emotional impulse of this satire. Sabine Wilke writes that "cultural destructions (negations) of bodies (such as in torture or in sadomasochistic beatings) are predicated on the prior construction of a body that is defined as a body that ceases to be" (208). This formulation is strikingly similar to Arntzen's comment that satire occurs from the production of the text's negativity, when that which is said or represented "gewissermaßen seine eigene Abschaffung mitproduziert" (essentially helps to facilitate its own elimination; 15). In *Ein ungeratener Sohn*, the boy's body is disciplined to be a body that is negated; the family creates the son's individual corporeal subjectivity in order to eradicate it. The more the stepfather attempts to control the son through violence, the more the son wishes to comply in utter devotion. However, that control simultaneously slips away from the stepfather, for the boy resembles a tree less and less, a fact that is read by the stepfather as violence enacted on him by the boy. This culminates in the bloody pruning of the son. The ultimate result is the creation of Kuno's "colossal" negative corporeal subjectivity, for in not becoming a tree, the boy becomes excessively human.

In "Coldness and Cruelty," Gilles Deleuze analyses masochism and sadism in terms of their shared yet different connections to family. He summarizes both impulses as follows: "Sadism stands for the active negation of the mother and the inflation of the father (who is placed above the law); masochism proceeds by a twofold disavowal, a positive, idealizing disavowal of the mother (who is identified with the law) and an invalidating disavowal of the father (who is expelled from the symbolic order)" (68). In Rasp's text, we see a strange conversion of each of these moments of negation and disavowal, for the father is inflated as in the case of sadism, but is also idealized even as he is disavowed, as is the case of the masochist's mother according to Deleuze. It is for this reason that the impulse behind the relationships forming the family nexus in this novel is one of submissive, willing, and docile love, but a love that is by the end violently aggressive, directed by the combined forces of masochism and sadism.[18]

Kneip says of the plan that while its content fails, its implication succeeds, particularly in relation to the stepfather (225). The manner in which the stepfather controls, cultivates, and disciplines the son does suggest success of the violent course of discipline. However, this reading is not entirely upheld by the end of the text. The final chapter, written in the present tense, portrays Kuno as a monolith. His parents wait on him, now fifty years old, as he sits in an armchair, not having moved for over twenty years (122–3). The parents, skittish and animal-like in their movements, continue training his body, though this time by cutting his toenails and bringing him food (123). In utter ambivalence and lethargy, he does not move and takes no interest in life (123). The boy who was to become a sturdy tree is now nothing more than a mound of flesh, a perversion of the inanimate object that the parents disciplined him to be. In this moment, however, he has also taken authority away from the parents: "Sometimes, doing nothing is the most violent thing to do" (Žižek, *Violence* 183). Kuno has turned around the violence enacted upon him to now be directed at his parents. He does so through the mere presence of his docile body as a reminder of that violence.

Doing nothing is of course the ultimate act of resistance, a total and radical process of disavowal akin to the "Great Refusal" (Marcuse, *One* 257). When taken together, the negation of the subject as well as the disavowal present in this closing menagerie has narrative-poetic repercussions. Deleuze considers both the sadistic and the masochistic impulse to have implications for narrative subjectivity and narrative structures. In his comparative analysis of the writings of the Marquis de Sade and Leopold von Sacher-Masoch, he claims:

> The fundamental distinction between sadism and masochism can be summarized *in the contrasting process of the negative and negation on the one hand, and of disavowal and suspense on the other*. The first represents a speculative and analytical manner of apprehending the Death Instinct ...[,] while the second pursues the same object in a totally different way, mythically, dialectically and in the imaginary. ("Coldness" 35; emphasis in orig.)

Here, Deleuze makes a distinction between a dialectical, and thus linguistic, mastery of the death drive and the approach to Thanatos through the realm of fantasy. Moreover, he explains that the sadistic hero is involved in "thinking out the Death Instinct (pure negation) in a demonstrative form," whereas the masochistic hero is engaged in a process of disavowal, which is an operation "radically contesting the validity of that which is" (31). The discrepancy between the two types of heroes describes the relationship of the narrator to the narrative here. In the novel, there is a combination between masochistic (narrator) and sadistic (narrative) principles. With regard to satire, negativity emerges from within the narrative fabric of the text itself. "Die satirische Textpraxis bringt nicht den alternativen Diskurs hervor, sondern ist im Akt der Destruktion selbst neuer Diskurs" (The satirical text praxis does not generate an alternative discourse, but instead constitutes a new discourse during the act of destruction; Rasper 298). The text is engaged not only in the negation of the subject Kuno, but also in a negation of all discourses related to the cultivation of the subject as located within the family, pure negation acting here as a utopian concept. The narrator, in turn, disempowers the negativity of the narrative by contesting its validity as satire: He embraces the plan. The reader is caught in the tension between these two forces. The reader is asked to sign the contract of masochism in that the reader is asked to believe and participate in the plan through the act of reading. The reader must also do the work of satire by inserting the critical consensus on the contextual discourses into the narrative during the act of reading in order to understand its politics. For these reasons, the violence that is incurred on the son is also enacted upon the reader.

The cover of the first edition of *Ein ungeratener Sohn* displaying the man transformed into a tree discussed above implies that the experiment does not fail and confronts the reader at each opening or closing of the book. It becomes the imaginary of what could have happened had the experiment been achieved. Bender's suggestion seems appropriate here: "Die Parabel soll so unausgeführt und durchlöchert bleiben, damit sie über die erste und letzte Seite des Buches hinausgreift, damit sie ergänzt werde vom Leser" (The parable is supposed to remain unexecuted and perforated, in order for it to reach beyond the first and last page of the book, in order for it to be supplemented by the reader; 182). Rasp utilizes the voice of satire, powered by violent love, to create a parable of discipline in the authoritarian family. This violent love is directed within the text at its familial objects, within the form at its narrator and narrative, and beyond the text at its context, which includes the interconnection between reader and discourse as extraliterary consensus.

Throughout this study the private sphere has been made public in a multiplicity of ways. Here it is the familial mechanisms surrounding the child's body that are politicized within public discourse. The radical understanding of how this is to be read ethically is seen in the critical consensus that was built on the longer trajectory of discourse on discipline, education, and the authoritarian or anti-authoritarian family. "Discourse about youth reveals not only the underpinnings of the adult subject and its collective forms – as a lightning rod for wider operations of control, discourse about youth and generation also reveals their veiling political mechanisms" (Fisher 274). Through the interplay between the textual satire of discipline in the authoritarian family and the background of the contextual trajectory of authority and anti-authority in the postwar family as a disciplinary institution, we see how youth – here in the figure of Kuno – unveils those (adult- and state-driven) political mechanisms. Rasp's satire thereby engenders a very pointed connection to the debate on the rearing of children, discourse, education, and family in West Germany.

Because of its demand for reader-participation, satire implicates the reader in its narrative structure, for it demands the reader recognize the extraliterary consensus found within the competing negative forces in the text's structure. Rasp engages a satirical poetics that are radically negative in that they contain a critical impulse to effect positive change in the reader's private experience. This text corresponds to Wolfgang Iser's reading of the negative and negativity, despite the lack of distance between reader and narrative subject (*Akt* 348; *Act* 226). The blanks in the text that Iser identifies as negation would be here the missing moral evaluation of the parable. In these blanks, the readers are asked to create their own text built from their repertoire, as Iser calls the discursive context, thus creating the double of satire in the form of negativity. This second text should be read as a political guidebook for the reader's transformation of the private sphere through eradication of authority and transformation of pedagogical practices.

Rasp's novel is the most explicitly political of all the literary texts examined here, in part because of her use of satire as her negative narrative vehicle. The 1960s New Left consensus on the ills of the authoritarian family, built on almost two decades of ideological discourse surrounding the political use-value of the child's body in the family, clarifies the revolutionary potential of this 1967 satire: The desire to change the way in which the child functions within the family and the family within society, and vice versa, the way society works on the family and the family works on the child. *Revolting Families* thus ends teetering on the brink of 1968, the year that stands in for West Germany's revolutionary tipping point. Rasp's satire displays how the family and with it the child was believed across many discourses and well after 1968 to be fundamental for the national identity-political transformation of the private sphere.

Conclusion

Since the publication of Renate Rasp's *Ein ungeratener Sohn* in November 1967, the phrase the "private is political" has become commonplace, in part perhaps because of its association with the seeming universality of 1968 social transformations. The two parts of the once-provocative battle cry are now often inseparable, and appear even as a tautology. However, if the private is always by default political, then the repression, inequalities, violence, or psychological damage occurring in the private sphere that have public consequences might go unquestioned. The public infiltration and control of the private, moreover, could be overlooked for its effect on individual experience. Literary authors and public intellectuals Ilija Trojanow and Juli Zeh write of this danger in *Angriff auf die Freiheit* (Attack on Freedom, 2009), warning readers that because of the standard pairing of private with political, the state is able to dismantle the private sphere in the name of the public good. They close with the following: "Ein autoritärer Staat kann jeden Protest im Keim ersticken, mit Hilfe von Gesetzen, die heute verabschiedet werden, um uns angeblich zu schützen. Wehren Sie sich. Noch ist es nicht zu spät" (An authoritarian state can quash every protest at its inception with the help of laws that are being passed today for our supposed protection. Fight back. It is still not too late; 138–9). This call to arms sounded in the first decade of the twenty-first century displays the continuing sense of urgency in Germany of critically questioning the politicization of the private sphere in order to incite social and intimate change. Trojanow and Zeh are first and foremost literary authors; therefore, literature continues to be a space that inspires this critical questioning.

This study has charted the long reach of the "private is political" in West Germany since the end of the Second World War. The trajectory begins already in the immediate postwar period and its discourses of social politics, pedagogy, psychology, and nationhood. With the rise of the counterculture and the New

Left in the 1960s, these normalizing discourses were joined by anti-authoritarian discussions on the private sphere, the family, and the child. Throughout the long Sixties (from the late 1950s to the early 1970s), the private sphere and the family found their place in political discussions ranging from their ethical importance in national identity tinged with Cold War rhetoric to Marxist understandings of social repression as formative for liberated subjects. This trajectory also finds its place in literature. Jaimey Fisher identifies a set of "fundamental bourgeois themes" that can be seen in the immediate postwar representation of generational difference in literature (57). He sees these themes to include "the family as bourgeois private sphere, the school as site of social reproduction, and youth as the social other making both of these conceivable as well as unstable" (57). This study of New and Black Realism has shown how these bourgeois themes remain key sites for the development of politically engaged literature in the 1960s as well.

The literary appearance of these contextual themes related to the private sphere appear in New and Black Realism in the nuclear family, which has as its task the development of subjectivity based in social normativity. The literary texts reveal this subjectivity to be deformed through and eradicated by these normative expectations that resonate in the literary texts as repression, authority, and violence. In Dieter Wellershoff's New Realist novel *Ein schöner Tag*, these expectations work negatively on both father and son, for they are hampered by their inability to communicate and circulate publically as subjects. This results in their physical neurotic symptoms, including hallucinations, feverish sweat, and catatonic paralysis. That this privately experienced repression has its roots in the personal trauma of the war through the loss of the wife and mother links up the historically based discourses on the continuing effect of the war in the present with the intimate sphere. On the other hand, Rolf Dieter Brinkmann's protagonists of "In der Grube" and *Die Umarmung*, texts also containing New Realist features, display an adverse relationship to sexuality and repressed feelings towards libidinal bodies because of their experience of *körperliche Starre* and physical entrapment created by the middle-class home. The negative effect of a controlled and managed sensuality is expressed in these short stories as disgust towards the libidinal body. This disgust is the result of repressive expectations of conforming to sexual and social mores of bourgeois respectability as perpetuated by the private sphere. The *körperliche Starre* therefore produces a *Starre* of subjectivity. Gisela Elsner's Black Realist novel *Die Riesenzwerge*, on the other hand, more broadly tackles institutional violence and absurd hierarchies through the consumption patterns of the post-economic-miracle family as an institution upholding all others of 1960s West Germany. This consumption is thematized through meat, but applies also to the unquestioning internalization of belief systems that perpetuate systemic violence. These systems eradicate individual subjectivity in its entirety. Finally, Renate Rasp's *Ein ungeratener Sohn*, also a Black Realist text, satirically presents the deforming consequences of the authoritarian family with regard to discipline and pedagogy by narrating a parabolic story of a child's intended transformation into a tree. In this novel, the child's body is highly politicized, a fact reflecting the contextual discourses on the family since the postwar period. New and Black Realist writings, therefore, engage with discussions on the political and national importance of the private sphere taking place in broad areas of importance at the time, including psychology, pedagogy, sexuality, and economics. These discourses concern social and sexual repression, consumption, uniform eradication of individuality, and deformation of subjectivity. The private, both in society and in literature, is the potential locus of revolt and social change.

Thus, this interest in the discursive context – a context shared by author, text, and reader alike – leads to the assumption of a critically conscious reader. The negative corporeal realisms display how the family, the intimate body, and the private home are sites for the new political subject that is emerging in the 1960s as one that is in revolt and revolting, or rather, that is politically engaged through negativity. The negativity is anchored primarily in the bodies of children and youth as they grapple with the effects of the nuclear family and the home. The visceral response elicited from the reader as he or she critically approaches the negative portrayal of bodies underscores the reader's own experience with intimate bodies in the private sphere. The corporeal negativity in these texts acts much like German Studies scholar Gerhard Richter's definition of a *Denkbild* (thought-image). It forces the reader to stop and think, because the reader becomes involved in untangling meaning that the *Denkbild* also resists providing, for "the image that the Denkbild gives us is a picture of this resistance" (13). The *Denkbild* is politically charged, as "it offers a mode of thinking, reading, and writing that allows us to inquire into the history and logic of aesthetic ideologies" (21). The reader of the New and Black Realist texts is halted in the reading process by the appearance of such negative physical manifestations as neurotic hallucinations, disgusting fluids, grotesque permutations, or violent disfigurement. He or she then must engage in a process of meaning making by inserting his or her own contextual experience into the blanks in the text, producing a second, personal text (Iser). Through negativity as a *Denkbild* the reader is asked to reconsider the standard modes for representation in literature and for categorizing private experience. In other words, the *Denkbild* in the form of negativity shakes up the reader's comfortable acceptance of the way things have always been represented in text and experienced in modes of living.

However, the critical engagement of the reader does not take place only through negativity as an emotion, but also through the text form and the writing/reading act itself. The negativity found in these literatures is, as Richter writes of the *Denkbild*, "woven from the material fibres of language" (13), for the negative bodies also work in narratological terms and define the language of the texts. The language emanates from the negative bodies. Wellershoff's writings on literature, as a professional reader of theory and literature in his role as theorist and editor, opened the first chapter of this study not only because he offers a blueprint for the examination of the private sphere in literature that also captures the narratological potential of corporeal negativity, but also because his literary essays provided the clearest link among the author, text, reader, and context through the writing/reading act. Literature must incite the reader to political and social action by becoming a simulation space for the reader to practise non-normative behaviours. Similarly, Brinkmann's essays on literature, poetics, and creativity display his understanding of the body in the creative process to be an instrument for the author's and the reader's shared sensual liberation. Elsner's use of endless repetitions in language that also reflect the repetitions of content shows, moreover, how the writing act can be transformed into a resistant reading act through the experience of stuplimity. Finally, Rasp's mobilization of satire as a very specific text form that demands the reader engage with the content of the critique through an understanding of extraliterary consensus sets the direct political potential of the writing and reading act into motion. For this reason, these corporeal realisms are in content and form negatively, creatively, and ethically utopian.

Finally, these literatures reflect what Lauren Berlant calls the "thick moment of ongoingness" that is the historical present, or the immediate experience of the everyday (*Cruel* 200). For this reason, the literary texts examined here have a very strong sense of specificity that is locatable in a moment in history through the incorporation of contextual discourses appearing or being read concurrently with the literary works. Because of this strong sense of a present, they continue to possess an urgent sense of "now" that is shared by other discourses of the decade. This understanding therefore returns to the "structure of feeling" that opened the introduction to this study. Raymond Williams uses the term in 1961 to describe a culturally dominant feeling; he explains that the possession of the structure of feeling is "a very deep and very wide possession, in all actual communities" (48). Similarly, fifty years later Berlant suggests for periods of intensely felt politics (as was the case for the 1960s) that there exists a "sense of political and social mutuality that is performed in moments of collective audition" (*Cruel* 224). It is because of such feeling tones in this period of intense social and political transformation that the aspects of negativity, the family, and corporeality resonate in aesthetics and structure, in poetic form and cultural content, in text and context, and in author and reader.

While the feeling that all levels of society must be politically engaged widely characterizes the radical and revolutionary 1960s, this notion can by no means be seen as possessed by mainstream society.[1] Moreover, within the political movement generally thought of as characteristic for a literary 1968, the works examined here should not be taken as dominant examples, neither because of their specific topical interest in the private sphere nor in their negative aesthetic approach to reality. These works and authors are, in a sense, outliers of a literary-political decade, outliers despite, or perhaps because of, their interplay with normative and counter-normative socio-psycho-political discourses of the time. By specifically focusing on intimate and subjective experiences and by clothing these in a narrative aesthetics guided by the distorted body and its disturbed emotions, these texts stand out as singular and minor examples of a long tradition of German literary realism. What makes these texts outliers is not that they see the private sphere to be politically engaged, for this dominates the decade. Nor are they outliers because they utilize negativity, for as has been shown this places them in line with the critical writing on negativity in intellectual circles from the Frankfurt School to the Konstanz School. These literatures are singular examples because their private spheres are disturbingly distorted, their politics corporeally displayed, and their negativity emotionally non-cathartic.

Sianne Ngai calls negative emotions "minor affects" (*Ugly* 354). By considering the negative corporeal realisms examined here as a literature of minor affects, we gain access to their larger potential beyond the scope of their own historical present. In their discussion of minor literature on the basis of Franz Kafka, Gilles Deleuze and Félix Guattari point to its three defining characteristics as "the deterritorialization of language, the connection of the individual to a political immediacy, and the collective assemblage of enunciation" (18). They explain further: "We might as well say that minor no longer designates specific literatures but the revolutionary conditions for every literature within the heart of what is called great (or established) literature" (18). New and Black Realism display similar features to this understanding of minor literature. The deterritorialization of language, or the "minor practice of major language" from within that major language, appears here in terms not of major and minor national linguistic identities, but of major and minor literary practices (18). Although created within the dominant or major discussions on the political representation of reality during the 1960s and using the language of the contextual discourse on the private sphere, the New and Black Realist texts depict that reality in a manner atypical of the decade's broad definition of realism by focusing on the (minor) subjective and private experiences as expressed by the textual bodies. Berlant uses the term "normative realism" to describe the subject's desire to understand present and past, public and private, and "distribution of sensibilities that discipline the imaginary about what the good life is and how proper people act" (*Cruel* 53). This is precisely what the realisms in this study work against. New and Black Realism fight all established concepts of literature, but also all acts of normativity and methods for meaning making; instead of the imaginary about the good life, these realisms create an imaginary about the uncomfortable life.

Moreover, the connection to contemporary political concerns is primary to minor literary texts, for "everything in them is political" (Deleuze and Guattari 17). The individual concern "becomes all the more necessary, indispensable, magnified, because a whole other story is vibrating within it. In this way, the family triangle connects to other triangles – commercial, economic, bureaucratic, juridical – that determine its values" (17). In New and Black Realism, the political force of the discursive context is communicated solely through the private individual's corporeal subjective experience as located in the family, from the individual's traumatic or repressed memories and sexual experience to their consumptive or pedagogical practices, through which public discourses vibrate. Further, the individual subjectivity of the reader becomes politically activated precisely by the interlocking private and public spheres identifiable within and beyond the texts.

Finally, in keeping with minor literature, the realisms examined in this study practise collective enunciation in that the individual bodies in the texts stand in for the collective national body, and the manner in which they speak to an imagined individual reader references a collective public readership. Most important, however, this literature of minor affects heeds Deleuze and Guattari's call to refuse all major functions, and instead to embrace being or becoming minor as a creative revolutionary process (27). This "Great Refusal" (Marcuse, *One* 257) as a creative process is how negative corporeal realism's engagement of the reader through emotional negativity, ambivalence, non-catharsis, or passivity is transformed into radical resistance.

Notes

Introduction: On Realism, Negativity, and Intimacy

1 All translations from German to English are my own (under initial consultation with Barbara Pausch) unless otherwise noted.

2 For an overview of the variety of countercultural movements taking place during this time period, see Nick Thomas. A rash of books came out during the forty-year commemoration of "68," including Routledge's launch of the journal devoted to the decade, *The Sixties*.

3 Langston identifies the "corporeal realism characteristic of post-fascist avant-gardes" as differing from pre-fascist realism that approached the "real signs of the damage that modern experience putatively inflicts on bodies" (*Visions* 19). He writes, further, that "corporeal wholeness" (19) communicates forgetting and denial, whereas "fractured bodies, both past and present, are flagged as the loci of real historical violence" (20).

4 In *Ugly Feelings*, Ngai uses the term "feeling tone," to refer to a text's organizing affect and its relation to its audience, for it describes not merely the reader's emotional response. Instead, tone is "a global and hyperrelational concept of *feeling* that encompasses attitude: a literary text's affective bearing, orientation, or 'set toward' its audience and world" (43).

5 The 1960s engaged in a self-analysis of the decade's literature well before the decade was out and immediately following its end.

6 This was by no means anything new; see the so-called Expressionism debate between Lukács and Brecht. For a closer examination of these earlier debates as they connect to New Realism see Powroslo. For a short overview of the issues of realism for the 1960s see Baßler.

7 Much of this discussion was begun a decade earlier by the French *nouveau roman*. The proponents of the *nouveau roman* most influential to New Realism were

Nathalie Sarraute and Alain Robbe-Grillet. Merkes examines New Realism and *nouveau roman*. See also Zeltner-Neukomm.

8 *Akzente* was understood at the time as examining shifts and changes related to literature and culture. For an English-language analysis of the journal contemporary to this discussion see Lass.

9 Reich-Ranicki also refers to this change in the relationship between reality and the everyday in literature, calling it in 1967 "Literatur der kleinen Schritte" (literature of small steps; 63).

10 An audio recording of the attack can be found at http://german.princeton.edu/landmarks/gruppe-47.

11 The quotes are from a reprint of the speech in Jaeckle.

12 Ten years later Powroslo writes: "Literatur von Rang befaßt sich durchweg mit negativen Phänomenen. In ihrem Mittelpunkt steht die Darstellung des Abstoßenden und Häßlichen; menschliche Verkümmerung und menschliches Elend sind ihr bevorzugter Gegenstand" (Literature of note does consistently deal with negative phenomena. The depiction of the repulsive and ugly is at its centre; human atrophy and human misery are its favourite subjects; 106–7).

13 See Adorno, "Kulturkritik und Gesellschaft" ("Cultural Criticism and Society").

14 While I have taken the English title from the 1972 translation by Morris, the translation itself represents my own.

15 This corresponds to what was called a fight against the *politischer Reinheitswahn* (political cleanliness mania) that saw anything that did not correspond to the system to be taboo; see Schmidtke.

16 The quotes are from the first publication of the essay in North America in *Playboy* (December 1969).

17 Not all were enthusiastic for the application to the West German context. Literary critic Reinhard Baumgart suggests in his response that in order for Fiedler's thoughts to become a political reality, West German literature's commitment to realism would have to be abandoned (25).

18 For various discussions of the viability of the literary category of New Realism, see Powroslo 23; Happekotte 26, 37, 54; Tschierske 2; Merkes 4; Geduldig 120.

19 Unlike Wellershoff, H.M. Enzensberger refuses to identify unifying tendencies of the texts he introduces, nor does he wish to apply any of the author's writing style to German literature as a whole (*Vorzeichen* 11). He does describe similarities, two of these being detail and simplicity (21, 23).

20 I have chosen to translate *Schwarzer Realismus* as Black Realism, and not dark realism, for it references also black humour. Dark would suggest a brooding aspect to this literature that does not exist.

21 Dujmić calls the textual product of New Realism a negative psychological portrait of societal reality (95). Puknus terms New Realism nonconformist (10).

22 These quotations are taken from the 1997 translation by Hullot-Kentor.

23 Founded by Hans Roberts Jauss along with other members including Iser and Peter Szondi, the group published seventeen volumes between 1963 and 1998 based on colloquia. See Wagner for a history of the group. Of special note is the 1968 volume called *Die nicht mehr schönen Künste: Grenzphänomene des Ästhetischen* (The No Longer Beautiful Arts: Aesthetics at the Margins), in which the discussants approach the issue of what they call the rise of the anti-aesthetic, divided along two general lines of interest: Christian art and the Middle Ages, and those pieces that begin in modernity.

24 This is a term coined by Wellershoff that is an extension of an earlier term, *Simulationsraum*, or space for simulation, found "Fiktion und Praxis," which is discussed in chapter 1.

25 The quotations here are from a 1978 English edition of the text.

26 See also Fluck 186–8.

27 See also *Languages of the Unsayable* (1989) by Iser and Budick.

28 For a discussion of Marcuse's importance during the decade, see Kellner's introduction to *Herbert Marcuse: The New Left and the 1960s* as well as DeKoven.

29 For an overview of studies on the postwar family up to the 1990s, see Joosten. For a summary of the sociological interest in the family since 1945 see Delille and Grohn.

30 The English quotations here are from a 2008 translation by Rendall.

31 Of course this is not just the case in Germany alone. As Moeller claims, the crisis of and rebuilding of the family was of national importance for all nations that were involved in the Second World War (2).

32 As Moeller notes, as late as 1950, there were still 130 women for every 100 men (28).

33 Moeller in *Protecting Motherhood* and Herzog in *Sex after Fascism* each claims that the concept of the normative family upheld by the paternal wage system did not exist as such in Germany before 1945.

34 Other studies contend that the equation of the role of the woman as mother degenders the specific problem by merging it into a social and societal problem (Joosten 7).

35 See also Annette F. Timm's *The Politics of Fertility in Twentieth-Century Berlin* for a discussion of family policy in terms of the discourse surrounding fertility, politics, and history in the 1950s and 1960s, including also writings by the counterculture.

36 In a revisionist essay from 1960 entitled "Familie in Gefahr?" (Families in Danger?) based on a talk at Innsbruck, Wuermeling claims that the family was not in crisis following the war, but rather the only institution still standing, equating the dangers the family faces today with those of the war (93).

37 Gender expectations are clarified in two specific essays, "Mutter sein in dieser Zeit" (Being a Mother Today) and "Hilfen für den Vater durch Kirche, Staat und Gesellschaft" (Help for the Father through Church, State, and Society), both from 1959.
38 See *Sexualität und Klassenkampf* (Sexuality and Class Struggle, 1968) and *Sexualität, Moral und Gesellschaft* (Sexuality, Morals, and Society, 1970).
39 A study of the subject as constituted in the private sphere of the family should actually reach back to the rise of the *Bürgertum*. Of particular note here is Jürgen Habermas's *Strukturwandel der Öffentlichkeit*, especially in light of its 1962 publication date. For the purposes of this study, the focus is on the postwar reaction to the rise of fascism and authoritarianism and the family's central role in 1950s and 1960s West Germany, the context of the novels studied here. One text not touched on here is the collection of writings on family and authoritarianism by members of the Frankfurt School, *Studien über Autorität und Familie* (*A Study on Authority*, 1936); this study, conducted by Max Horkheimer, Herbert Marcuse, Erich Fromm, and others, was influential to many New Left intellectuals writing in the West German 1960s.

1. Trauma, Neurosis, and the Postwar Family

1 A portion of an earlier version of this chapter was published as "Masculinities in Trauma: The Male Body in Dieter Wellershoff's 1960s Writings and New Leftist Psychological Discourse," in *Über Gegenwartsliteratur: Interpretationen und Interventionen. Festschrift für Paul Michael Lützeler zum 65. Geburtstag / About Contemporary Literature: Interpretations and Interventions. A Festschrift for Paul Michael Lützeler on his 65th Birthday*, ed. Mark Rectanus (Bielefeld: Aisthesis, 2008), 315–31. Smaller portions of earlier versions of this and chapter 2 are brought together in "Kölner Realismus Redux? The Legacy of 1960s Realism in Postunification Literature," in *Closing Borders, Bridging Gaps? Deutscher Pop an der Jahrtausendwende*, ed. Anke Biendarra, spec. issue of *Literatur für Leser* 31.2 (2008): 81–93.
2 The English quotations are from a 1971 translation by Shapiro.
3 Laing uses the term "family nexus" throughout his writings to refer to patterns of relations that determine how individual family members function as a system.
4 See Moeller for a discussion of the female-dominated public sphere and the backlash against this in the postwar period.
5 In a very early essay on the text, Burns explains that the father, unlike the son, does not experience total breakdown because he has a past (21).
6 This wording broadly references Derrida's *Archive Fever*.
7 Bügner calls this a "vergangenheitsauslöschende Purifikationsstrategie" (purification strategy that extinguishes the past; 210); I see these moments of purification to have an ontological purpose.

8 Following the definition of the two terms set out by Laplanche and Pontalis, neurosis represents the symptomatic effects of the symbolic representation of psychic conflict that has its roots in childhood, often oscillating in the attempt to find a balance between desire and refusal. Psychosis is the manifestation of neurosis that ultimately displays a primary (libidinal) disconnect to reality.

9 Wellershoff's interest in schizophrenia and Laing's writings is seen in his second novel.

10 The English quotations and references are from the 1975 translation by Placzek.

11 The term "anti-psychiatry" was coined by David Cooper in 1967. He identifies two stages of psychiatry he sees as problematic. In the first stage, the schizophrenic person is labelled as ill, and in a second move, everything the person does is ruled invalid (x). Psychiatry in this understanding is violence and demands conformism to social norms. The schizophrenic illness always occurs within a microsocial crisis situation, which is the familial.

12 Fredric Jameson reminds us in *Archaeologies of the Future* that the "Utopian remedy must at first be a fundamentally negative one, and stand as a clarion call to remove and to extirpate this specific root of all evil from which all the others spring" (12).

13 This is an uncharacteristically positive approach to utopia by Marcuse. In the essay "Zum Begriff der Negation in der Dialektik" (On the Term Negation in the Dialectic), published in 1969, Marcuse warns that negativity, which must develop and exist within the system, is almost impossible to find today (185). It is hard to avoid the neutralization or incorporation of negativity, which would merely reproduce that system and not change it (188).

14 See also Raulet 117.

2. Repression, Disgust, and Adolescent Memories

1 Langston calls Brinkmann among the "youngest and certainly earliest champions of French realism in Germany" and claims: "Within a year, Brinkmann had advanced beyond Kiepenheuer and Witsch's legendary Böll as the press's rising star" (*Visions* 107).

2 Critics and literary historians are of two minds as to whether Brinkmann's early work can be assigned to New Realism. Vormweg mentions that Brinkmann refuses to be aligned with the "Kölner Schule" group of New Realists cultivated by his editor Wellershoff ("Portrait" 9). Späth in her monograph also thinks Brinkmann's literary work has to do, not with New Realism, but instead with the *nouveau roman* (34). On the other hand, Schäfer says of Brinkmann's "In der Grube" that it is an exemplary text of New Realism (64). Merkes includes both of Brinkmann's short story collections in the rubric of New Realism. See also Mortiz Baßler and Langston's discussion of Brinkmann in *Visions of Violence*.

3 Sutherland calls this phase part of his poetics of the global.

4 Brinkmann continues to apply this to the artists and writers: "Und es ist das Klischee vom 'Mann,' wie es das Klischee von der 'Frau' ist, wie das vom 'Romancier,' wie das vom 'Lyriker,' wie das vom 'Bildhauer,' wie undsoweiter, worauf sich der Großteil installierter Kritik weiterhin abstrakt verläßt: der unsichtbare Käfig jeweiliger Zuständigkeit kann nicht verlassen werden" (The majority of established criticism still abstractly depends upon the cliché of "man" and the cliché of "woman," just like that of "novelist," that of "poet," that of "sculptor," that of and so on: the invisible cage surrounding each area of responsibility cannot be left; "Film" 243). He makes the offhand comment: "Ein Beispiel: angesichts des überraschenden Erfolgs einer jungen deutschen Autorin, deren Prosa 'camp-ig' kalt und obszön kalkuliert ist, wurde in einer Besprechung gefragt: 'Was ist heute mit unseren Frauen los?'" (An example: in light of the surprising success of a young female German author, whose prose is campy-cold and obscenely calculated, the question was posed in a review: "What is wrong with our women today?"; "Film" 243). This statement could very well be in reference to Renate Rasp.

5 For other recent specific examinations of sexuality in this period see also Elizabeth Heinemann, *Before Porn Was Legal: The Erotica Empire of Beate Uhse* (2011); Josie McLellan, *Love in the Time of Communism: Intimacy and Sexuality in the GDR* (2011); Sybille Steinbacher, *Wie der Sex nach Deutschland kam: Der Kampf um Sittlichkeit und Anstand in der frühen Bundesrepublik* (2011).

6 Herzog remarks that Reich's texts were bootlegged more than any other author of the time, the first being *Massenpsychologie des Faschismus* (*The Mass Psychology of Fascism*) in 1965 (159).

7 The English quotation is taken from a 1970 translation by Carfagno.

8 The English quotations are taken from a 1973 translation by Carfagno.

9 The absolute importance of Reich and Marcuse for Reiche and others is discussed by Reiche in his disillusioned 1988 essay "Sexuelle Revolution – Erinnerung an einen Mythos" (Sexual Revolution – Memory of a Myth). In it he claims: "Das idiotische Theorem von der 'sexuellen Revolution' lebt weiter in einem mittlerweile weitgehend entpolitisierten sexologischen Dauerargument der Linken" (The idiotic theorem of the "sexual revolution" continues to live on in the form of a now mostly depoliticized perpetual sexological argument of the Left; 69). He remembers the slogan "sexuelle Revolution" (sexual revolution) but also the "Zerschlagung der autoritären Kleinfamilie" (destruction of the authoritarian nuclear family) as empty catchphrases (52). See also Timm for a discussion of Marcuse, the counterculture, and the Nazi past.

10 See also Boothe.

11 In the essay "Raw Matter," Ngai sees desire to be at odds with or negated by disgust (165).

12 Baßler suggests that the negative experiences resonating in the home town originate in a negative childhood experience that takes place even earlier than the first sexual encounter, even colouring that encounter with violence (27). This negative experience is described in the text as a torturous form of play, whereby the children bind each other up and torture each other physically. The narrator himself recounts having been the object of just such a game, thrown into the ditch that is a recurring image of disgust in the novel and forms the title of the story.

13 And, as Langston notes, the past is also a problem for his body (*Visions* 116).

14 See Menninghaus 12 and in particular Freud's letter to Fließ on 14 November 1897.

15 This fits with Langston's suggestion that waste elimination is experienced as "forward progress," while sex is experienced as pollution (*Visions* 116).

16 See Menninghaus's discussion of Bataille's phrase the "ontology of male desire" (375).

17 See Bordo's *The Male Body* (47). Langston also calls the metaphors used by Brinkmann "patently feminine," arguing that they reinforce a gender confusion in the protagonist (*Visions* 118).

18 Wuermeling's 1963 essay outlines very well the extent of the family political support of single-family homes and apartments in the postwar period, beginning in 1953. Wuermeling sees the *Eigenheim* or single-family home to provide the family with stability and pride, but by the late 1960s it represented entrapment, as will be explored in chapter 3.

19 It is into this trench that the protagonist was thrown as a child, and the memory of that violent game follows him in the image of the ditch and, as Baßler contests, colours his experience of the town. While this chapter is focused on the sexually repressive aspects of family in childhood, the violence incurred on the boy compounds the violence also present in the experience of the libidinal self.

20 Schreyer suggests that this imagery results from the italicized middle section of the text. He writes that the narrator, returning to the train station after his meal, is followed by images of his past that erupt from his body like flatulence (67).

21 See Freud's letter to Fließ on 22 December 1897.

22 See Lacan, *Seminar XX*.

23 For a discussion of this phrase, see Menninghaus 375.

24 This reading does not encompass the stories in the collection, but has instead chosen representative examples from among the six stories.

25 Punday makes this statement in an analysis of Bakhtin's understanding of how narratives elucidate the "gap between exterior world and private space" (102).

26 Ngai reads this resistance in terms of Marcuse's understanding of "repressive tolerance," which is the negative of the plural system (*Ugly* 340).

27 Boothe reminds us that disgust's object, dirt and defilement, also should be seen as an act of rebellion, citing the 1960s generation's embrace of that which produces disgust (10).

28 Or as Boyken sees in Brinkmann's early prose, the body is the "Medium der direkten Wahrnehmung" (medium of immediate perception; 121).

3. Consumption, Vertigo, and Childhood Visions

1 The original German highlights in language the title of Renate Rasp's short novel, *Ein ungeratener Sohn*. Another wayward daughter, of course, from the Austrian context would be Elfriede Jelinek. See also Jelinek's essay on Elsner in the *Konkret* special issue on Elsner.

2 For an overview of Elsner's life and work, see Künzel's introduction "Einmal im Abseits, immer im Abseits?" (Once Off-Side, Always Off-Side) to number 49 of *Konkret* (2009), devoted to Elsner, as well as her 2012 book on Elnser.

3 Flitner has compiled the most comprehensive look at Elsner's appearance in the press in comparison to Jelinek. More recently, Künzel has examined Elsner's reception and performative masquerade. See Künzel's essays on these subjects in *Meisterwerke* (Masterworks, 2005) and *Autorinszenierungen* (Author Performances, 2007). See also my comparison of Elsner's and Rasp's reception in "Böser Blick, entblößte Brust" (Evil Eye, Bared Breast) in which some of the examples presented here also appear.

4 When she committed suicide in 1992, her publishing house Rowohlt had long since auctioned off her books and cancelled her contract; Elsner was never able to achieve the success she saw with her first text.

5 Künzel, who sees Elsner to be one of the most important female satirists in contemporary German literature, is the primary scholar in Germany working on correcting this problem. See her many publications on Elsner, as well as her editing and championing of the republishing of Elsner's work in *Verbrecher Verlag*, and her foundation of an international Gisela Elsner Society. See also the study by Mindt and the special issue of *Konkret* entitled *Die letzte Kommunistin* (The Last Communist), edited by Künzel. The near disregard for Elsner continues to apply to North American German studies.

6 Elsner herself was highly critical of those women writing "Frauenliteratur" (women's literature) or who were expressed feminist authors. See the second volume of critical essays edited by Künzel, entitled *Im literarischen Ghetto* (Gisela Elsner: In the Literary Ghetto) from 2011.

7 This closer consideration of the language of the reception of her work provides underlying commentary on Elsner's (not entirely singular) status as a female author who criticizes and satirizes West German society – a task normally reserved for the male members of the Gruppe 47. Elsner and Rasp are most often cited as the paramount examples of Black Realism. That they are both female has broader-reaching implications for the study of the female satirist in contemporary German literature.

8 Another aspect making Black Realism difficult to define in particular with relation to these two women is that fact that they did not write on the aesthetic-creative act, as did Brinkmann and Wellershoff. However, Elsner wrote many critical essays on literature, the literary market, culture, and politics, all of which have at their centre a concern for power structures in society. Elsner writes in 1989 that there are two issues that determine reality: the class struggle and atomic armament ("Band-würmer" 249). Künzel suggests that these essays can be read as a type of literary program that comes back again and again to the political base of reality through satire ("Schriftsteller" 346). While this chapter does not read Elsner's early novel as a satire, there are satirical elements – most specifically related to the depiction of reality. Perhaps a better label than Black Realism for these two authors would be, in the end, Satirical Realism.

9 This English quotation is taken from a 1963 translation by Weisstein.

10 For a broader placement of the novel in the context of the grotesque and satirical tradition see Mindt.

11 This narrative perspective caused many contemporary reviewers to see Oskar Mazerath in Lothar.

12 Silverman uses this phrase to discuss the manner in which Rainer Werner Fass-binder often does not film his characters head-on, but instead trains the camera at their mirrored reflections or through windowpanes.

13 Baudrillard identifies the serial reproduction of the real as a type of hyperreal-ism propagated by the *nouveau roman*. Baudrillard writes of the *nouveau roman*: "Irreality no longer belongs to the dream or the phantasm, to a beyond or hidden interiority, but to *the hallucinatory resemblance of the real to itself*. To gain exit from the crisis of representation, the real must be sealed off in a pure repetition" ("Order" 72; emphasis in orig.). Pure repetition allows for the construction of the reader's objectivity through the "blind relay of the gaze," which in turn explains the "vertigo of realistic simulation" (ibid.). In *Die Riesenzwerge*, the repetitive simulation of the bodies and the organic parts slows down the reader's metabolism of the text; it becomes impossible to distinguish the original object from its representation.

14 Mindt compares this feature of the tapeworm to the centipede in Robbe-Grillet's *La Jalousie*.

15 The destabilization of meaning is best seen in the *Beitrag* "Der Herr" (The Lord), which finds Lothar describing the letters of the sentence "Gott spricht die Wah-rheit" (God speaks the truth).

16 Meyer continues to lend a strong feminist spin to the scene that it does not entirely contain. The mother's own guilt at refusing to stop or see the act and the reversal of the gender roles assigned to cannibal and victim in the final wedding scene prove that violence is not reserved for men. Mindt also writes that matriarchy is for Elsner not an alternative to patriarchy (75).

17 See also Moeller's extensive discussion of this (210).
18 This being one year after the publication of Elsner's second novel, *Der Nachwuchs*, in 1968 that features the issue of the single-family home and suburbia. See my article "Satirizing the Private as Political."
19 See Freud's *Totem und Tabu*.
20 Laplanche and Pontalis explain that in the primal scene the sexual relations of the parents are seen or fantasized by the child and generally assumed by the child to be an act of violence by the father. For Freud, the primal scene occurs around anal sex.
21 The bag of candy is given to him by one of the restaurant guests who consumed the father.
22 Meyer also notes the sexual aspect of this scene. "This self-referential move, which turns phallic power against its owner, negates and destroys the myth of male power based on ever increasing violence and patricide" (56). This lends a strong feminist spin to the text that I elsewhere suggest does not exist.
23 In the ninth *Beitrag*, children take part in the sex act between their parents, creating their eighth sibling.
24 For a reading of this scene with relation to the mother's task, see Polt-Heinzl, "Alltagsrituale unter dem Mikroskop" (Everyday Rituals under the Microscope).
25 Silverman makes this statement with reference to Fassbinder.

4. Discipline, Love, and Authoritative Child-Rearing

1 A portion of an earlier version of this chapter appeared as "Satirizing the Private as Political: 1968 and Postmillennial Family Narratives," *Women in German Yearbook* 25 (2009): 76–99.
2 The English title comes from a 1970 translation of the text by Figes; the translations are my own.
3 See the November 1968 edition of *Der Spiegel*, "Wohin rollt die Sex-Welle?" (Where Is the Sex-Wave Going?), connecting Rasp's political move to many other advertising strategies that utilize the female body.
4 In an interview in 1978, Elsner suggested that the writing of satire, like visiting a brothel, is primarily a male domain, and in 1985 she added: "Ich war die erste Frau, die eine Satire, nämlich *Die Riesenzwerge* schrieb" (I was the first woman to write a satire, and that was *The Giant Dwarfs*; quoted in Künzel, "Autorschaft" 180). Künzel also discusses the manner in which Elsner relates satire written by women to a woman going to a prostitute ("Schriftsteller" 348). The formulation is found in the interview "Vereinfacher haben es nicht leicht" (Simplifiers Do Not Have It Easy): "Satiren ... galten wie Bordellbesuch auschießlich als Männersache"

(Satires ... were seen, like brothels, to be masculine territory; 34). See also Künzel's discussion of satire and gender in English, "The Most Dangerous Presumption."

5 The citations for the English references are from a 1974 translation by Jephcott.

6 In a turn on Adorno, Elsner writes: "Ich schreibe meistenteils Satiren und muß oft feststellen, daß die Wirklichkeit meine satirischen Einfälle überrundet, daß ich oft hinter der Wirklichkeit herhinke" (I mostly write satires and must often realize that reality speeds past my satirical ideas, that I am often limping after reality; "Bandwürmer" 248).

7 Designed for Kiepenheuer & Witsch by Hannes Jähn.

8 The German translation of the title reads: *Orthopädie, oder die Kunst, bei den Kindern die Ungestaltheit des Leibes zu verhüten und zu verbessern. Alles durch solche Mittel, welche in der Väter und Mütter, und aller der Personen vermögen sind, welche Kinder zu erziehen haben* (Orthopedics, or the art of preventing and correcting deformities of the body in children. This through such means that the fathers and mothers, and all other guardians possess.)

9 The image is also reprinted in Foucault's *Discipline and Punish*.

10 The understanding of authority as ultimately part of German nature is confirmed later by West German radicals who believed that "German culture was especially *kinderfeindlich* [anti-children]" and thus utilized the child as a site to "remake German/human nature" (Herzog 165).

11 These findings are underscored two decades later by the Mitscherlichs.

12 The English quotations are from a 1969 translation by Mosbacher.

13 For a history of authoritarian and anti-authoritarian education and discipline, see Schroedter.

14 However, this was not long lasting, as men quickly began to also be involved in the *Kinderläden* project. See Herzog and the Authors' Collective. See also Nick Thomas for a discussion of the feminist movement in Germany. Rasp herself was clearly engaged in the burgeoning feminist movement, as exemplified by the Frankfurt Book Fair stunt. It is therefore of interest here to note that the radicalizing of the politicization of the child came hand-in-hand with women's political mobilization.

15 Hille makes this reference with regard to the portrayal of prosthetics following the First World War.

16 Rasp's poems are distinctly in line with the North American dirty speech movement.

17 Her 1973 text *Chinchilla: Leitfaden zur praktischen Ausübung* (Chinchilla: Guidance for Practical Application), a satirical handbook for budding prostitutes, takes love as commodity a step further.

18 Mitscherlich warns in *Auf dem Weg zur vaterlosen Gesellschaft* that sadism exists throughout 1960s West German society (220).

Works Cited

Adelson, Leslie A. *Making Bodies, Making History: Feminism and German Identity.* Lincoln: U of Nebraska P, 1993.

Adorno, Theodor. *Aesthetic Theory.* Trans. Robert Hullot-Kentor, ed. Gretel Adorno and Rolf Tiedemann. Minneapolis: U of Minnesota P, 1997.

Adorno, Theodor. *Ästhetische Theorie.* Vol. 7 of *Gesammelte Schriften.*

Adorno, Theodor. *Gesammelte Schriften.* Frankfurt/M: Suhrkamp, 1970–97. 10 vols.

Adorno, Theodor. "Kulturkritik und Gesellschaft." Vol. 10 of *Gesammelte Schriften,* 11–30.

Adorno, Theodor. "Juvenal's Error." *Minima Moralia.* 1951. Trans. E.F.N. Jephcott. London: Verso, 2005. 209–12.

Adorno, Theodor. "Juvenals Irrtum." *Minima Moralia.* Vol. 4 of *Gesammelte Schriften,* 239–41.

Adorno, Theodor. *Negative Dialektik.* Vol. 6 of *Gesammelte Schriften.*

Alexander, John. "Beatle-Haired Writer Attacks Group 47 Style." *The Daily Princetonian,* 27 Apr. 1966: 3.

Andry, Nicolas. *Orthopädie, oder die Kunst, bey den Kindern die Ungestaltheit des Leibes zu verhüten und zu verbessern.* Trans. Philopädon (1744). Ed. D. Wessinghage. Bad Abbach: Deutsche Bibliothek, 1987.

Armanski, Gerhard. *Fränkische Literaturlese: Essays über Poeten zwischen Main und Donau. Max Dauthendey, Elisabeth Engelhardt, Gisela Elsner, Friedrich Rückert, Süsskind von Trimberg, Moritz August von Thümmel, Leo Weismanter.* Würzburg: Königshausen & Neumann, 1998.

Arntzen, Helmut. *Satire in der deutschen Literatur: Geschichte und Theorie.* Darmstadt: Wissenschaftliche Buchgesellschaft, 1989.

Authors' Collective. *Storefront Day Care Centers: The Radical Berlin Experiment.* Trans. Catherine Lord and Renée Neu Watkins. Boston: Beacon Press, 1973.

Bakhtin, Mikhail. *Rabelais and His World*. Trans. Hélène Iswolsky. Bloomington: Indiana UP, 1984.

Barnes, Linda Horvay. *The Dialectics of Black Humor, Process and Product: A Reorientation Toward Contemporary American and German Black Humor Fiction*. Bern: Lang, 1978.

Baßler, Moritz. "*In der Grube*: Brinkmanns Neuer Realismus." *Medialität der Kunst: Rolf Dieter Brinkmann in Der Moderne*. Ed. Markus Fauser. Bielefeld: Transcript, 2011. 17–31.

Bataille, Georges. *Erotism: Death & Sensuality*. Trans. Mary Dalwood. San Francisco: City Lights Books, 1986.

Baudrillard, Jean. "The Order of the Simulacra." *Symbolic Exchange and Death*. London: Sage, 2004. 50–86.

Baudrillard, Jean. *Simulacra and Simulation*. Trans. Sheila Faria Glaser. Ann Arbor: U of Michigan P, 2006.

Bauer, Thomas. *Schauplatz Lektüre: Blick, Figur und Subjekt in den Texten R. D. Brinkmanns*. Wiesbaden: Deutscher Universitäts-Verlag, 2002.

Baumgart, Reinhart. "Die Enkel von Thomas Proust und Marcel Mann Zehn Anmerkungen zu Thesen von Leslie Fiedler." *Grenzverschiebungen: Neue Tendenzen in der deutschen Literatur der 60er Jahre*. Ed. Renate Matthaei. Cologne: Kiepenheuer & Witsch, 1970. 1–47.

Bender, Hans. "Ein ungeratener Sohn: Kuno wird kupiert." *Der Spiegel*, 20 Nov. 1967: 180–2.

Bender, Hans, et al. *Der Zürcher Literaturstreit: Eine Dokumentation*. Spec. issue of *Sprache im technischen Zeitalter* 22 (1967).

Berghahn, Volker R. "Recasting Bourgeois Germany." *The Miracle Years: A Cultural History of West Germany, 1949–1968*. Ed. Hanna Schissler. Princeton: Princeton UP, 2001. 326–40.

Berlant, Lauren. *Cruel Optimism*. Durham, NC: Duke UP, 2011.

Berlant, Lauren. "Intimacy: A Special Issue." *Intimacy*. Ed. Lauren Berlant. Chicago: U of Chicago P, 2000. 1–8.

Biess, Frank. "Survivors of Totalitarianism: Returning POWs and the Reconstruction of Masculine Citizenship in West Germany, 1945–1955." *The Miracle Years: A Cultural History of West Germany, 1949–1968*. Ed. Hanna Schissler. Princeton: Princeton UP, 2001. 57–82.

Blöcker, Günter. "Ausgeliefert an eine Übermacht. Nach dem Höllensturz." *Frankfurter Allgemeine Zeitung*, 4 Apr. 1964: 5.

Blöcker, Günter. "Kummer mit dem Nachwuchs." *Süddeutsche Zeitung*, 19–20 Oct. 1968: 106.

Bodamer, Joachim. *Der Mann von Heute: Seine Gestalt und Psychologie*. Stuttgart: Curt E. Schwab, 1956.

Bookhagen, Christel, Eike Hemmer, Jan Raspe, et al. "Kindererziehung in der Kommune." *Kursbuch* 17 (1969): 147–78.

Boothe, Brigitte. "Die Psychoanalyse des Schmutzes: Das Ekelregime." *Figurationen* 2.1 (2008): 7–25.

Bordo, Susan. *The Male Body: A New Look at Men in Public and in Private*. New York: Farrar, Straus, and Giroux, 1999.

Boyken, Thomas. "'Die Umrisse verloren sich darin, die Körper wie aufgeweicht': Körperdarstellungen in der frühen Prosa Rolf Dieter Brinkmanns." *Neue Perspektiven auf Rolf Dieter Brinkmann. Orte – Helden – Körper*. Ed. Thomas Boyken et al. Munich: Fink, 2010. 109–23.

Breiteneicher, Hille Jan, Rolf Mauff, and Manfred Triebe, and the Autorenkollektiv Lankwitz. *Kinderläden: Revolution der Erziehung oder Erziehung zur Revolution?* Reinbek: Rowohlt, 1971.

Brinkmann, Rolf Dieter. "Einübung einer neuen Sensibilität." *Rolf Dieter Brinkmann: Literaturmagazin Sonderheft*. Ed. Maleen Brinkmann. Reinbek: Rowohlt, 1995. 147–55.

Brinkmann, Rolf Dieter. *Erzählungen*. Reinbek: Rowohlt, 1985.

Brinkmann, Rolf Dieter. *Der Film in Worten*. Reinbek: Rowohlt, 1982.

Brinkmann, Rolf Dieter. "Der Film in Worten." *Der Film in Worten*, 223–47.

Brinkmann, Rolf Dieter. *Godzilla*. Cologne: Hake, 1968.

Brinkmann, Rolf Dieter. "In der Grube." *Erzählungen*, 7–67.

Brinkmann, Rolf Dieter. *Keiner weiß mehr*. Berlin: Kiepenheuer & Witsch, 1968.

Brinkmann, Rolf Dieter. "Nachweis über Erstveröffentlichungen." *Erzählungen*, 408–10.

Brinkmann, Rolf Dieter. "Notizen 1969 zu amerikanischen Gedichten und zu dieser Anthologie." *Silverscreen: Neue amerikanische Lyrik*. Frankfurt/M: Buchergilde Gutenberg, 1969. 8–32.

Brinkmann, Rolf Dieter. "Notizen und Beobachtungen vor dem Schreiben eines zweiten Romans 1970/74." *Der Film in Worten*, 275–95.

Brinkmann, Rolf Dieter. *Die Umarmung*. Cologne: Kiepenheuer & Witsch, 1965.

Bügner, Torsten. *Lebenssimulationen: Zur Literaturtheorie und fiktionalen Praxis von Dieter Wellershoff*. Wiesbaden: Deutscher Universitäts-Verlag, 1993.

Bühler, Hans Harro. *Familienpolitik als Einkommens- und Eigentumspolitik*. Berlin: Duncker & Humblot, 1961.

Burns, Robert. "Ein schöner Tag – Neuer Realismus oder psychologisierter Naturalismus?" *Der Schriftsteller Dieter Wellershoff: Interpretationen und Analysen*. Ed. R. Hinton Thomas. Cologne: Kiepenheuer & Witsch, 1975. 15–40.

Carius, Karl-Eckhard, Wilfried Kürschner, and Olaf Selg, eds. *Brinkmann: Schnitte Im Atemschutz*. Munich: Edition Text + Kritik, 2008.

Claßen, Ludger. *Satirisches Erzählen im 20. Jahrhundert: Heinrich Mann, Bertolt Brecht, Martin Walser, F. C. Delius*. Munich: Fink, 1985.

Coole, Diana. *Negativity and Politics: Dionysus and Dialectics from Kant to Poststructuralism*. London: Routledge, 2000.

Cooper, David. *Psychiatry and Anti-Psychiatry*. London: Tavistock Publications, 1967.

Cowie, Elizabeth. "Pornography and Fantasy: Psychoanalytic Perspectives." *Sex Exposed: Sexuality and the Pornography Debate*. Ed. Lynne Segal and Mary McIntosh. New Brunswick, NJ: Rutgers UP, 1993. 132–52.

Cremer, Dorothe. *"Ihre Gebärden sind riesig, ihre Äußerungen winzig": Zu Gisela Elsners Die Riesenzwerge. Schreibweise und soziale Realität der Adenauerzeit*. Herbolzheim: Centaurus, 2003.

DeKoven, Marianne. *Utopia Limited: The Sixties and the Emergence of the Postmodern*. Durham, NC: Duke UP, 2004.

Deleuze, Gilles. "Coldness and Cruelty." *Masochism*. Trans. Jean McNeil. New York: Zone Books, 1991. 9–138.

Deleuze, Gilles. *The Fold: Leibnitz and the Baroque*. Trans. Tom Conley. London: Continuum, 2006.

Deleuze, Gilles, and Félix Guattari. *Kafka: Toward a Minor Literature*. Trans. Dana Polan and Réda Bensmaïa. Minneapolis: U of Minnesota P, 1986.

Delille, Angela, and Andrea Grohn. *Blick zurück aufs Glück: Frauenleben und Familienpolitik in den 50er Jahren*. Berlin: Elefanten Press, 1985.

Derrida, Jacques. *Archive Fever: A Freudian Impression*. Trans. Eric Prenowitz. Chicago: U of Chicago P, 1995.

Dujmić, Daniela. *Literatur zwischen Autonomie und Engagement: Zur Poetic von Hans Magnus Enzensberger, Peter Handke und Dieter Wellershoff*. Konstanz: Hartung-Gorre, 1996.

Dujmić, Daniela, and Dietrich Harth. "Zur Poetic des 'wilden Denkens': Träume, Bewußtseinsdämmerungen, Halluzinationen und Verstörungen in Dieter Wellershoffs Erzählprosa." *Dieter Wellershoff: Studien zu seinem Werk*. Ed. Manfred Durzak. Hartmut Steinecke, and Kieth Bullivant. Cologne: Kiepenheuer & Witsch, 1990. 278–96.

Elsner, Gisela. "Autorinnen im literarischen Ghetto." *Im literarischen Ghetto. Kritische Schriften 2*. Ed. Christine Künzel. Berlin: Verbrecher, 2011. 41–59.

Elsner, Gisela. "Bandwürmer im Leib des Literaturbetriebs." *Im literarischen Ghetto*. Ed. Christine Künzel, 247–53.

Elsner, Gisela. *Flüche einer Verfluchten. Kritische Schriften 1*. Ed. Christine Künzel. Berlin: Verbrecher, 2011.

Elsner, Gisela. *Im literarischen Ghetto. Kritische Schriften 2*. Ed. Christine Künzel. Berlin: Verbrecher, 2011.

Elsner, Gisela. *Der Nachwuchs*. Reinbek: Rohwohlt, 1968.

Elsner, Gisela. *Die Riesenzwerge: Ein Beitrag*. Berlin: Aufbau, 2001.

Elsner, Gisela. "Vereinfacher haben es nicht leicht." *Im literarischen Ghetto*. Ed. Christine Künzel, 33–40.

Elsner, Gisela, and Klaus Roehler. *Wespen im Schnee: 99 Briefe und ein Tagebuch*. Berlin: Aufbau, 2001.

Enzensberger, Christian. *Größerer Versuch über den Schmutz*. Munich: Carl Hanser, 1968.

Enzensberger, Christian. *Smut: An Anatomy of Dirt*. Trans. Sandra Morris. New York: Seabury Press, 1972.

Enzensberger, Hans Magnus. "Einführung." *Vorzeichen: Fünf neue deutsche Autoren*. Frankfurt/M: Suhrkamp, 1962. 7–24.

Enzensberger, Hans Magnus. "Gemeinplätze, die Neueste Literatur betreffend." *Kursbuch* 15 (1968): 187–200.

Enzensberger, Hans Magnus, ed. *Vorzeichen: Fünf neue deutsche Autoren. Christian Grote, Hans Günter Michelsen, Gisela Elsner, Ror Wolf, Jürgen Becker*. Frankfurt/M: Suhrkamp, 1962.

Ernst, Thomas. *Popliteratur*. Hamburg: Europäische Verlagsanstalt/Rotbuch, 2001.

Esselborn, Karl. "Neuer Realismus." *Literatur in der Bundesrepublik Deutschland bis 1967: Hansers Sozialgeschichte der deutschen Literatur vom 16. Jahrhundert bis zur Gegenwart 10*. Ed. Ludwig Fischer. Munich: DTV, 1986. 460–8.

Evans, Jennifer V. *Life among the Ruins: Cityscape and Sexuality in Cold War Berlin*. New York: Palgrave Macmillan, 2011.

Faulstich, Werner. *Die Kultur der 60er Jahre. Kulturgeschichte des zwanzigsten Jahrhunderts*. Munich: Fink, 2003.

Fauser, Markus, ed. *Medialität der Kunst: Rolf Dieter Brinkmann in der Moderne*. Bielefeld: Transcript, 2011.

Fiedler, Leslie. "Cross the Border, Close the Gap." *Playboy*, December 1969: 151, 230, 252–54.

Fisher, Jaimey. *Disciplining Germany: Youth, Reeducation, and Reconstruction after the Second World War*. Detroit: Wayne State UP, 2007.

Flitner, Christine. *Frauen in der Literaturkritik: Gisela Elsner und Elfriede Jelinek im Feuilleton der Bundesrepublik Deutschland*. Pfaffenweiler: Centaurus-Verlagsgesellschaft, 1995.

Fluck, Winfried. "The Search for Distance: Negation and Negativity in Wolfgang Iser's Literary Theory." *New Literary History* 31.1 (2000): 175–210. http://dx.doi.org/10.1353/nlh.2000.0004.

Foucault, Michel. *Discipline and Punish: The Birth of the Prison*. Trans. Alan Sheridan. New York: Vintage Books, 1977.

Freud, Sigmund. *The Complete Letters of Sigmund Freud to Wilhelm Fließ 1887–1904*. Trans. Jeffrey Moussaieff Masson. Cambridge: Harvard UP, 1985.

Freud, Sigmund. "From the History of an Infantile Neurosis." *The Complete Psychological Works of Sigmund Freud*. Vol. 17, trans. James Strachey. London: Hogarth, 1955. 7–124.

Freud, Sigmund. "Das ökonomische Problem des Masochismus." *Gesammelte Werke.* Vol. 13. Frankfurt/M: Fischer, 1969. 371–83.

Freud, Sigmund. *Studienausgabe.* Ed. Alexander Mitscherlich, Angela Richards, James Strachey. 10 vols. Frankfurt/M: Fischer, 2000.

Freud, Sigmund. *Totem und Tabu. Studienausgabe.* Vol. 8. Ed. Mitscherlich, Richards, and Strachey.

Freud, Sigmund. *Zur Psychopathologie des Alltagslebens: Über Vergessen, Versprechen, Vergreifen, Aberglauben und Irrtum.* Frankfurt/M: Fischer, 1990.

Freud, Sigmund. *Zwei Kinderneurosen. Studienausgabe.* Vol. 8. Ed. Mitscherlich, Richards, and Strachey.

Freyberg, Doris, and Thomas von Freyberg. *Zur Kritik der Sexualerziehung.* Frankfurt/M: Suhrkamp, 1971.

Fuß, Peter. *Das Groteske: Ein Medium des kulturellen Wandels.* Cologne: Böhlau, 2001.

Geduldig, Gunter. "'… Ein großes Problem, in der Welt zu sein': Ein Gespräch mit Dieter Wellershoff." *Too Much: Das lange Leben des Rolf Dieter Brinkmann.* Ed. Gunter Geduldig and Marco Sagurna. Aachen: Alano-Verlag, 1994. 111–25.

Gehlen, Arnold. *Der Mensch: Seine Natur und seine Stellung in der Welt.* Wiesbaden: Akademische Verlagsgesellschaft Athenaion, 1978.

Gehlen, Arnold. *Urmensch und Spätkultur: Philosophische Ergebnisse und Aussagen.* Wiesbaden: Athenäum, 1964.

Gerhardt, Marlis. "Gisela Elsner." *Neue Literatur von Frauen.* Ed. Heinz Puknus. Munich: Beck, 1980. 88–93.

Gross, Thomas. *Alltagserkundungen: Empirisches Schreiben in der Ästhetik und in den späten Materialbänden Rolf Dieter Brinkmanns.* Stuttgart: Metzler, 1993.

Habermas, Jürgen. *Erkenntnis und Interesse.* Frankfurt/M: Suhrkamp, 1973.

Habermas, Jürgen. *Knowledge and Human Interests.* Trans. Jeremy J. Shapiro. Boston: Beacon Press, 1971.

Habermas, Jürgen. *Strukturwandel der Öffentlichkeit.* Frankfurt/M: Suhrkamp, 1990.

Haensch, Dietrich. *Repressive Familienpolitik: Sexualunterdrückung als Mittels der Politik.* Reinbek: Rowohlt, 1969.

Handke, Peter. "Zur Tagung der Gruppe 47 in USA." *Positionen des Erzählens: Analysen und Theorien zur Literatur der Bundesrepublik.* Ed. Heinz Ludwig Arnold and Theo Buck. Munich: Beck, 1976. 181–5

Happekotte, Bernd. *Dieter Wellershoff – rezipiert und isoliert: Studien zur Wirkungsgeschichte.* Frankfurt/M: Lang, 1995.

Heineman, Elizabeth. *Before Porn Was Legal: The Erotic Empire of Beate Uhse.* Chicago: U of Chicago P, 2011.

Hermand, Jost. "Pop oder die These vom Ende der Kunst." *Die deutsche Literatur der Gegenwart: Aspekte und Tendenzen.* Ed. Manfred Durzak. Stuttgart: Reclam, 1971.

Herrmann, Karsten. *Bewußtseinserkundungen im "Angst- und Todesuniversum": Rolf Dieter Brinkmanns Collagebücher.* Bielefeld: Aisthesis, 1999.

Herzog, Dagmar. *Sex after Fascism: Memory and Morality in Twentieth-Century Germany*. Princeton: Princeton UP, 2005.

Highmore, Ben. "Bitter after Taste: Affect, Food, and Social Aesthetics." *The Affect Theory Reader*. Ed. Melissa Gregg and Gregory J. Seigworth. Durham, NC: Duke UP, 2010. 118–37.

Highmore, Ben. *Ordinary Lives: Studies in the Everyday*. London: Routledge, 2011.

Hille, Karoline. "'... über den Grenzen, mitten in Nüchternheit': Prothesenkörper, Maschinenherzen, Automatenhirne." *Puppen Körper Automaten: Phantasmen der Moderne*. Ed. Pia Müller-Tamm and Katharina Sykora. Cologne: Oktagon, 1999. 140–59.

Höllerer, Walter. "Veränderung." *Akzente* 11.5–6 (1964): 386–98.

Horkheimer, Max, Erich Fromm, Herbert Marcuse, et al. *Studien über Autorität und Familie*. 1936. Lüneburg: Klampen, 2005.

Iser, Wolfgang. *The Act of Reading: A Theory of Aesthetic Response*. Baltimore: Johns Hopkins UP, 1978.

Iser, Wolfgang. *Der Akt des Lesens: Theorie ästhetischer Wirkung*. Munich: Fink, 1976.

Iser, Wolfgang. "Negativität als tertium quid von Darstellung und Rezeption." *Positionen der Negativität*. Ed. Harald Weinrich. Munich: Fink, 1975. 530–3.

Iser, Wolfgang. "The Play of the Text." *Languages of the Unsayable*. Ed. Wolfgang Iser and Sanford Budick. New York: Columbia UP, 1989. 325–39.

Iser, Wolfgang, and Sanford Budick. "Introduction." *Languages of the Unsayable*. Ed. Wolfgang Iser and Sanford Budick. New York: Columbia UP, 1989. xi–xxi.

Jaeckle, Erwin. *Der Zürcher Literaturschock*. Munich: Albert Langen–Georg Müller, 1968.

Jaeger, Joachim. *Realismus und Anthropologie: Eine Studie zum Werk Dieter Wellershoffs*. Frankfurt/M: Lang, 1990.

Jameson, Fredric. *Archaeologies of the Future: The Desire Called Utopia and Other Science Fictions*. 2005. London: Verso, 2007.

Jauss, Hans Robert. *Literaturgeschichte als Provokation der Literaturwissenschaft*. Ed. Gerhard Hess. Konstanz: Universitäts-Druckerei, 1967.

Jauss, Hans Robert. Ed. *Die nicht mehr schönen Künste: Grenzphänomene des Ästhetischen*. Munich: Fink, 1968.

Jelinek, Elfriede. "Ist die Schwarze Köchin da? Ja, ja, ja!" *Die letzte Kommunistin: Texte zu Gisela Elsner*. Ed. Christine Künzel. Spec. issue of *Konkret*, 49 (2009): 23–8.

Jerome, Roy. "An Interview with Tilmann Moser on Trauma, Therapeutic Technique, and the Constitution of Masculinity in the Sons of the National Socialist Generation." *Conceptions of Postwar German Masculinity*. Ed. Roy Jerome. Albany: SUNY Press, 2001. 45–62.

Jeziorkowski, Klaus. "Pflanzschule." *Frankfurter Allgemeine Zeitung*, 31 Oct. 1967: Literaturblatt 1.

Joosten, Astrid. *Die Frau, das segenspendende Herz der Familie: Familienpolitik als Frauenpolitik in der Ära Adenauer*. Pfaffenweiler: Centaurus, 1990.

Jost, Claudia. *Die Logik des Parasitären: Literarische Texte. Medizinische Diskurse. Schrifttheorien.* Stuttgart: Metzler, 2000.

Jung, Werner. *Im Dunkel des gelebten Augenblicks: Dieter Wellershoff – Erzähler, Medienautor, Essayist.* Berlin: Erich Schmidt, 2000.

Kaiser, Joachim. "Zu viele Zwerge." *Süddeutsche Zeitung*, 16–18 May 1964.

Kayser, Wolfgang. *Das Groteske in Malerei und Dichtung.* Reinbek: Rowohlt, 1960.

Kellner, Douglas. "Introduction: Radical Politics, Marcuse, and the New Left." *Herbert Marcuse: The New Left and the 1960s. Collected Papers of Herbert Marcuse.* Ed. Douglas Kellner. Vol. 3. London: Routledge, 2005. 1–37.

Kellner, Douglas. "Marcuse and the Quest for Radical Subjectivity." *Herbert Marcuse: A Critical Reader.* Ed. W. Mark Cobb. New York: Routledge, 2004. 81–99.

Klimke, Martin. "'The struggle continues': Revisiting the German Sixties." *Sixties* 1.2 (2008): 247–52. http://dx.doi.org/10.1080/17541320802486862.

Kneip, Birgit. *Zwischen Angriff und Verteidigung: Satirische Schreibweise in der deutschen Erzähl- und Dokumentarprosa 1945–75.* Frankfurt/M: Lang, 1993.

Koepnick, Lutz. *Framing Attention: Windows on Modern German Culture.* Baltimore: Johns Hopkins UP, 2007.

Kramberg, K.H. "Vorstellung einer Bestie: Das erste Buch von Renate Rasp." *Die Zeit* (Hamburg), 13 Oct. 1967: 26.

Kristeva, Julia. *Intimate Revolt: The Powers and Limits of Psychoanalysis.* Trans. Jeanine Herman. Vol. 2. New York: Columbia UP, 2002.

Kristeva, Julia. *Powers of Horror: An Essay on Abjection.* Trans. Leon S. Roudiez. New York: Columbia UP, 1982.

Kristeva, Julia. *Revolution in Poetic Language.* Trans. Margaret Waller. New York: Columbia UP, 1984.

Krüger, Ingrid. "Pflanzengarten. Der erste Roman von Renate Rasp." *Die Welt der Literatur*, 21 Dec. 1967: 4.

Künzel, Christine. "Einmal im Abseits, immer im Abseits? Anmerkungen zum Verschwinden der Autorin Gisela Elsner." *Die letzte Kommunistin: Texte zu Gisela Elsner.* Ed. C. Künzel. 7–20.

Künzel, Christine. "Es gibt solche Schriftsteller und solche ..." *Im literarischen Ghetto.* Ed. C. Künzel. Berlin: Verbrecher Verlag, 2011. 345–64.

Künzel, Christine. "Gisela Elsner: *Die Riesenzwerge* (1964)." *Meisterwerke – Deutschsprachige Autorinnen im 20. Jahrhundert.* Ed. Claudia Benthien and Inge Stephan. Cologne: Böhlau, 2005. 93–109.

Künzel, Christine. *"Ich bin eine schmutzige Satirikerin": Zum Werk Gisela Elsners (1937–1992).* Taunus: Ulrike Helmer, 2012.

Künzel, Christine. "Leben und Sterben in der 'Wirtschaftswunder-Plunderwelt': Wirtschafts- und Kapitalismuskritik bei Gisela Elsner." *"Denn wovon lebt der Mensch?": Literatur und Wirtschaft.* Frankfurt/M: Lang, 2009. 169–92.

Künzel, Christine, ed. *Die letzte Kommunistin: Texte zu Gisela Elsner.* Spec. issue of *Konkret*, 49 (2009).

Künzel, Christine. "The Most Dangerous Presumption: Women Authors and the Problems of Writing Satire." *Gender Forum: An Internet Journal for Gender Studies* 35 (2011). http://www.genderforum.org/issues/gender-and-humour-ii/the-most-dangerous-presumption.

Künzel, Christine. "Satire und Groteske als Mittel der Dekonstruktion (klein-)bürgerlicher Rituale und Mythen. Gisela Elsner." *Brüche und Umbrüche. Frauen, Literatur und soziale Bewegungen.* Ed. Margrid Bircken, Marianne Lüdecke, and Helmut Peitsch. Potsdam: Universitätsverlag Potsdam, 2010. 403–25.

Künzel, Christine. "Eine 'schreibende Kleopatra': Autorschaft und Maskerade bei Gisela Elsner." *Autorinszenierungen: Autorschaft und Literarisches Werk im Kontext der Medien.* Ed. Christine Künzel and Jörg Schönert. Königshausen & Neumann, 2007. 177–90.

Lacan, Jacques. *Écrits: A Selection.* Trans. Alan Sheridan. New York: W.W. Norton, 1977.

Lacan, Jacques. *The Seminar XX, Encore: On Feminine Sexuality, the Limits of Love and Knowledge.* Ed. Jacques-Alain Miller. Trans. Bruce Fink. New York: W.W. Norton, 1998.

Laing, R.D. *The Divided Self: An Existential Study in Sanity and Madness.* London: Routledge, 1999.

Laing, R.D. *The Politics of Experience.* New York: Pantheon, 1967.

Laing, R.D. *The Politics of the Family and Other Essays.* New York: Pantheon, 1968.

Laing, R.D. *Self and Others.* London: Routledge, 1999.

Langston, Richard. "Roll Over Beethoven! Chuck Berry! Mick Jagger! 1960s Rock, the Myth of Progress, and the Burden of National Identity in West Germany." *Sound Matters: Essays on the Acoustics of Modern German Culture.* Ed. Nora M. Alter and Lutz Koepnick. New York: Berghahn, 2004. 183–96

Langston, Richard. *Visions of Violence: German Avant-Gardes after Fascism.* Evanston, IL: Northwestern UP, 2008.

Laplanche, J., and J.-B. Pontalis. *The Language of Psycho-Analysis.* Trans. Donald Nicholson-Smith. New York: Norton, 1973.

Laplanche, J., and J.-B. Pontalis. *Das Vokabular der Psychoanalyse.* Frankfurt/M: Suhrkamp, 1972.

Lass, R.H. "Accent on the Sixties." *Modern Language Review* 61.3 (1966): 455–66. http://dx.doi.org/10.2307/3721490.

League, Kathleen. *Adorno, Radical Negativity, and Cultural Critique: Utopia in the Map of the World.* Lanham, MD: Lexington Books, 2011.

Lieskounig, Jürgen. *Das Kreuz mit dem Körper: Untersuchungen zur Darstellung von Körperlichkeit in ausgewählten westdeutschen Romanen aus den fünfziger, sechziger und siebziger Jahren.* Frankfurt/M: Lang, 1999.

Lorenz, Dagmar C.G. "Humor bei zeitgenössischen Autorinnen." *Germanic Review* 62.1 (1987): 28–36. http://dx.doi.org/10.1080/00168890.1987.9935419.

Lukács, Georg. "Zur Frage der Satire." 1932. *Probleme des Realismus I*. Vol. 4. Neuwied: Luchterhand, 1971. 83–107.

Marcuse, Herbert. "Cultural Revolution." *Toward a Critical Theory of Society: Collected Papers of Herbert Marcuse*. Ed. Douglas Kellner. Vol. 2. London: Routledge, 2001. 121–62.

Marcuse, Herbert. *Eros and Civilization: A Philosophical Inquiry into Freud*. Boston: Beacon Press, 1955.

Marcuse, Herbert. *An Essay on Liberation*. Boston: Beacon Press, 1969.

Marcuse, Herbert. "Foreword." *Negations: Essays in Critical Theory*. Boston: Beacon Press, 1968. xi–xx.

Marcuse, Herbert. *One-Dimensional Man*. Boston: Beacon Press, 1964.

Marcuse, Herbert. "Zum Begriff der Negation in der Dialektik." *Ideen zu einer kritischen Theorie der Gesellschaft*. Frankfurt/M: Suhrkamp, 1969. 185–90.

Matthaei, Renate. *Grenzverschiebung: Neue Tendenzen in der deutschen Literatur der 60er Jahre*. Cologne: Kiepenheuer & Witsch, 1970.

McLellan, Josie. *Love in the Time of Communism: Intimacy and Sexuality in the GDR*. Cambridge: Cambridge UP, 2011.

Menninghaus, Winfried. *Disgust: Theory and History of a Strong Sensation*. Trans. Howard Eiland and Joel Golb. Albany: SUNY Press, 2003.

Merkes, Christa. *Wahrnehmungsstrukturen in Werken des Neuen Realismus: Theorie und Praxis des Neuen Realismus und des nouveau roman – Eine Gegenüberstellung*. Frankfurt/M: Lang, 1982.

Meyer, Franziska. "Women Writing in the 1950s and 1960s." *Post-War Women's Writing in German: Feminist Critical Approaches*. Ed. Chris Weedo. Providence: Berghahn, 1997. 45–60.

Michel, Karl Markus. "Ein Kranz für die Literatur." *Kursbuch* 15 (1968): 169–87.

Mindt, Carsten. *Verfremdung des Vertrauten: Zur literarischen Ethnografie der "Bundesdeutschen" im Werk Gisela Elsners*. Frankfurt/M: Lang, 2009.

Mitscherlich, Alexander. *Auf dem Weg zur vaterlosen Gesellschaft: Ideen zur Sozialpsychologie*. Berlin: Beltz, 2003.

Mitscherlich, Alexander. *Society without the Father: A Contribution to Social Psychology*. Trans. Eric Mosbacher. New York: Harcourt, Brace & World, 1969.

Mitscherlich, Alexander, and Margarete Mitscherlich. *The Inability to Mourn: Principles of Collective Behavior*. Trans. Beverly R. Placzek. New York: Grove, 1975.

Mitscherlich, Alexander, and Margarete Mitscherlich. *Die Unfähigkeit zu trauern: Grundlagen kollektiven Verhaltens*. Munich: Piper, 2004.

Moeller, Robert G. *Protecting Motherhood: Women and the Family in the Politics of Post-War West Germany*. Berkeley: U of California P, 1993.

Moser, Tilmann. "Paralysis, Silence, and the Unknown SS-Father: A Therapeutic Case Study on the Return of the Third Reich in Psychotherapy." *Conceptions of Postwar German Masculinity*. Ed. Roy Jerome. Albany: State U of New York P, 2001. 63–90.

Neidhardt, Friedhelm. *Die Familie in Deutschland: Gesellschaftliche Stellung, Struktur und Funktionen*. Opladen: C.W. Leske, 1966.

Ngai, Sianne. "Raw Matter: A Poetics of Disgust." *Telling It Slant: Avant-Garde Poetics of the 1990s*. Ed. Mark Wallace and Steven Marks. Tuscaloosa: U of Alabama P, 2002. 161–90.

Ngai, Sianne. *Ugly Feelings*. Cambridge: Harvard UP, 2005.

Politische Akademie Eichholz. *Familienpolitik in der Industriegesellschaft*. Bonn: Eichholz, 1964.

Polt-Heinzl, Evelyne. "Alltagsrituale unter dem Mikroskop, oder Wie Gisela Elsner aus dem Nähkästchen plaudern läßt." *Die letzte Kommunistin: Texte zu Gisela Elsner*. Ed. Christine Künzel. Spec. issue of *Konkret*, 49 (2009): 47–61.

Powroslo, Wolfgang. *Erkenntnis durch Literatur: Realismus in der westdeutschen Literaturtheorie der Gegenwart*. Cologne: Kiepenheuer & Witsch, 1976.

Punday, Daniel. *Narrative Bodies: Toward a Corporeal Narratology*. New York: Palgrave Macmillan, 2003.

Puknus, Heinz. "Ordnung und Realität: Zu Wellershoffs Theorie einer nonkonformen Literatur." *Dieter Wellershoff*. Ed. Heinz Ludwig Arnold. Munich: Text + Kritik, 1985. 3–11.

Rasp, Renate. *Chinchilla: Leitfaden zur praktischen Ausübung*. Reinbek: Rowohlt, 1973.

Rasp, Renate. *A Family Failure*. Trans. Eva Figes. London: Calder & Boyars, 1970.

Rasp, Renate. *Eine Rennstrecke: Gedichte*. Cologne: Kiepenheuer & Witsch, 1969.

Rasp, Renate. "Der Spaziergang nach St. Heinrich." *Wochenende: Sechs Autoren variieren ein Thema*. Cologne: Kiepenheuer & Witsch, 1967. 149–90.

Rasp, Renate. *Ein ungeratener Sohn*. Berlin: DTV, 1970.

Rasper, Christiane. "Lust-Mörderinnen in der Sprache: Satirische Texte von Frauen und ihr kämpferisches Potential." *Frauen – Literatur – Revolution*. Ed. Helga Grubitzsch, Maria Kublitz, Dorothea Mey, and Ingeborg Singendonk-Heublein. Pfaffenweiler: Centaurus, 1992. 291–99.

Raulet, Gérard. "Marcuse's Negative Dialectics of Imagination." *Herbert Marcuse: A Critical Reader*. Ed. W. Mark Cobb. New York: Routledge, 2004. 114–27.

Reich, Wilhelm. *The Function of the Orgasm: Sex-Economic Problems of Biological Energy*. Vol. 1 of *The Discovery of the Orgone*. Trans. Vincent R. Carfagno. New York: Farrar, Straus, and Giroux, 1973.

Reich, Wilhelm. *Die Funktion des Orgasmus: Sexualökonomische Grundprobleme der biologischen Energie*. Cologne: Kiepenheuer & Witsch, 2004.

Reich, Wilhelm. *Genitality: The Theory and Therapy of Neurosis*. Trans. Philip Schmitz. *Early Writings* 2. New York: Farrar, Straus and Giroux, 1975.

Reich, Wilhelm. *Die Massenpsychologie des Faschismus*. Cologne: Kiepenheuer & Witsch, 1971.

Reich, Wilhelm. *The Mass Psychology of Fascism*. Trans. Vincent R. Carfagno. Ed. Mary Higgins and Chester M. Raphael. New York: The Noonday Press, 1970.

Reich, Wilhelm. *Die sexuelle Revolution*. 4th ed. Frankfurt/M: Fischer, 1971.

Reiche, Reimut. *Sexualität und Klassenkampf: Zur Abwehr repressiver Entsublimierung*. Frankfurt/M: Fischer, 1974.

Reiche, Reimut. *Sexualität, Moral und Gesellschaft. Arbeitshefte* 8. Wiesbaden: Hessische Landszentrale für politische Bildung, 1970.

Reiche, Reimut. "Sexuelle Revolution – Erinnerung an einen Mythos." *Die Früchte der Revolte: Über die Veränderung der politischen Kultur durch die Studentenbewegung.* Berlin: Klaus Wagenbach, 1988. 45–70.

Reich-Ranicki, Marcel. "Deutsche Schriftsteller und deutsche Wirklichkeit." *Der Monat* 19.229 (1967): 56–63.

Richter, Gerhard. *Thought-Images: Frankfurt School Writers' Reflections from Damaged Life*. Stanford: Stanford UP, 2007.

Robbe-Grillet, Alain. *Argumente für einen neuen Roman*. Trans. Marie-Simon Morel. Munich: Hanser, 1965.

Rölli-Alkemper, Lukas. *Familie im Wiederaufbau: Katholizismus und bürgerliches Familienideal in der Bundesrepublik Deutschland 1945–1965*. Paderborn: Ferdinand Schöningh, 2000.

Salzinger, Helmut. "Diesmal ein Zwergriese. Gisela Elsners zweiter Roman." *Die Zeit*, 20 Sept. 1968: LIT 3.

Sarraute, Nathalie. *Zeitalter des Argwohns: Über den Roman*. Trans. Kyra Stromberg. Darmstadt: Moderner Buch-Club, 1965.

Sass, Jan. *Der magische Moment: Phantasiestrukturen im Werk Dieter Wellershoffs*. Tübingen: Stauffenburg, 1990.

Scarry, Elaine. *The Body in Pain: The Making and the Unmaking of the World*. New York: Oxford UP, 1985.

Schäfer, Jörgen. *Pop-Literatur: Rolf Dieter Brinkmann und das Verhältnis zur Populärkultur der sechziger Jahre*. Stuttgart: M & P Verlag für Wissenschaft und Forschung, 1998.

Schissler, Hanna, ed. *The Miracle Years: A Cultural History of West Germany, 1949–1968*. Princeton: Princeton UP, 2001.

Schmidtke, Michael. "The German New Left and National Socialism." *Coping with the Nazi Past: West German Debates on Nazism and Generational Conflict, 1955–1975*. Ed. Philipp Gassert and Alan E. Steinweis. New York: Berghahn, 2006. 176–93.

Schnell, Ralf. *Geschichte der deutschsprachigen Literatur seit 1945*. Stuttgart: Metzler, 2003.

Schreyer, Robert. "Aus den leeren Wiederholungen, die blendende Helligkeit vor Augen ...: Über die frühe Prosa Rolf Dieter Brinkmanns." *Rolf Dieter Brinkmann.* Ed. Heinz Ludwig Arnold. Munich: Text + Kritik, 1981. 65–75.

Schroedter, Thomas. *Antiautoritäre Pädagogik: Zur Geschichte und Wiederaneignung eines verfemten Begriffes.* Stuttgart: Schmetterling, 2007.

Schwalfenberg, Claudia. *Die andere Modernität: Strukturen des Ich-Sagens bei Rolf Dieter Brinkmann.* Münster: Agenda, 1997.

Sedoun, Katia, Valeria Schmidt, and Eberhard Schultz. "Introduction." *Storefront Day Care Centers: The Radical Berlin Experiment.* Trans. Catherine Lord and Renée Neu Watkins. Boston: Beacon Press, 1973. xi–xxiii.

"Sieg der Zwerge." *Der Spiegel,* 13 May 1964: 123.

Siepmann, Eckhard, ed. *CheSchahShit: Die sechziger Jahre zwischen Cocktail and Molotow.* Berlin: Elefanten Press, 1984.

Silverman, Kaja. *Male Subjectivity at the Margins.* New York: Routledge, 1992.

Smith-Prei, Carrie. "Böser Blick, entblößte Brust: Der Autorinkörper als Gegenstand des literarischen Skandals. Gisela Elsner und Renate Rasp." *Literatur als Skandal.* Ed. Stefan Neuhaus. Göttingen: Vandenhoeck & Ruprecht, 2007. 549–58.

Smith-Prei, Carrie. "Kölner Realismus Redux? The Legacy of 1960s Realism in Postunification Literature." *Closing Borders, Bridging Gaps? Deutscher Pop an der Jahrtausendwende.* Ed. Anke Biendarra. Spec. issue of *Literatur für Leser,* 31.2 (2008): 81–93.

Smith-Prei, Carrie. "Masculinities in Trauma: The Male Body in Dieter Wellershoff's 1960s Writings and New Leftist Psychological Discourse." *Über Gegenwartsliteratur: Interpretationen und Interventionen. Festschrift für Paul Michael Lützeler zum 65. Geburtstag. / About Contemporary Literature: Interpretations and Interventions. A Festschrift for Paul Michael Lützeler on his 65th Birthday.* Ed. Mark Rectanus. Bielefeld: Aisthesis, 2008. 315–31.

Smith-Prei, Carrie. "Satirizing the Private as Political: 1968 and Postmillennial Family Narratives." *Women in German Yearbook* 25 (2009): 76–99.

Sofsky, Wolfgang. *Privacy: A Manifesto.* Trans. Steven Rendall. Princeton: Princeton UP, 2008.

Sofsky, Wolfgang. *Verteidigung des Privaten: Eine Streitschrift.* Munich: Beck, 2009.

Späth, Sibylle. *Rolf Dieter Brinkmann.* Stuttgart: Metzler, 1989.

Steinbacher, Sybille. *Wie der Sex nach Deutschland kam: Der Kampf um Sittlichkeit und Anstand in der frühen Bundesrepublik.* Munich: Siedler, 2011.

Sutherland, Marielle. "'Globale Empfindsamkeit': Rolf Dieter Brinkmann's Poetics of the Global." *Local/Global Narratives.* Ed. Renate Rechtien and Karoline von Oppon. Amsterdam: Rodopi, 2007. 201–27.

Sywottek, Arnold. "From Starvation to Excess? Trends in the Consumer Society from the 1940s to the 1970s." *The Miracle Years: A Cultural History of West Germany, 1949–1968*. Ed. Hanna Schissler. Princeton: Princeton UP, 2001. 340–58.

Timm, Annette F. *The Politics of Fertility in Twentieth-Century Berlin*. Cambridge: Cambridge UP, 2010.

Thomas, Calvin. *Male Matters: Masculinity, Anxiety, and the Male Body on the Line*. Urbana: U of Illinois P, 1996.

Thomas, Nick. *Protest Movements in 1960s West Germany*. New York: Berg, 2003.

Thomas, R. Hinton, and Keith Bullivant. *Literature in Upheaval: West German Writers and the Challenge of the 1960s*. New York: Manchester UP, 1974.

Trojanow, Ilija, and Juli Zeh. *Angriff auf die Freiheit: Sicherheitswahn, Überwachungsstaat und der Abbau bürgerlicher Rechte*. Munich: Hanser Verlag, 2009.

Tschierske, Ulrich. *Das Glück, der Tod und der "Augenblick": Realismus und Utopie im Werk Dieter Wellershoffs*. Tübingen: Max Niemeyer, 1990.

"Vom Fleisch und Blut. Buchbesprechung." *Der Spiegel*, 29 Apr. 1964: 118–19.

Vormweg, Heinrich. "Portrait Rolf Dieter Brinkmann." *Rolf Dieter Brinkmann 16. April 1940–23. April 1975 zum 50. Geburtstag*. Bremen: Antiquariat Beim Steirnenen Kreuz, 1996. 7–12.

Vormweg, Heinrich. "Zwischen Realismus und Groteske." *Die Literatur der Bundesrepublik Deutschland*. Ed. Dieter Lattmann. Zürich: Kindler, 1973. 309–21.

Wagner, Julia. "Anfangen. Zur Konstitutionsphase der Forschungsgruppe 'Poetik und Hermeneutik.'" *Internationales Archiv für Sozialgeschichte der deutschen Literatur* 35.1 (2010): 53–76. http://dx.doi.org/10.1515/iasl.2010.005.

Warner, Michael. *Publics and Counterpublics*. New York: Zone Books, 2005.

Wellershoff, Dieter. "Destruktion als Befreiungsversuch. Über Rolf Dieter Brinkmann." *Akzente* 23 (1976): 277–86.

Wellershoff, Dieter. *Ein schöner Tag*. Cologne: Kiepenheuer & Witsch, 1966.

Wellershoff, Dieter. "Fiktion und Praxis." *Literatur und Veränderung*, 9–32.

Wellershoff, Dieter. *Das Geschichtliche und das Private: Aspekte einer Entzweiung*. Wiesbaden: Franz Steiner, 1986.

Wellershoff, Dieter. "Identifikation und Distanz." *Positionen der Negativität*. Ed. Harald Weinrich. Munich: Fink, 1975. 549–51.

Wellershoff, Dieter. "Instanzen der Abwehr und das totale Environment." *Literatur und Veränderung*, 46–62.

Wellershoff, Dieter. *Literatur und Veränderung*. Cologne: Kiepenheuer & Witsch, 1969.

Wellershoff, Dieter. "Nachausekommen." *Literatur und Veränderung*, 148–71.

Wellershoff, Dieter. "Neuer Realismus." *Essays, Aufsätze, Marginalien. Werke*, vol. 4. Cologne: Kiepenheuer & Witsch, 1997. 843–4.

Wellershoff, Dieter. "Objektverlust." *Literatur und Veränderung*, 180–5.

Wellershoff, Dieter. *Die Schattengrenze*. Cologne: Kiepenheuer & Witsch, 1969.

Wellershoff, Dieter. "Die Verneinung als Kategorie des Werdens." *Positionen der Negativität: Harald Weinrich.* Munich: Fink, 1975. 219–33.

Wellershoff, Dieter. "Wiederherstellung der Fremdheit." *Literatur und Veränderung,* 82–96.

Wellershoff, Dieter. *Wochenende: Sechs Autoren variieren ein Thema.* Cologne: Kiepenheuer & Witsch, 1967.

Wellershoff, Dieter. "Zu privat: Über eine Kategorie der Verdrängung." *Literatur und Veränderung,* 33–45.

Widmer, Walter. "Die Züchtung von Riesenzwergen: Von der kalten Wut der Gisela Elsner." *Die Zeit* 29 May 1964: 17.

Wilke, Sabine. *Ambiguous Embodiment: Construction and Destruction of Bodies in Modern German Literature and Culture.* Heidelberg: Synchron Wissenschaftsverlag der Autoren, 2000.

Williams, Raymond. *The Long Revolution.* London: Chatto & Windus, 1961.

Wingen, Max. *Die Familie heute: Erster Bericht der Bundesregierung über die Lage der Familien.* Spec. issue of *Bulletin,* 27 (1968).

"Wir, Zöglinge." *Der Spiegel,* 8 Apr. 1968: 198.

"Wohin rollt die Sex-Welle?" *Der Spiegel,* 18 Nov. 1968: 46–67.

Woolley, Jonathan. *The Ethical Project in Rolf Dieter Brinkmann's Westwärts 1&2.* Berlin: Weidler, 2005.

Wuermeling, Franz-Josef. "Acht Jahre Familienpolitik." *Familie – Gabe und Aufgabe,* 156–70.

Wuermeling, Franz-Josef. "Die Aufgabe der Familie." *Familie – Gabe und Aufgabe,* 11–14.

Wuermeling, Franz-Josef. "Der besondere Schutz der Familie durch die Staatliche Ordnung." *Familie – Gabe und Aufgabe,* 85–91.

Wuermeling, Franz-Josef. *Familie – Gabe und Aufgabe.* Cologne: Luthe-Verlag, 1963.

Wuermeling, Franz-Josef. "Familie in Gefahr?" *Familie – Gabe und Aufgabe,* 92–107.

Wuermeling, Franz-Josef. "Familienpolitik um der Gerechtigkeit willen." *Deutsches Pfarrerblatt* 20.58 (1958): 457–60.

Wuermeling, Franz-Josef. "Die Kinder von heute sind die Ernährer von morgen." Katholisches Männerwerk der Erzdiözese. Speech. Freiburg, November 1963.

Wuermeling, Franz-Josef. "Wohnungsbau als angewandte Familienpolitik." *Familie – Gabe und Aufgabe,* 142–55.

Wuermeling, Franz-Josef. "Zur inneren Ordnung der Familie." *Familie – Gabe und Aufgabe,* 15–23.

Zeltner-Neukomm, Gerda. *Die eigenmächtige Sprache: Zur Poetik des Nouveau Roman.* Olten: Walter-Verlag, 1965.

Žižek, Slavoj. *The Plague of Fantasies.* London: Verso, 1997.

Žižek, Slavoj. *Violence.* London: Profile Books, 2008.

Index

corporeal subjectivity, 6, 19, 23–5, 31,
    38–9, 82, 89, 94, 97, 129, 135, 153,
    155, 157. *See also* Marcuse, Herbert
counterculture, 68, 161, 172n9
counter-revolutionary, 30
Cowie, Elizabeth, 84
creativity, 11, 88, 164
Cruel Optimism (Berlant), 24, 164–6

Daily Princetonian, 8
DeKoven, Marianne, 5–6, 19, 21, 61,
    169n28
Deleuze, Gilles: "Coldness and Cruelty,"
    157–8; *The Fold*, 111
Deleuze, Gilles, and Félix Guattari,
    165–6
Delille, Angela, and Andrea Grohn,
    169n29
Denkbild, 163–4
Derrida, Jacques, 62, 170n6
desire: and consumption, 114; and fam-
    ily, 46–8, 57–8; management of, 20,
    40, 104, 123; repression of, 12, 40–1,
    82, 84, 97; sexuality and, 73, 78, 84–6,
    88, 154; and symptoms, 40–1, 43,
    53–4; theory of, 70–1, 172n11, 173n16
dirty speech, 177n16
disavowal, 157–8
discipline: critique of, 129, 134, 150–1,
    153, 160; as deforming, 136, 138–9,
    152, 157; in family, 129, 135, 140,
    143–5, 148–9, 151, 159; institutional,
    130, 134, 140; language of, 120, 140–1;
    organization of, 136–8; in postwar
    period, 143–5, 147
disgust: as affect, 70, 75, 88; and desire,
    70, 172n11; toward food, 115; grammar
    of, 71, 74, 79; toward life processes,
    80–1, 84, 154; as poetics, 69–71, 83–4,
    87, 94; and private sphere, 74; of the
    reader, 85; and the sexual body, 32, 64,
    69, 71–3, 78–9, 82, 85–7, 162; as social
    critique, 70, 87–8, 94, 173n27
docile body, 152, 157–8

Dujmić, Daniela, 168n21
Dujmić, Daniela, and Dietrich Hart, 151

economic miracle, 14, 32, 89, 115, 117,
    120, 123, 162
education, 42, 68, 97, 114, 119, 124, 130,
    133–4, 143–53, 159, 160, 177n13
ejaculate, 78, 85–6, 123
Elsner, Gisela: "Bandwürmer im Leib
    des Literaturbetriebs," 126; and Black
    Realism, 32, 97, 100–3; debut of,
    14, 98, 101; as first female German
    satirist, 126; reception of, 99–100, 128;
    Die Riesenzwerge, 32, 97–8, 103–26,
    131, 162, 175n13, 176n4
ennui, 70, 80–1
Enzensberger, Christian, 9, 88
Enzensberger, Hans Magnus, 10, 14, 98,
    102, 168n19
Erhard, Ludwig, 14, 118
ethics: creativity as, 63, 65, 88–9, 93;
    in family, 28–30, 159, 162; towards
    readers, 4, 88, 93–4, 97, 103
Eros, 19–21, 42, 67–8, 70
Eros and Civilization (Marcuse), 19–20,
    40, 42, 67
Esselborn, Karl, 102
excess, 14, 26, 70–1, 80–1, 83, 85, 97,
    103, 111, 113, 115, 123
excrement, 9, 83, 154. *See also* faeces;
    urine
extraliterary consensus, 132, 153, 159,
    160, 164
Evans, Jennifer V., 65
everyday, 5, 7–9, 11–14, 39, 89–92, 97,
    100–3, 110, 125–6, 131, 139, 156, 164,
    168n9. *See also* realism

faeces, 75, 82–3
family: consumption of, 118–20, 126;
    as hierarchical institution, 97, 105,
    115, 122, 124–5, 134, 148; and na-
    tional identity, 13, 26; and postwar
    period, 26–7, 45, 65, 144, 146, 169n29,